STEM to STORY

ENTHRALLING *and* EFFECTIVE LESSON PLANS *for* GRADES 5–8

By 826 National

Edited by Jennifer Traig

With generous support from Time Warner Cable

Time Warner Cable®   826 NATIONAL   JB JOSSEY-BASS
A Wiley Brand

Cover Design by Lauryn Tom

Measurement Tool: © pio3 | Shutterstock

Feather Image: © iStockphoto | OlgaLIS

Published by Jossey-Bass

A Wiley Brand

One Montgomery Street, Suite 1000, San Francisco, CA 94104-4594—www.josseybass.com

Jossey-Bass books and products are available through most bookstores. To contact Jossey-Bass directly call our Customer Care Department within the U.S. at 800-956-7739, outside the U.S. at 317-572-3986, or fax 317-572-4002.

Wiley publishes in a variety of print and electronic formats and by print-on-demand. Some material included with standard print versions of this book may not be included in e-books or in print-on-demand. If this book refers to media such as a CD or DVD that is not included in the version you purchased, you may download this material at http://booksupport.wiley.com. For more information about Wiley products, visit www.wiley.com.

Library of Congress Cataloging-in-Publication Data is available on file with the Library of Congress.

ISBN 978-1-119-00101-0 (pbk.), 978-1-119-00103-4 (epdf), 978-1-119-00102-7 (epub)

Printed in the United States of America

FIRST EDITION

PB Printing   10 9 8 7 6 5 4 3 2

CONTENTS

LESSON PLANS

1 THE SCIENCE OF SAVING DAYLIGHT 1

Students learn the fundamentals of the scientific method as they write
zany hypotheses to explain daylight saving time.

2 TECHNICALLY SPEAKING 10

A challenge to make a high-performing paper airplane introduces
students to the basic principles of both technical writing and engineering.

OBSERVATIONS *by* LORETTA "ALETA" JACKSON.

3 IT'S (PARTIALLY) ROCKET SCIENCE AND (MOSTLY) ICE CREAM 26

Students explore physical properties and engineering principles by trans-
forming a liquid into a solid—ice cream!—and then designing a structure to keep it cool.

OBSERVATIONS *by* MAYIM BIALIK.

APPENDIX

PREFACE

WHEN PEOPLE THINK OF SCIENCE, TECHNOLOGY, ENGINEERING, AND MATH—OR STEM—the relationship to creative writing is not the first thing that comes to mind. STEM brings up visions of hard science—beakers, syringes, computer code, and strands of DNA. Think of creative writing, and you probably think of feather-tipped quill pens, coffee shops, and angst. But we see something different. Creativity is the cornerstone of science in all its forms, regardless of the discipline, and writing is common to all subjects. It is a well-known fact that many of the inventions we use today—the cell phone, the electric car, the Internet—were first imagined by creative writers of science fiction. Yes, you have a creative writer to thank every time you make that phone call while taking pictures on vacation.

Somewhere along the way, the ability to think creatively and express new ideas in all forms (writing being the one most central to 826 National) got separated from the STEM discussion. This book is our effort at reconciliation. How did we start? Well, like many good stories, ours begins with a woman and a man (the writers of this preface, Tessie Topol and Gerald Richards) from two organizations, a ridiculously bold plan, and a room full of mad scientists. Perhaps the scientists weren't mad, but there was a room full of them, and representatives of foundations and corporations as well, all looking for ways to engage young people in STEM.

826 National's partnership with Time Warner Cable (TWC) began at Clinton Global Initiative (CGI) America in 2011 with a basic question: How do we make STEM more engaging, especially to students in low-income and underresourced communities? At that meeting, we made a commitment to action, to bring together 826 National's proven creative writing model and TWC's Connect a Million Minds, an initiative dedicated to connecting young people to the wonders of STEM through hands-on learning (*www.connectamillionminds.com*).

The result was a four-week STEM and creative writing pilot program conducted in summer 2012 at 826 National chapters in Los Angeles and New York, where more than sixty students engaged in hands-on learning around a range of inquiry-based topics, including the science behind ice cream and deep space exploration. In one lesson, kids designed their own experiments to determine whether salt or sugar made ice melt faster. The resulting discussion around the properties of salt led to a creative writing exercise in which students each composed a short story about a scientist who wakes up one morning in a world without salt. This original lesson was published in 826 National's book of writing lessons *Don't Forget to Write*, and parts are adapted here in this book.

The initial pilot was so successful that we decided to build on that and conduct workshops in summer 2013. Once again STEM and creative writing workshops were carried out at 826LA and 826NYC. But we were left with another question. Would these workshops work outside the walls of an 826? If you took away 826LA's Time Travel Mart or 826NYC's Brooklyn Superhero Supply Co., would students still be interested? So the pilot was expanded to include other TWC partners, Operation Breakthrough in Kansas City, Missouri, and the YMCA of Greater New York. Beyond examining the science of salt, that summer students donned lab coats and protective goggles to build landing gear for touching down on fictional planets, then put pen to paper to create stories about alien landscapes. And once again we had success on our hands, so much so that the YMCA expanded the number of students using the lessons from twenty to eighty-one!

The results of the pilot projects encouraged our two organizations to work together to create the STEM and creative writing book that you have in your hands. Filled with workshops on such topics as the physics of music, writing science fiction, and the science of superpowers, this book is meant to encourage kids to get their hands dirty, to be curious and ask questions, and to use what they've learned to spark their imagination. And to love every minute of it. Who knows? The next Gene Roddenberry or Madeleine L'Engle may be in your midst, dreaming of the next invention or innovation that could change the world.

You may be thinking, *I don't know much about science,* or *I haven't worked on a math problem in years!* That's okay. This book is for you as much as it's for your students. We wanted to make the lessons here easy enough to understand that your science proficiency, or lack thereof, would not be a barrier to use. The book is meant to be used in after-school and out-of-school settings, as well as in the classroom, by teachers, parents, and nonprofit staff.

This book is the result of an unexpected but wonderful partnership, and we'd like to thank all the people who helped make it possible. First and foremost, thanks to President Bill Clinton, who had the insight to bring people together to create partnerships that build lasting change; Dave Eggers and Nínive Calegari, whose idea of partnering an unusual storefront and a writing center has flourished into a global movement; TWC leadership, who got behind a sustained philanthropic commitment concerning an issue important not only to the success of their business but also to the nation at large; and all of the 826 volunteers and staff who created and piloted these lessons. Finally, thanks to you for picking up this book and believing that STEM and creative writing can help foster the next generation of creative thinkers, problem solvers, and innovators.

Have fun!

Tessie Topol
Vice President, Corporate Social Responsibility
Time Warner Cable

Gerald Richards
Chief Executive Officer
826 National

HOW TO USE THIS BOOK

WELCOME! MAYBE YOU'RE HERE BECAUSE YOU'RE A MAJOR STEM FAN WHO CAN'T GET enough science, technology, engineering, and math. Or maybe you're a, let's say, more *artistically* inclined person, who, for some reason or other, suddenly has to teach some science. Whether you're in your element or over your head, you're in the right place. We've got twelve easy, fun, engaging lesson plans that combine the STEM fields and writing, and we're here to walk you through every step. As the catalyst said to the chemical compound, let's get started!

Our goal is, we hope, the same as yours: to inspire students to love the STEM fields and writing, too. One of the most exciting parts of science—of any kind of learning—is discovering something new. When students are exploring and figuring out how the world around them works, they are discovering something new to them—which is just as important and exciting as a Nobel Prize–winning discovery. Such an opportunity to explore and discover can ignite a passion for deeper learning.

This book's aim is to create moments of inspiration for students. We want students to be able to explore and discover, and to tap into their creativity along the way. We want to engage students who might not otherwise think of themselves as "science types." And we want to highlight the many elegant connections between the arts and science.

So, how do you use this book?

Pick a lesson, any lesson. The different lessons each can stand alone. Together, they provide an opportunity for students to become deeply immersed in the practices of science and engineering. The lessons were designed and piloted in out-of-school environments, but we've adapted them to be used both in and out of the classroom. To make things easy, we've estimated the time needed for each section of every lesson, allowing educators to plan breaks in lessons based on their own unique time considerations. In addition, each lesson is indexed to both the Common Core State Standards for English language arts and the Next Generation Science Standards.

And if you're not a classroom teacher, there's plenty for you here, too. The lessons are designed to be taught by just about anyone: after-school educators; parents; and, yes, classroom teachers, from new to veteran. Each instructor will have a different level of experience. For those who want them, we provide some tips for teaching science. These tips are based on research, both cognitive science findings on how students learn as well as research that has looked at the impacts of instructional practices on students' learning. They're best practices that will bring a lot to your teaching.

We've also compiled a handy-dandy glossary: the Science-O-Pedia. Each entry covers the big, BIG ideas in the doing of science, from evidence and hypotheses to iteration and models. Read it first, or consult it just when needed.

Throughout this book, you will find opportunities for your students to question, explore, investigate, build, analyze, and create. They will be challenged to support their ideas with evidence and to communicate their ideas clearly. They will envision new worlds and explain how this one works. In the process, they will gain firsthand experience with revising: their writing, their scientific ideas, and the systems they have engineered.

Science and Writing

Writing is our bread and butter at 826, and it's integral to each lesson here. We cover two broad forms of writing: the documenting-your-work, sciencey kind of writing, and creative, imaginative Writing with a capital *W*.

Let's talk about the documenting-your-work kind of writing first. Documentation is an important piece of science, but admittedly it can seem boring to students who are in the middle of an exciting investigation. Why should your students do it? A few reasons:

◇ It provides an anchor, allowing students to keep track of their ideas and how they are changing as they are confronted with new evidence.

◇ It ensures students record what they have done and how they have done it, so that they, or someone else, can repeat it later.

◇ It gets students to describe (both qualitatively and quantitatively) the results of each investigation.

Basically, until someone invents a way to broadcast the great ideas in our brains directly to the world, writing is a necessary and useful part of the scientific process. Maybe one of your students will be that inventor, but for now, like the rest of us, they'll use the written word.

As much as possible, we've tried to make the science writing assignments authentic (especially because we cannot capture all the different types of science writing here). Different formats are suggested in different lessons. Sometimes we ask for an instructor to capture students' ideas on chart paper. In other lessons we have data sheets (not worksheets) to scaffold the data collection and reflection for students. There are no lab reports—in classrooms, these are often prescriptive, and we want to provide students with ample space and flexibility to figure out what is important through their writing.

Now, about the creative, capital *W* kind of Writing: that also has a place here. Writing leverages the science theme of a lesson to give students the opportunity to explore different genres—students write science fiction, explore origin poems, write songs, tell tales of a journey by ship, hone their technical writing skills, and more. They use the science that they have learned in the lesson as source material for their writing, reinforcing their science learning.

Students also learn about things that science and writing have in common. Both are creative processes that involve trial and error. Just like in writing, scientists often revise their work—they design an experiment, but after trying it, they regularly have to change the mechanics of the experiment to get data that can be understood and interpreted. Clear communication is important in both science and writing. Writers share their work in writing workshops, with editors, and through publication; scientists share their work in conferences, on collaborative online forums, in popular science books, and in journals.

There is one big difference between creative writing and science, however. In creative writing you can invent worlds, and the impossible is possible (as long as you build a rich enough foundation for the story). In contrast, scientists can't invent evidence—that's fraud. Any scientific conclusions have to be backed up by evidence. Science and fiction only go together in science fiction; and we'll be doing a little of that here, too.

What Is STEM?

Science, technology, engineering, and math are often lumped together. There are good reasons for this—there's a lot of overlap between these fields, and collaboration between their respective professionals—but a clearer picture of each area can't hurt.

Science aims to expand human knowledge, and it does so by testing and falsifying hypotheses, and then building on theories about how the world works—figuring out everything from what the tiniest building blocks of the universe are, to exactly how much universe there is. Technology refers not only to actual physical equipment but also to its invention and the training of people to use it. Engineering is the use of scientific principles to solve problems—often by developing technology—including how to get across the country (in cars, over highways), and how to do so more conveniently and safely (robot drivers). Mathematics, and its analysis of the relationships between quantities, underpins all of the above. (This usually refers to applied mathematics, which includes branches of calculus, logic, and statistics. The many, many branches of "pure" or "theoretical" math, however, which develop mathematical understanding for its own sake, continue to find practical use in science, engineering, and technology.)

Like we said, most of these fields overlap. Developing the technology that powers the graphics in Pixar movies and PlayStation games requires some pretty complicated abstract math—matrices and quaternions. And a lot of the most exciting research in particle physics depends on a marvelous feat of engineering—the Large Hadron Collider, a particle accelerator (or "atom smasher") seventeen miles around. These days, the STEM professionals who are proficient across disciplines are the ones doing some of the most exciting work.

And wow are we jazzed about that. But we also believe that STEM education needs to be even more interdisciplinary. It needs to include the arts; it needs to be STEAM.

Throughout much of history, it was. Although we think of science and art as being very different—in fact, opposite—disciplines now, that wasn't always the case. During the Renaissance, for instance, painters belonged to the same trade guild as physicians and apothecaries, the Arte dei Medici e Speziali. It's no coincidence that this was the period when both art and science saw some of their greatest advances, particularly in the realm of anatomical drawings, which required talent in both areas.

Today, iterative STEM processes are essential in art and design, and a lot of the creativity traditionally associated with the arts is necessary for STEM as well. By bridging the false art-versus-science dichotomy with STEAM, not only do we help students cultivate important skills in different fields, but also we help students with an affinity for one subject or another discover much more that they can be engaged and successful in.

Best of all, when STEM and writing are combined, students actually learn better. Research has shown that students grasp STEM concepts faster, and remember them longer, when they learn them not as rote facts, but through a story. Stories stimulate parts of the brain that straight memorization doesn't, and when we use them, we can harness more brain power. Cool!

Science Teaching

If you're new to teaching STEM subjects—or even if you're an old hand—you may find the following tips useful (we certainly do!). These best practices are based on research and results, and we've found them to be enormously helpful.

Let Discovery Motivate Learning

We started by discussing the power of discovery. We want to reemphasize that here. The decision not to front-load lessons with content or vocabulary was deliberate. We know that leading with discovery is contrary to practice that has been promoted in schools for the past several years. It is, however, very much in line with the Next Generation Science Standards (2013) and *A Framework for K–12 Science Education* (2012). If you're not already doing it, we encourage you to give it a try.

Keep Your Hands in Your Pockets

In the 1980s researchers observed science classrooms and found a shocking disparity. When boys asked for help on an activity, the teacher was likely to give them some pointers and move on. When girls asked for help, the teacher, whether male or female, was likely to take over the materials and show them how to do it.[1]

What are the implications of this? As this happens to a student repeatedly over her educational career, she comes to expect to be rescued, either consciously or subconsciously. In practice this means that girls learn that they do not need to struggle and persist to complete a task, as someone else will do it for them. Although this may make getting through school appear easier, it has some real downsides. In many cases the reward is greater for the struggle—you learn more, and you feel a stronger sense of accomplishment. Learning persistence is a valuable skill—one that will help any student be successful, not only in school but in work and in life in general. One very practical tip to prevent yourself from rescuing a student, of any gender, is to keep your hands in your metaphorical pockets as you circulate around the room. With this stance, you can still ask great questions to promote thinking and provide practical tips or instruction, but it ensures that all students will have the opportunity to complete their own work, in the process building skills in persisting through difficult challenges.

Questions Are the Answer

It's tempting to provide lots of information up front—giving students vocabulary words and telling them what they will see in the investigation they are about to complete. When we organize a lesson this way, we have taken away our students' chance to explore and discover something for themselves. Where is the excitement in that? Instead, ask questions like the following:

◇ What have you tried? followed by What else could you try? (or, if the student is really stuck, Have you tried . . . ?)

◇ What did you observe or notice?

◇ How do you think it works?

◇ How do you know that? or Why do you think that? or What is your evidence for that?

◇ What do you think will happen if you change X?

◇ Why do you think that happens?

◇ Can you think of any additional explanations for what you observed?

---

1. Tobin, K., & Garnett, P. (1987). Gender related differences in science activities. *Science Education, 71,* 91–103.

We would argue that answering your students' questions with questions is the intellectual equivalent of keeping your hands in your pockets. Both are hard to do. Both require students to struggle and persist. And both are worth the effort, as they can have a profound impact on students' learning.

What does this mean? It means that when a student asks, for example, "Why does this happen?" you pause and, rather than giving the answer, respond by asking something like, "Why do you think that happens?" There are benefits both for you as a teacher and for your students when you respond this way: you get the opportunity to hear students' thinking, to understand where they are in their understanding of a concept, and to help them put their new learning in the context of their prior understanding. You can use a series of questions to guide students, in effect scaffolding their thought process; you can also use questions to redirect students' thinking. This is a flexible strategy, too, one you can use in one-on-one, small group, and whole group settings.

The Power of Prior Knowledge, Ideas, and Experience

Humans have been building on their scientific knowledge for millennia, progressing from early findings like "Fire hot!" to the more advanced implications of string theory physics. It's a process that's taken thousands of years, and it can often be very hard for huge shifts in scientific thought to take hold. The transition from an Earth-centered (geocentric) view of the cosmos to a sun-centered (heliocentric) view is a great example of this shift. Placing Earth in the center of the cosmos is consistent with what we see when we look up at the sky. Earth appears fixed, and the sun appears to move around us. This view, that the earth was the center, took hold powerfully in the ancient world. Over time, astronomers made more and more detailed observations of the movement of celestial bodies relative to Earth. Despite the fact that these newer observations were not consistent with the geocentric model, that view held for more than 1,500 years. It took what is now called a revolution (the Copernican Revolution) for the heliocentric model to begin to gain acceptance (and resistance continued . . .).

Humans are stubborn, and when a scientific idea appears to contradict our own experience or our "narrative" about how the world works, it takes work to make sense of and integrate that new idea. This is as true for individuals as it is for societies.

All students arrive at the classroom with their own framework for how the world around them works. This framework is based on their prior knowledge and experiences—developed both in and out of classrooms. Students' ideas about the world can be both powerful and persistent—much like the geocentric theory of the cosmos. New ideas and knowledge are not incorporated into a student's framework overnight. And, much as early astronomers created more and more complicated models to make their data fit the existing geocentric model, students will also try to fit conflicting information into their existing framework. Sometimes shifting their thinking requires the equivalent of a scientific revolution.

Some concrete steps to support students as they develop their understanding of a concept and to help shift their thinking consist of the following:

◇ **Solicit students' prior knowledge.** This step is helpful for both teachers and students: teachers gain insight into their students' current understanding, and students have a chance to articulate their thinking and identify questions they have about a topic. In addition, this process can build interest and engagement in a lesson. Finally, when done in a group setting, it gives students an opportunity to hear different ideas about the same topic, which in turn can further stimulate interest, raise additional questions, and help students begin to confront their assumptions. The lessons in this book use a variety of strategies to solicit prior knowledge.

◇ **Have students take a side.** Creating scenarios in which students can wrestle with their ideas can help them see that their mental model for a phenomenon may need some revision. One way to do this is to have students make and document their predictions (state what they think will happen—take a side). To make a good prediction (or a more formal hypothesis), students need to synthesize their current understanding of a phenomenon and apply that knowledge to the investigation at hand. Following the experiment, they then need to analyze whether their results were consistent or inconsistent with their predictions, and come up with a revised explanation for the phenomenon. Another strategy is to use something called a "discrepant event." Discrepant events have an unexpected, often puzzling outcome. In the lesson "Tinfoil Shipbuilding," for example, we suggest including a pumice stone in the collection of objects that you use to demonstrate objects that float or sink. Pumice behaves unlike other rocks. It floats. This forces students to think about the reasons something might float or sink beyond, *Well, it's a rock, and I know that rocks sink.*

◇ **Save time for sense-making.** Despite careful planning, science investigations often take longer than anticipated. As a result, what gets squeezed in many classrooms is time for students to make sense of the experience they have just had. This sense-making is, however, a critical piece of learning. It can occur in discussions with whole or small groups. In a discussion, the goal is for the instructor not to "recap" and tell the students what they "should" have learned, but rather to provide opportunities for the students to explain their current understanding and, even more important, share and build knowledge together. Note also that these discussions don't have to occur only at the end of a lesson—they can be integrated throughout. Sense-making can also happen through student writing, whereby students integrate and explain their new understanding of how or why a phenomenon occurs. There are examples of both sense-making discussions and sense-making writing in this book.

"Mistakes" Are Normal

Many students who have been in very prescriptive learning environments will want to know everything before they begin—every step they should take, even the conclusion they should reach. Quite a few would rather not start than possibly make a mistake. This approach is not conducive to scientific learning.

Science is all about learning by doing, and that includes making "mistakes." Practicing scientists make mistakes all the time, and so will your students over the course of these lessons. You should turn these mistakes into teachable moments and help students learn what they can. If it seems like a procedure went wrong (which is likely to happen when students are doing something for the first time), it's at the very least an opportunity to improve the procedure. More than you'd expect, though, difficulty with a procedure opens the door to unexpected observations and new lines of inquiry. (Where would the world be if Alexander Fleming had berated himself and thrown out the petri dish he accidentally allowed to be contaminated with mold? We might not have the antibiotics we do today if he hadn't discovered penicillin.)

If a student's hypothesis turns out to be wrong, it can feel to him or her like an especially huge mistake, a failure. But very few predictions prove to be entirely correct. In fact, the goal is not to prove a hypothesis, but to test it. A hypothesis helps scientists articulate, "This is where my thinking is now," so that they can ask good questions, learn more, and revise their thinking accordingly. There should be no stigma attached to being "wrong"—it's part of the process of learning what's "right" (as determined by the best information at the time). Always remind your students of this, and make your classroom a safe environment for mistakes and the wonderful learning that comes with them.

"YOU MUST NEVER FEEL BADLY ABOUT MAKING MISTAKES," EXPLAINED REASON QUIETLY, "AS LONG AS YOU TAKE THE TROUBLE TO LEARN FROM THEM. FOR YOU OFTEN LEARN MORE BY BEING WRONG FOR THE RIGHT REASONS THAN YOU DO BY BEING RIGHT FOR THE WRONG REASONS."

—NORTON JUSTER, *The Phantom Tollbooth*

Sesquipedalianism Masquerading as Erudition (or Long Words Dressed Up as Knowledge)

Science words are fun—long and complicated and like a secret language (more on this to come). Students and adults alike will often use science terms in a discussion, and we certainly want to encourage students to practice using these words, as this will ultimately build fluency. That said, we encourage you to challenge students when they introduce a science word, because it's important to be sure that everyone in the room understands what the word means, including the student who used the word in the first place. For example, many students will have heard of **density** (an important concept in "Tinfoil Shipbuilding") and will know that it has a relationship to floating and sinking. A student may well respond to the question "How do ships, which are really, really, really massive, float in water?" by saying, "It has to do with density." The student would be correct—it does have to do with density—but it is possible to give that answer without having any understanding of the concept of density. In this situation, and with almost all science words, we recommend saying to the student, "Will you please clarify what you mean by density? That's an important concept, and we want to be sure that everyone in the room understands what you mean." If the student responds at this point that she "can't really explain," don't make a big deal out of it; instead just point out that through the investigation, everyone will have a chance to explore the concept of density, and that the group can come up with a definition together later.

Science and Language Learning

The big science words just mentioned can make science learning very abstract, particularly when science is taught through a lecture or a textbook. In these situations, students are confronted with lots of new vocabulary at once and have few hands-on opportunities to really connect with the words. Researchers have analyzed high school–level science textbooks and found that they frequently require students to master more vocabulary than is recommended for secondary school foreign language courses—meaning that ninth-grade biology has more vocab to learn than Spanish I.[2] Memorizing a word is very different from understanding a concept. We want students to understand concepts and in parallel learn how to effectively communicate them.

To this end, the lessons in this book provide rich opportunities to develop students' English language skills (both for those who learned English as a first language and for those who may be English language learners). Throughout the book you will find opportunities for your students to talk (both formally and informally), listen, and write. The concrete experiences students have with materials will help them develop their conceptual understanding of science topics while also providing a mental scaffold onto which they can attach the language that they practice in the workshops.

2. Groves, F. (1995). Science vocabulary load of selected secondary science textbooks. *School Science and Mathematics, 95*(5), 231–235.

The Cat's Out of the Bag

Although we have designed these lessons to emphasize student discovery, there is always the chance that someone in the workshop will already know (or worse, will blurt out) "the answer." It is important to view this situation as a positive one, as it presents a wonderful teachable moment in which "the answer" should be challenged. An "answer" has an air of finality to it—what's the point of continuing with the investigation if you already know the "why"? Yet in science, even when a researcher finds an answer, that answer often leads to further questions and subsequent investigations. Perhaps more relevant to working with students, though, is that "the answer" is often rife with assumptions or information that some but not all of the students in the workshop have access to (such as from a prior school experience). When students present an answer, follow up with them by asking questions like these:

◇ How do you know? ("I learned it in class" doesn't count! See the next question.)

◇ What is your evidence for that?

◇ Is there an experiment you could do to test your idea?

◇ Is that the only explanation?

A Word on Materials

To simplify your lesson prep, we introduce each lesson with a list of the materials you'll need. Some are short and consist of things you likely already have on hand; others are a bit more involved. Feel free to adapt these lists to suit your own class's needs. The lists don't include the things you probably already use every day—like paper, pencils, a chalkboard, and so on—though you'll need those too. More fanciful supplies like lab coats and hero capes are optional (but very fun).

Using Science Notebooks or Lab Journals

Though not every lesson plan calls for it, we recommend that students use science notebooks or lab journals whenever possible, for a whole list of reasons. Using them helps students keep track of what they've done, and it helps them plan what they should do next. It instills good observation and data-keeping habits. It encourages them to *write*, which is always a good thing. Plus it's just good science practice, and it's what real scientists do.

An Important Note on Safety

The lessons in this book are designed to be applicable—and accessible—in a variety of settings, and the activities involve household items, with a few easily attainable exceptions. (If you have a cache of owl pellets lying around your house, we're coming over!) The activities and the materials involved should be perfectly safe if conducted and used properly. That said, it is important for instructors to note any precautions mentioned, and, above all, to always follow standard science safety procedures (wear goggles and gloves when appropriate; wash your hands and equipment; have a fire extinguisher handy; don't drink weird-colored, boiling liquids handed to you by a guy with a maniacal laugh; and so on). A helpful overview, provided by the National Science Teachers Association, may be found at *www.nsta.org/docs/SafetyInTheScienceClassroomLabAndField.pdf.*

FOR YOU TO KNOW (AND YOUR STUDENTS TO DISCOVER)

This book covers a wide array of science, technology, engineering, and mathematics topics, and we recognize that few educators will be comfortable with all of them. The lessons were designed to focus on discovery and exploration, so we encourage you to explore and learn alongside your students. To bring you up to speed quickly, each lesson includes this section, which provides some background on the subject at hand. This is to give you a solid foundation before you teach. Because it's all very interesting, this section is also useful at parties, letting you dazzle your fellow guests with your knowledge of STEM facts and trivia.

This section is for you—and not the students. You shouldn't feel like you have to read it, and you certainly shouldn't feel like you have to teach it. If you do choose to teach this material to students, we've found it's best not to introduce these ideas or vocabulary words at the beginning of a lesson. As a lesson progresses and students are sharing their observations and ideas, it will usually become clear that they have discovered many of these concepts for themselves. You can then help them by providing labels (the vocabulary words) to hang on the scientific ideas they have already described in their observations. As you do this, try to draw on students' own language in connecting their observations and ideas to the "scientific" language. If, at the end of the lesson, your students haven't learned what they were "supposed" to, resist the urge to give it to them. Their questions and curiosity will do a better job of motivating learning over the long term. Waiting is powerful—and you will see the results in what your students do and learn.

STEM@HOME

We hope these workshops will inspire your students' interest in STEM, and we want them to be able to continue their investigations. To provide a catalyst, we've included STEM@Home take-home pages to accompany every lesson. These pages include follow-up investigations closely linked to the STEM topic of the workshop that can be completed with common household materials, as well as extras like fun facts about the workshop topic. The STEM@Home pages also give parents a window into the corresponding workshop, and can be used to seed conversations between parents and their children about the science and writing done during the workshop session.

And Finally, a Roundup of Our Best Tips

We've found the following practices to be incredibly helpful in every workshop we do, from writing fairy tales with first graders to isolating DNA with high school seniors. We suggest that you always try to . . .

Use the Socratic Method

In brief: don't give the answer; help each student arrive at the answer for him- or herself. Suggestions and corrections are ideally made by asking questions, as in, "What happened when we added the salt?" When the student replies, "This liquid started to solidify," continue with another question: "Why do you think that happened?" Such guidance can definitely help students navigate their way to a solution or a proven or disproven hypothesis; it can also simply encourage exploration of new ideas. This same technique can be used in working with writing and revision. It's not always possible, of course, to teach the whole lesson through questions. But students will gain and retain the knowledge better if they come to realizations for themselves.

Give Your Students Time to Create

Students can be very product oriented, and may be thinking about what they will be getting out of their time with you. Honor the creative process, make sure to emphasize what the workshop will ideally produce for them in the end, and give them time during the workshop to work toward this goal.

Be Flexible

Each workshop session is based on a solid lesson plan, usually broken into basic time frames for the day. That said, remember that it's okay—and in fact encouraged—to cater timing and activities to your own parameters, your own time frames, and what you think will be most effective for your students. Don't be afraid to switch things up if something isn't working as planned, or if you're having an incredible workshop breakthrough. If you need to move on to an alternate activity, or put more time into an activity you thought would be shorter, go for it. Come in with an open mind about timing whenever timing permits.

Give Your Students Time to Revise

Wherever possible, we'd like students to remember that revision is an important and rewarding part of the writing process. While not shortchanging students in terms of the time needed to experience the creative process or the fun involved in discovering new things in your workshop, try to find time for students to revisit their writing and work on improving it: lengthening a piece, adding more details, checking for major spelling errors, making verb tense consistent, or focusing on a literary device introduced in the workshop. Let students know how good their writing will be with some work! Giving students an idea of just how great their work will be after a few revisions will give them the strength and endurance to follow through: "Wow, this has tons of potential! When we get some of this punctuation fixed up, and maybe fiddle with that conclusion, you'll really have something fantastic here!" Students will be ready for the work ahead if they know they'll have something great when they're done.

Make Time for Reflection

Active teaching leads right up to the final minute of every lesson. At the end of each session, and the lesson as a whole, make sure to allow time for students to reflect—individually and as a group. Lead the students through a recap and ask what they remember. Articulating takeaways gives staying power to the students' discoveries.

SCIENCE-O-PEDIA: A GLOSSARY

AMONG THE SPECIALIZED WORDS USED IN SCIENCE ARE WORDS THAT CONVEY integral ideas of how scientific knowledge is built. Some of these words seem very similar to "English" words (as opposed to words from the language of science), but they have in fact been co-opted and in science have very specific meanings that are different (in both subtle and not so subtle ways) from how they are used in everyday English. The process of science makes a lot more sense when you understand how these words are used in the scientific context.

Assumptions

It's next to impossible to engage in scientific practice without being aware of assumptions. When scientists generate a hypothesis, it needs to be specific enough to be testable. Everything else outside the scope of that hypothesis is an assumption. Assumptions can be parts of generally accepted theories, or untested hypotheses that are assumed to be true to make the hypothesis you are focusing on sufficiently narrow and testable.

When a hypothesis is tested, the underlying assumptions are also tested. It's much better if the assumptions are generally well supported; that way, the core hypothesis is easier to accept or reject. (If we do an experiment to test the density of some new-fangled gas, we should change our prediction of the density based on the experiment, rather than question well-tested assumed values for the force of Earth's gravity or the density of water.) If the assumptions aren't backed by evidence, then they should be under as much scrutiny as a rejected hypothesis.

Being aware of assumptions makes for better science. A researcher could do an experiment on the difficulty of learning Esperanto, or any other language, and determine that learning a foreign language is basically impossible because test subjects can't recognize any spoken words, even after studying an extensive vocabulary sheet. Or this researcher could recognize that his experiment contained an embedded assumption—that visual recognition of words leads to auditory recognition of words. Recognizing this assumption would help the researcher realize that the experiment should be done differently. Similarly, someone could create a perfect dragon skeleton out of some found bones and conclude that dragons were real—if he does not identify his assumptions (that the bones are bones, rather than replicas of bones, such as realistic parts of a plastic toy).

Recognizing assumptions isn't always easy. You can help your students gain this skill by regularly asking them how they know things, or whether there are alternative explanations, even crazy ones. With more questions going around, there's more of an opportunity for you and your students to see if you've been relying on assumptions that might not actually be true. Over time you may even find that your students begin to question each other's.

Evidence

Most students have probably heard the word "evidence" in the context of a crime scene or a trial. Police collect evidence (clues) from the crime scene, and the prosecutor uses these clues to build a case against the accused. A single piece of evidence, however, rarely tells the whole story—and evidence is often collected gradually. Thus, over time the "story" of what happened can change, often dramatically, and the emergence of new evidence can lead to new suspects and rule out others.

Scientists also use evidence to build a case. The evidence helps them develop an understanding of (the case for) how something in the natural world works. Just like at a crime scene, the evidence often builds gradually, and as a result, scientific understanding can change over time. A new piece of evidence, just like in the criminal case, can help scientists discover that the way they thought something worked was wrong, and can help point them in new directions.

Where does scientific evidence come from? There are many possible sources. The best scientific evidence is direct observations—quantitative or qualitative descriptions of objects or events. But sometimes we can only obtain indirect evidence. For example, when astronomers observe "wobble" in a star's orbit, it provides indirect evidence that there may be a planet nearby. However, the astronomers cannot say that they have found a planet until they have accumulated other direct evidence—ideally a direct observation—of an actual planet. The "wobble" helps the astronomers to know where to look, but it is the direct observation that makes the discovery. Closer to home, if a physician can detect antibodies in a patient, we could take that as evidence that there was an infection earlier, even if we couldn't observe the infection before, because we know that infections cause the immune system to produce antibodies.

Planned experimental investigations, in either the field or the laboratory, aim to produce direct and indirect evidence. Depending on the field, evidence can also come from observation of unplanned events or phenomena (for example, every time there is an earthquake, scientists learn a great deal about what happens when tectonic plates move relative to each other). Most important, because scientific understanding is built over time, there exists a body of knowledge and evidence that helps us define our current understanding of the world. Scientists access this prior knowledge in a variety of ways: they do background research, they read scientific papers that detail the evidence from other scientists' experiments, and they talk with other scientists, in the process coming to know what the accepted understandings are in their field. Connections formed between existing pieces of evidence can themselves be evidence (for example, in the case of a meta-analysis that uses statistics to combine the data from multiple studies or experiments).

It is critical that every new piece of evidence a scientist gathers be weighed against the "case" the scientist is building to explain how something works. Sometimes the evidence strengthens the case, whereas other times it contradicts it and requires the scientist to begin to think of other possible explanations that fit all the evidence.

Iteration

Scientists and even more frequently engineers use the term "iterative" to refer to the way they revise and refine their scientific ideas (scientists) or design solutions (engineers). For a revision process to be iterative, it must take into account feedback or information that you have gathered through science experiments or design tests, or new information you have obtained in some other way (for example, from other scientists or engineers). Iterative processes are cyclical and ongoing. A scientist may repeat similar experiments many times to disprove possible scenarios and fine-tune a hypothesis, or an engineer may tweak the shape of a wing bit by bit between experiments to find out how to minimize drag.

Models

Scientists frequently rely on models to help them conduct their work. Here are a few examples:

◇ Engineers often use scale models of structures or machines to test them.

◇ Many STEM professionals use mathematical models (often as simple as a few equations) to make predictions about satellite motion or population change.

◇ Computer models that simplify real-life systems help us study things like the weather, climate change, brain function, and proteins that can help cure cancer.

◇ Biologists use model systems—other organisms whose biology is in some way similar to our own—to learn how we as humans work. They've learned about human development from observing fruit flies, and have even learned how to cure some human diseases by studying rats and mice.

Why use models? Often, testing the real thing is impossible or impractical. It would be a waste if civil engineers had to repeatedly rebuild a skyscraper until they got it right; and if we waited for an earthquake to test a bridge, we'd be too late. Sometimes we use models because the alternative is unethical. Infecting humans to study disease development or disease spread falls under this category. (Regrettably, such experiments on humans were actually performed before the scientific community understood that the desire to gain knowledge did not trump the value of human [or animal] lives. Fortunately, we have learned better.)

Theories and Hypotheses

The difference between a theory and a hypothesis can be confusing—perhaps more so because in conversation we often use them interchangeably. In science, these terms are very different. It is important to help students learn to use these terms correctly, as their misuse contributes to misunderstandings about the solidity of scientific understanding in regard to such topics as evolution and human-caused climate change.

Theories

In science, a theory is an explanation for how or why something occurs. Theories take into account a large accumulation of scientific evidence. They are in effect our best explanations given the body of evidence we have at the time. Theories are dynamic: new evidence can provide support for a theory, force us to refine and revise a theory (make our explanation better), or lead us to reject a theory altogether and replace it with a new one that is consistent with all the evidence. Although it is big news when an important piece of evidence emerges that supports or refutes (calls into question) a theory, it should not be a surprise. Scientists seek important evidence like this, as the ultimate goal of science is to have the strongest explanations (theories) possible. There are many examples from the history of science where new evidence enabled us to strengthen theories, and similarly there are examples where new evidence caused scientists to propose a new theory—one that fit the evidence better. Following are a few famous examples:

◇ The ultimate goal of many physicists is a theory of everything. One of the steps along the way is verifying the Standard Model, which is a theory that goes into the tiniest particles we know and the forces between them, like electromagnetism. The Standard Model predicted the existence of a particle called the Higgs boson (nicknamed the "God particle"), and the existence of the Higgs boson explains why the building blocks of matter have mass. Theories that predicted the Higgs boson emerged in the 1960s, and it wasn't until half a century later that new technology (the Large Hadron Collider mentioned earlier) allowed us to verify the existence of the Higgs boson—and strengthen the Standard Model.

◇ The Copernican Revolution, which established that Earth orbits the sun, spanned centuries. For a long time, people believed that everything in the sky—sun, moon, and stars—orbited Earth in circles. Then some astronomers noticed that some things in the sky, like the planet Mars, didn't exactly move in circles—these celestial bodies even appeared to reverse direction at times. Astronomers weren't ready to give up the Earth-centric model and, to make the evidence fit their model, they had to go so far as to propose strange orbit shapes that kept Earth at the center of the universe. One of the most important pieces of evidence to dent the old geocentric theory was Galileo's discovery and observation of four of Jupiter's moons. The paths these moons traveled in Earth's sky were so irregular that many astronomers changed their mind. There was no geocentric hypothesis they could sensibly propose that would take into account these orbits, thus they came to accept the idea that these moons orbited Jupiter, and Jupiter orbited the sun.

Hypotheses

Like theories, hypotheses also seek to explain phenomena. They differ from theories in many ways, however. Whereas a theory is a broad explanation of some aspect of how the world works (such as evolution), a hypothesis is much more specific (for example, the hypothesis that chickens are related to dinosaurs). Theories are based on an accumulation of evidence, whereas hypotheses are much more tentative—they help us formulate the logical next step in an investigation designed to further our knowledge.

There are some key features of hypotheses:

◇ **Hypotheses must be testable.** Testing a hypothesis gives us important information that may support or refute the hypothesis. Although it can seem like splitting hairs, we want to move away from the language that a hypothesis is "wrong." The evidence either does or does not support a hypothesis, and if it doesn't, we come up with a new hypothesis and test that one.

◇ Put another way, **hypotheses must be falsifiable.** In science, everything must be questionable as we take into account new evidence. Because of this principle, we can't prove anything as absolutely true. We can, however, prove things as false (which then leads us to consider an alternative theory as closer to the truth). So, when we say we should be able to test a hypothesis, we mean that we must be able to show that it is false.

◇ **Hypotheses should be as simple as possible.** The idea that hypotheses should be simple dates back to the Middle Ages (or earlier). It is famously attributed to William of Occam, who argued that when deciding among competing hypotheses, one should select the simplest (the hypothesis that relies on the fewest assumptions). This idea is an important one and continues into modern times. (Occam's razor, as the principle is known, is often stated as, "All things being equal, the simplest explanation tends to be the right one." This particular phrasing was popularized by the movie *Contact,* based on Carl Sagan's novel.)

◇ Albert Einstein put a limit on Occam's razor when he said, "It can scarcely be denied that the supreme goal of all theory is to make the irreducible basic elements as simple and as few as possible without having to surrender the adequate representation of a single datum of experience." There is irony in the fact that Einstein used this decidedly not simple sentence to say that **hypotheses (and theories) should be consistent with all observations.** A theory too simple to explain observations is no good, and a hypothesis inconsistent with any previous observation is invalid from the start. (The saying "Everything should be made as simple as possible, but no simpler" may have come from Einstein's statement just given, and is often called Einstein's razor.)

Returning to the idea of specificity of language, you may commonly hear people say something like, "This batch of cookies did not turn out right. My theory is that I added too much butter." But this statement is not a theory because it is very limited in scope and is not based on much evidence (though perhaps it is based on prior observation). It is testable, however, and so is a reasonable hypothesis for why the cookies did not turn out as hoped. We encourage you to be specific in your language when using the terms "hypothesis" and "theory"—in both scientific and nonscientific contexts. This will help your students understand these terms and appropriately apply them to their work.

Variables

Understanding variables is a critical part of doing science and engineering. In short, variables are the things that can be varied or changed in an experiment. An experiment typically seeks to test whether changing A has an effect on B. As an example, students could test whether changing the time they leave their house in the morning has an effect on the time they arrive at school. To make any conclusions from such an experiment, it is important that students (as much as possible) only change one variable—the time they leave. If, in addition to changing the time they leave, they take a different route, they will not be able to make conclusions about the impact of changing the time on the time they arrive at school, because they will not—in this experiment—be able to distinguish between the effect of changing the time and the effect of changing the route.

Although the example just given is fairly obvious, there are lots of other little variables that can be harder to control for in any experimental system. With arrival time, these include walking alone or with friends, climbing a tree, stopping at a convenience store, and more. It is a useful exercise to identify possible variables before starting any experiment, and to explicitly think about ways to isolate or limit the number of variables that will be changed in the experiment.

The terms "independent variable" and "dependent variable" are an important part of the scientific vocabulary, but are often confusing. In an experimental system, the independent variable is the one that is changed by the experimenter (in the earlier example, it is the time the student leaves the house). The experimenter then tests whether the independent variable has an effect on the dependent variable. In the preceding example, we are asking whether the arrival time (dependent variable) depends on the departure time (independent variable).

ACKNOWLEDGMENTS

LIKE ALL 826 NATIONAL PROJECTS, THIS BOOK WAS MADE POSSIBLE BY THE contributions of an incredibly creative and generous group of people who were kind enough to share their time and talents. Everything starts somewhere, and we should start by thanking the leadership and staff (current and former) at the Clinton Global Initiative (CGI), which brought 826 National and Time Warner Cable (TWC) together. Many thanks to President Bill Clinton; Alex Reeves, Director of CGI America; Hayley Kallenberg, correspondence and marketing senior associate at CGI; and Nate Madsen, formerly of CGI and current Chief of Staff at US2020. We're especially grateful to our project partners at TWC for their shared vision for and support of the project, including Dave Borchardt, Tara DeGeorges, Iris Duran, Jon Hulsey, Shamicka Jones, Karen Lacava, Kim Latour, Vickie Minor, and Maryanne Ravenel. Special thanks to Tessie Topol and Leah Gutstadt, our lead partners throughout the project.

For her work and advising on the pilot projects at 826 chapters in 2012, including collaboration on "It's (Partially) Rocket Science and (Mostly) Ice Cream," we thank Carol Tang and the Coalition for Science After School. In piloting these workshops outside of 826 chapters, we had the pleasure of working with Ajibola Adepoju and her team at Operation Breakthrough in Kansas City, Missouri, and we are grateful for all of their enthusiasm and communication throughout the collaboration. We are similarly grateful to Shakira O'Kane of the YMCA of Greater New York and to Shakima Figuera-Collins and her team at Flushing YMCA Beacon Center, where a summer pilot was also launched.

Thanks, also, to the executive directors of all the 826 chapters, and to the many staffers who helped and contributed, especially Erin Archuleta, Jen Benka, Lauren Broder, Catherine Calabro, Zach Duffy, Jessica Drench, Pedro Estrada, Jorge Garcia, Joan Kim, Ryan Lewis, Mariama Lockington, Kristin Lorey, Karen Sama, Kait Steele, Eric Stensvaag, and Amy Sumerton. For his epic and inspired work throughout the project, including original lessons and thoughtful revisions, we thank 826LA Director of Education Julius Diaz Panoriñgan. We also thank Rebecca Smith, PhD, and the Science & Health Education Partnership at the University of California, San Francisco, for input and expertise throughout the project, from pilot collaboration on "It's (Partially) Rocket Science and (Mostly) Ice Cream" and "The Science of Superpowers," her work on the background content for instructors, to the contribution of our STEM@Home activities, which we can't get enough of. Truly, we could not have asked for better lab partners.

Thanks to the visionary volunteers who help us offer innovative and engaging programming at all of our chapters. A special thanks to those who led new iterations of the STEM and creative writing workshops and offered valuable input in preparation for the book, including Aneesha Badrinarian, Jim Ottaviani, Jeff Shi, and Jaci Thomas. Thanks to the very talented Kersey Barrett-Tormey for her artwork. Great thanks to everyone at Jossey-Bass, especially Kate Gagnon, Tracy Gallagher, Justin Frahm, and Francie Jones. Finally, thanks to our brilliant lesson plan contributors, the ultimate catalysts of creativity. We tip our beakers and take off our pen caps to each of them, and to all their work that continues to inspire.

THE AUTHORS

826 NATIONAL IS A NETWORK OF NONPROFIT ORGANIZATIONS DEDICATED TO supporting students, ages six to eighteen, through opportunities to explore their creativity and writing skills. 826 chapters are located in San Francisco, New York, Los Angeles, Chicago, Ann Arbor/Detroit, Boston, and Washington, DC. The services of each 826 chapter are based on the understanding that great leaps in learning can happen with one-on-one attention, and that strong writing skills are fundamental to future success. 826 offers innovative and dynamic project-based learning opportunities, building on students' classroom experience and strengthening their ability to express ideas effectively, creatively, confidently, and in their own voice. Each 826 chapter offers after-school tutoring, field trips, workshops, and in-school programs—all free of charge—for students, classes, and schools.

Jennifer Traig is the author of the memoirs *Devil in the Details* and *Well Enough Alone,* and the editor of *The Autobiographer's Handbook.* A longtime 826 volunteer, she has a PhD in literature and lives in Ann Arbor, where she serves on the board of directors for 826michigan.

826's History

Since its founding in San Francisco in 2002 by award-winning author Dave Eggers and award-winning educator Nínive Calegari, 826 has sparked students' imaginations. 826 Valencia, our flagship chapter, grew out of a desire to partner the professional literary and arts community of San Francisco with local students in need of engaging learning opportunities. The tutoring and writing center was designed to be a vibrant setting for rigorous educational activities. Connecting students with local authors, artists, and college students while providing a space that is whimsical and fun has proved to be an excellent model for achieving results, and the idea was replicated in cities nationwide.

Each of our writing and tutoring centers welcomes students through a unique storefront with a fanciful theme. These inviting spaces create an exciting and safe learning environment in which students feel encouraged to be creative. Although each center has a different theme (in Los Angeles students are encouraged to dabble in time travel, whereas in Chicago they may begin their future career as a spy), the 826 model always holds true: if you offer students rigorous and fun learning opportunities and one-on-one attention, they will make great strides in their writing skills and confidence.

In 2008 a national office was established to serve the growing network of chapters by maintaining the brand, developing evaluation systems, coordinating national press and marketing initiatives, building a base of national supporters, ensuring programmatic quality and consistency, and overseeing replication of the 826 model. 826 National is the hub of the 826 network. It is an independent nonprofit organization that provides strategic leadership, administration, and other resources to ensure the success of its network of writing and tutoring centers.

Our Student Programming

Each year, 826 collectively provides more than thirty thousand students from underresourced families and low-performing school districts with one-on-one tutoring, writing instruction, classroom support, and a wide variety of publishing opportunities. We give students high-quality, engaging, and hands-on literary programming. The result: better writing, improved grades, stronger community ties between young people and professional adults, and brighter futures.

All 826 chapters offer the following:

◇ After-school tutoring: Neighborhood students receive free, one-on-one tutoring up to five days a week in all subject areas at each center. 826 National's tutoring program is designed to inspire learning, foster creativity, and help students understand and complete their homework each day. We accomplish this by giving youth—particularly low-income youth—free access to invaluable academic assistance.

◇ Workshops: Our free workshops foster creativity and strengthen writing skills in a variety of areas. All offerings directly support classroom curricula while engaging students with imaginative and often playful themes. Workshops are project based and taught by experienced, accomplished literary professionals. Examples of workshops include "Writing for Pets" (just what it sounds like!); "Mad Science," in which students, wearing lab coats, isolate strands of their own DNA and then write stories about their DNA mutating in strange ways; "How to Persuade Your Parents, or: Whining Effectively"; "Spy Training"; and "How to Write a Comic Book," taught by a professional cartoonist.

◇ Publishing: 826 publishes an array of student-authored literary quarterlies, newspapers, books, chapbooks, and anthologies, which are displayed and sold in the retail shops that front our writing centers and also are distributed and sold nationwide. We use professional editors and designers to allow the students' work to shine. Our most significant student collaboration each year, the Young Authors' Book Project, partners a local high school classroom with professional writers and editors. The students spend three to four months crafting essays around a particular theme, continuously collaborating with adult tutors through the editing and publishing process. When the project is complete, we celebrate the release with a festive party. The final book is a stunning reflection of months of hard work, engagement, and dedication on the part of the students and tutors.

◇ Field trips: Several times a week, entire public school classes journey to our writing centers for two-hour, interactive, high-energy writing events, like our signature Storytelling and Bookmaking program. As a group, students compose an original story, crafting plot points and characters. Students return home with personalized books, not to mention a deepened understanding of storytelling, bookmaking, and collaboration.

◇ In-school projects: We dispatch teams of volunteers into local, high-need public schools to support teachers and provide students with one-on-one assistance as they tackle various writing projects, such as school newspapers, research papers, oral histories, and college entrance essays. We know the quality of student work is greatly enhanced when it will be shared with an authentic audience, so 826 is committed to publishing our students' work in quarterlies, chapbooks, and 'zines.

Our five thousand volunteers make our work possible and our programs free of charge. They are local community residents, including professional writers, artists, college students, parents, bankers, lawyers, and retirees from a wide range of professions. These passionate individuals are found at our centers throughout the day, sitting side by side with our students after school, supporting morning field trips, and helping entire classrooms of students learn the art of writing. Our volunteers actively connect with youth every day.

If you would like to get involved in programs as a tutor or as a donor, please go to the 826 National website, *www.826national.org*, to find out more, or visit one of our chapter websites (the full list can be found in the appendix).

THE CONTRIBUTORS

KERSEY BARRETT-TORMEY grew up in Mill Valley, California, drawing and writing her own short stories from an early age. In 2010 she graduated from California Institute of the Arts with a BFA in Experimental Animation. She currently resides in the Bay Area, popping up in galleries from San Francisco all the way down to LA. When she isn't working from her big imagination, writing songs, illustrating her own children's books and making short animated films, she enjoys going on adventures with her friends and inspiring others to make art! You can see more of her work at www.kerseybarrett-tormey.com.

LAUREN BRODER is the Director of Research and Evaluation at 826 National, where she helps promote the growth of the organization through developing and administering evaluation metrics to understand the impact of the inspiring programming occurring nationwide. Lauren has always been drawn to helping children and young adults realize their full potential, which led her to pursue and earn her doctorate in developmental psychology. Her everyday superpowers include statistical analysis skills, data management prowess, and precision yoga-ing.

EMILY CLADER received her PhD in mathematics from the University of Michigan in May 2014. In addition to her work in a research program that delves into connections between geometry and string theory, she loves to communicate math through teaching and writing, as well as to create music in a variety of ways. Her latest adventure is moving to Switzerland, where she is doing a postdoctoral fellowship at the ETH Zürich.

CORY DOCTOROW (*www.craphound.com*) is a science fiction author, activist, journalist, and blogger. He is the coeditor of *Boing Boing* (*www.boingboing.net*) and the author of young adult novels like *Homeland, Pirate Cinema,* and *Little Brother,* and novels for adults like *Rapture of the Nerds* and *Makers.* He is the former European director of the Electronic Frontier Foundation, and he cofounded the UK Open Rights Group. Born in Toronto, Canada, he now lives in London.

KEVIN HAINLINE is an astronomer whose work focuses on galaxy evolution and supermassive black holes. He explores how the light and energy released as gas falls onto a black hole can affect the surrounding galaxy, both nearby and at vast cosmic distances. He also brings science education to the public through planetarium and museum outreach, and writes and records podcasts about science at *www.thestarsconnectus.com.* He's very enthusiastic.

PETER CALHOUN HALL is an artist and law student based in Brooklyn, New York, where he leads the Building Workshop at 826. Alex Trebek seemed to like his art program when they discussed it on *Jeopardy.* More important, John Hodgman spoke to Peter at least twice during the 826 Trivia Night. Everything Peter knows about good teaching he learned from Jess Berenblum,

Sam Otter, and Walter Shandy. His hobbies include diagrams, poems and experiments, illustration, repeating himself, sentences, graph paper, blue pencils, pinnipeds, repeating himself, the codevelopment of the nineteenth-century scientific episteme and Anglo-American legal theory on the validity of evidence, dogs, pizza, and cool tree branches.

DANIEL JOHNSON is a poet, an educator, and the founding Executive Director of 826 Boston and the Greater Boston Bigfoot Research Institute. He served as a bilingual elementary teacher in Phoenix, Arizona, with Teach For America, where, in the name of science, he lit money on fire, mummified chickens, and dissected cow eyeballs with his fifth and sixth graders. Daniel has worked in arts education for over a decade, including stints at Snow City Arts Foundation and Association House of Chicago. He is the author of *How to Catch a Falling Knife,* a collection of poems published by Alice James Books.

MAI LE grew up interested in math, science, art, and reading. Her favorite books were *A Wrinkle in Time,* the Harry Potter series, *Ender's Game,* and any historical fiction where a young heroine got to go on an adventure. Mai studied electrical engineering at Stanford, where she joined the Society of Women Engineers (SWE), leading engineering activities for K–12 students. During this time, she served as an editor for a campus literary arts magazine and learned how powerful creative writing can be. She then joined the University of Michigan PhD program, and now serves as outreach cochair for Grad SWE. Their partnership with 826michigan has been fantastic, and they are excited to keep working with 826.

MARIAMA J. LOCKINGTON is a writer and educator living in Brooklyn, New York. She is the former Operations Manager for 826 National and currently works as the Director of Education for 826NYC. Mariama has a master's in education from Lesley University, and an MFA in poetry from San Francisco State University. In addition to her work with youth, Mariama is a published poet and performer.

JULIUS DIAZ PANORIŃGAN graduated from Stanford University with a degree in mathematical and computational science; he is now Director of Education at 826LA. He isn't sure whether his time in these seemingly radically different backgrounds is a cause or a symptom of his affinity for interdisciplinary education. Julius helps cook up 826LA's madcap writing workshops, which interconnect as many fields as possible. As of late, he's enjoyed working with everyone at 826LA and 826 National on curricula interweaving STEM and writing, two things near and dear to his heart.

CHRIS PECK was a program intern at 826 Boston in 2012 while attending Emerson College. In 2013 he earned his BFA in writing, literature, and publishing with a concentration in short fiction. Chris has a tremendous sense of pride over the work he did with 826 Boston and the youth the chapter serves. His fondest memories have to do with the curricula he was able to develop, whether it was his lesson on water filtration at the Summer Science Camp or his lesson on writing a survival guide as part of a series on creative writing. Chris currently is working on his master's degree in English education and will be certified to teach English in 2015. He can't thank 826 enough for inspiring him to instill passion for writing and reading in our youth.

DANIEL RECK is a PhD student in economics at the University of Michigan in Ann Arbor. His research concerns the importance of information, attention, and perception in the design of public policy, especially tax policy. He lives in Ann Arbor and volunteers at 826michigan. Prior to coming to Michigan, Daniel studied economics, mathematics, and psychology at the University of Oklahoma.

A. REID is an artist, writer, and educator in Worcester, Massachusetts, operating under the idea that making art can be a rigorous way of learning and doing work—even when it is fun. A 2010 alum of the Studio for Interrelated Media at MassArt, she has participated in residencies with Cabin Time, Grin City, and Have Company, among others, and has exhibited work throughout the United States. She is a Worcester Farm to School volunteer, an American Pie Council amateur-level member, a letterpress printer at AS220, a household fermentation specialist, and a maple syrup producer. She currently works as an audio describer for the Museum of Fine Arts, Boston.

GERALD RICHARDS is the CEO of 826 National, with more than twenty years of management and development experience at national nonprofit organizations. His nonprofit career has included positions with the Network for Teaching Entrepreneurship; the United Negro College Fund; the University of California, San Francisco; the J. David Gladstone Institutes; Chicago Panel on Social Policy; and the Cradle Foundation. Gerald is a respected trainer and sought-after speaker on topics of youth and education access. He has also served as an education expert for national marketing campaigns promoting creativity in and outside the classroom. He currently serves on the boards of the International Development Exchange (IDEX), Mission SF Community Financial Center, and the Woodland School, and previously served on the boards of Juma Ventures and KIPP SF Bay Academy. Gerald has a BA in film studies from Wesleyan University and an MFA in writing from the School of the Art Institute of Chicago.

KAREN SAMA grew up in Queens, New York, holds a bachelor's degree in religion, and worked with preschoolers with special needs for eight years in Denver, Colorado. She is a Program Manager in her sixth year at 826 Boston in Roxbury. Her favorite student achievements from Science and Writing Camp include peacefully solving international conflicts between newly formed countries via water balloon wars using homemade catapults; building platypus-proof temporary shelters in the rain during the Survival Games; writing incantations to protect newly buried, mummified chickens; and exposing a cryptozoological huckster using knowledge of the evolutionary adaptations of birds. She's a lucky lady.

REBECCA SMITH is codirector of the Science & Health Education Partnership (SEP) at the University of California, San Francisco, where she supports science teaching and learning in public schools. She has extensive experience developing and implementing teacher-scientist partnership programs, teaching doctoral students and postdoctoral fellows, and leading professional development for teachers. Through her work with SEP, Rebecca has designed innovative learning experiences that engage students, from youths to adults, as scientists in the classroom, helping them discover big ideas in science and learn how to think critically and make conclusions using evidence. She has also served as an adviser to out-of-school programs seeking to incorporate opportunities for STEM learning into their programming.

KAIT STEELE is the Director of Field Operations at 826 National. Kait was a founding member of 826CHI, serving as the organization's first Programs Coordinator and later as Director of Education. Prior to joining 826, she studied creative writing at Northwestern University and worked at Woodstock School in India. Kait spends much of her time being awed and inspired by the profound, hilarious, and powerful words of student writers, and by the volunteers and staff who support their creativity each day. Of note, at the time of this publication there are 814 documents containing the word "zombie" on her computer.

TESSIE TOPOL is Vice President of Corporate Social Responsibility (CSR) at Time Warner Cable (TWC), where she is responsible for the company's overall CSR strategy and programs, including TWC's signature philanthropic initiative, Connect a Million Minds (CAMM). CAMM is the company's $100 million cash and in-kind commitment to inspire student interest in science, technology, engineering, and math. The initiative has won multiple awards and in 2013 was inducted into *PR News Magazine*'s Hall of Fame as a Best-in-Class Communications Initiative. Before TWC, Tessie served as director of strategic partnerships and public affairs at MTV, which she joined after ten years in the nonprofit and government sectors. Tessie holds a master's degree in international affairs from the School of International and Public Affairs and a certificate from the Harriman Institute of Russian, Eurasian, and Eastern European Studies, both at Columbia University. She received her undergraduate degree in political science from the University of Pennsylvania, where she graduated magna cum laude and Phi Beta Kappa.

THE SCIENCE OF SAVING DAYLIGHT

BASED ON THE ORIGINAL WORKSHOP BY KEVIN HAINLINE

1 SESSION, 2 HOURS OR MORE
STEM DISCIPLINES: *General introduction to science, communication, the scientific method, and science writing*
WRITING ACTIVITY: *Technical writing*

MANY STUDENTS ARE TURNED OFF BY science classes that overemphasize the memorization of facts. Now, a lot of people (including those of us at 826) think that knowing these established scientific tidbits is supercool. What's even cooler, though, is discovery: the use of this information to solve problems (as in engineering), or to further advance our knowledge (via the sciences).

In this lesson, we take a step back from the facts and focus instead on the process: the scientific method. As an added bonus, students will work on another essential scientific practice: communication, both written and oral.

This lesson introduces students to the scientific method and the fun of making discoveries. To make things easy for you, we've provided a subject (daylight saving time) and slides to guide the lesson, but you should feel free to change things up as you see fit. Follow the steps as suggested or do them in a completely different order. The slides can be printed and photocopied, or downloaded and then projected from a computer. Skip the slides or customize them. Investigate daylight saving time or another important scientific subject, like why dogs kick when you scratch their belly, or whether the five-second rule for dropped food is valid. The point is just to get students to generate and test hypotheses and talk about their findings.

> **MATERIALS**
>
> ☐ Slides (See the thumbnails; slides are also available for download at *www.wiley.com/go/826stem*)
>
> ☐ A computer to show video clips
>
> ☐ Digital projector (optional, but helpful)
>
> ☐ Lab coat (optional)

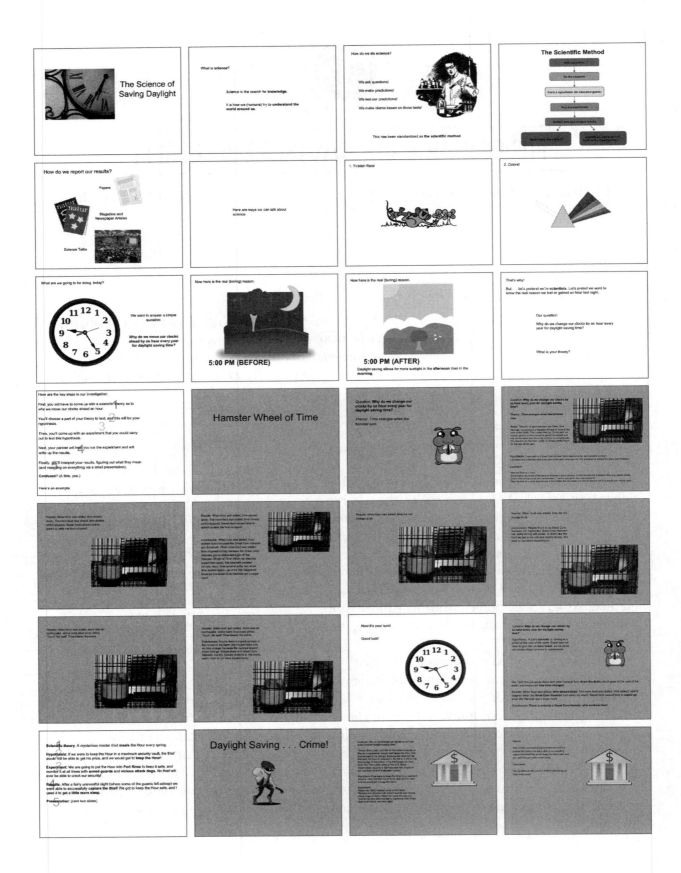

Introduction (15 minutes)

Using the slides as a guide, start by talking about science, the scientific method, and how scientists "do" science: a scientist's job is to observe, make a hypothesis about the way the world works, create and run an experiment to test this hypothesis, and finally interpret and present the results in some way. (Note that the common use of "theory" lines up better with the scientific use of "hypothesis." You'll want to use the right terms at the right times throughout this lesson. For more on theories and hypotheses, see the Science-O-Pedia.) Make sure to emphasize the last point—describing how scientists write up results in academic papers and magazine and newspaper articles, and also give talks—to make sure your budding scientists know that they need to be able to communicate the things they discover.

Next, show the students two video examples of science experiments.[1] Then ask them to identify the hypothesis in either one, and explain how the "experiments" looked at these hypotheses.

Scientific Challenge Accepted! (5 minutes)

Then, introduce the big problem that students are going to tackle: Why do we move our clocks by an hour for daylight saving time? Give them the real reason (to increase the length of daylight during waking hours), but then challenge them to come up with a new and interesting hypothesis, and a test for this hypothesis. The slides offer a sample hypothesis (the Hamster Wheel of Time theory).

Developing Theories and Hypotheses (20 minutes)

Now the students will think up their own theory for why time changes at the beginning and end of daylight saving time. Hopefully, the Hamster Wheel of Time theory (or an alternate theory) has gotten the students excited about this activity. Having students work in groups here will help, especially if you don't have extra adults. Individual creativity can spur the creativity of other group members. Encourage students to think of lots of possible theories, and to be as out there as possible. Really, they can come up with almost anything they want as an explanation, and even the most ridiculous things will work out (and provide some valuable insight into hypothesis formulation and experiment design).

When writing a theory, students should be as specific and descriptive as possible, particularly about the mechanisms of the theory. They can and should refine their theory to make it better (as with the "theory" and "better theory" examples in the slides). The more specific and detailed the theory, the easier it will be to identify parts to test!

Once that's done, it's time for the students to make a hypothesis about their theory, and design an experiment to test it (each student should do this individually, rather than in groups). Things start to get tricky here. One of the most important qualities of a scientific theory, and of a hypothesis by extension, is that it is testable and falsifiable—that it can be proven wrong. When devising a hypothesis, its scope must be sufficiently narrow; otherwise, it's hard to test. The whole of the theory of evolution, for example, is not a good hypothesis. The hypothesis that hippos and manatees have a common ancestor is,[2] however, and testing a hypothesis like this would add either evidence to

---

1. We recommend these two videos: (1) tickling rats for science (*www.youtube.com/watch?v=j-admRGFVNM*), and (2) Bill Nye the Science Guy on prisms (*www.youtube.com/watch?v=gtgBHsSzCPE*).

2. Actually, current research shows that hippos are closely related to whales, and manatees are closely related to elephants, relatively speaking.

support a given theory or evidence against it. (In the latter case, the theory would change and potentially even be discarded entirely, should sufficient evidence be built up.)

To help your students pick one part of their theory from which to make a hypothesis, ask them the following questions:

◇ Which part of your theory are you the least sure of?

◇ Which part of your theory is most likely to be questioned by others, or is hardest to believe?

◇ Which part of your theory is the most fantastic or interesting?

Often, but not always, hypotheses take on an "If . . . then . . ." format: "If I do *this* test, then *this* will happen." Note that there's actually a second, assumed "if": "If I do this test—*and if this part of the theory is true*—then this will happen." Put another way, the hypothesis says what will happen assuming the underlying theory is true, so if the hypothesis is falsified, the related parts of the theory will need to be reexamined.

Designing an experiment often goes hand in hand with making a hypothesis. When we design an experiment, we want to clearly spell out the steps we will take to verify or falsify the hypothesis, and we want to specify the results we'd expect if our hypothesis were true or false.

"Running" the Experiment (10 minutes)

At this point, stop. Return to the slides, and ask students what they thought would happen in the Hamster Wheel of Time (or other) experiment. The slides give a couple of different scenarios for things that might happen when the experiment is "run," including possible interpretations of each.

The more unpredictable this section of the lesson is, the better. You can ask your students to supply alternate interpretations of the results provided in the slides. They can give you different results for the experiment, and you can work on interpreting those results on the spot. (Struggling through this is okay; it'll model what your students will do, and what scientists do.) You can also suggest wild results, and have your students suggest interpretations!

After the discussion, have students hand over their experiment design to a partner, who will "run" the experiment and give his or her partner details on the "results" of the experiment. This segment illustrates the collaborative nature of science (it's really important for scientists to be able to run other scientists' experiments for themselves), and will help create more variables that will make the rest of the procedure more exciting. Let students know that sometimes experiments will generate the expected results (time slowed down!), and sometimes the exact opposite is what they will get (there was no change in time). And sometimes there will be a seemingly random result (like a giant "Ouch!" from the core of the earth).

Coming to Conclusions (10 minutes)

This next part teaches the kids the importance of figuring out what the results actually mean. (*Science secret:* This is what scientists spend 99.99 percent of their time doing. It takes time to run experiments and gather observations, but figuring out what those results actually mean is much more difficult and time consuming.) Students should now return the data to the original student who devised the experiment. Each student will then interpret the results written up by his or her partner and come up with a conclusion that explains everything. If students have time, they can and should draw a figure that will help illustrate and explain their results.

Presentations (60 minutes or more)

We suggest that you spend at least an hour on student presentations, which should fill whatever time you have left. Communication is a critical part of science, but one to which students often have little exposure. We suggest using a "scientific conference" format that will give every student a chance to present his or her work. This will probably take an entire class period (or more). Decide on how much time each presenter will have, and remind students of the structure of scientific presentations (present the question or hypothesis you were studying, present your experimental approach, summarize data without interpretation so others can draw their own conclusions, then share the conclusions you derived from the data). This is a great opportunity for students to develop their oral communication skills, and to use evidence to back up their conclusions.

Isaac Newton once remarked, "If I have seen further it is by standing on the shoulders of giants," meaning that his contributions to science relied on those of others before him. Science builds on itself, and good communication makes that process much easier. Good communication allows scientists to check and validate others' work, and it enables collaboration that yields new hypotheses and theories.

In this part of the lesson, students practice their scientific communication skills. Students can place their results on chart paper, which they can use to present their findings, or they can just present them verbally. In general, they'll report on some of the key points in their process, making sure to emphasize any surprising results and resultant interesting conclusions. During these talks, you get to act as moderator and emcee.

Introduce each student (give students an option to wear a lab coat, if you've got one available), and turn the floor over to him or her, putting up or pulling down chart paper if necessary. Students get a kick out of presenting their whimsical hypotheses, experiments, and conclusions. After each student finishes, open up the floor for questions (this allows for both more silliness and more critical thought). Don't forget that you can ask questions yourself, as moderator. Ask for better explanations, with questions along the lines of the following:

◇ What made you want to do this experiment?

◇ Can you tell me more about this part of your experiment?

◇ This portion of your experiment is very interesting. How did you come up with it?

◇ Why, and how, did you do this part of your experiment?

◇ How did you come up with your (scientific) method?

For example, say a student proposed that the reason we move the clocks ahead by a certain amount is that the sun is actually changing mass, causing a shift in Earth's orbit around the sun, thus resulting in the need to correct our clocks. Say that the student's proposed experiment involved looking at Jupiter to see if it was also changing. A question that fits into the first camp would be, Can you explain how you measured Jupiter's position, and how you know how far away it is?

You can help students digest the science behind their presentations and take the next step, with questions like these:

◇ What is your evidence for your conclusion?

◇ What doesn't your conclusion explain about [some ignored result]?

◇ Your results could also be explained by [some alternate conclusion]. What made you decide on your conclusion rather than [some alternate conclusion]?

◇ Your conclusion seems to imply [this]. What kind of experiment could you run to test that?

◇ How would your results translate to similar situations?

◇ What do your findings imply for the future?

◇ What other questions about your theory do you want to answer?

◇ What are your next steps in this investigation?

Again, going with the Jupiter experiment, some good questions to ask might be, Do you think that this is happening to any other stars? What do you think will happen in the far distant future? Do you think that this will get worse or better?

These queries neatly echo the types of questions that generally come up in science talks. Students tend to be good with the first kind of question (the explaining kind); the second (of the big picture and next steps variety) is more of a challenge that appropriately gets at the heart of the scientific method.

Please note that when you're modeling questions and comments, you should be as constructive as possible. In science, questions are a necessity; they can help the asker understand things, and also help the askee reassess his or her thinking. It's important to recognize the difference between questioning an idea and questioning the person who came up with the idea; the former is scientific, the latter, not so much. To help make this distinction clear to students, be sure to specifically address positives in their fictional experiments whenever you challenge other parts of their process. That way, it's less likely that they'll perceive such challenges as personal attacks, and more likely that they'll see them as invitations to further the scientific exchange.

Don't forget to applaud each scientist after the Q&A!

FOR YOU TO KNOW (AND YOUR STUDENTS TO DISCOVER)

It is likely that you remember, probably sometime between third and sixth grade, having to memorize the scientific method (at least once) at the start of the school year. At the time, your teacher (or a textbook) presented a linear sequence of steps that was something like this: Question → Research → Hypothesis → Experiment → Data collection → Data analysis → Conclusions. Done.

As it turns out, this sequence is really a boiled-down version of the scientific method. Scientists don't use just one "method," and they don't always follow the steps in the same linear order. But most scientists would agree on the core ideas.[3]

Scientists ask questions—lots of them. These questions can come out of their own experiments and observations, from looking at other scientists' data, from conversations with other scientists, or . . . the list goes on and on. From a question, scientists will try to figure out an answer.

3. An interactive graphic that provides more details about how the scientific method works is available at *http://undsci.berkeley.edu/article/scienceflowchart*.

This process can involve research of the kind students do all the time—looking up what is known about the topic. It can involve observing the world around them, or collecting specimens (as a botanist or paleontologist might do); sometimes it leads to a hypothesis, or it can lead directly to an experiment.

When scientists do experiments, they always collect data, and they have to analyze the data to understand what an experiment is telling them (to come to a conclusion). Few sets of experimental data fit the original hypothesis perfectly, and it is the scientists' job to explain why: Was the original hypothesis fundamentally flawed? Did we make a mistake in the way we ran the experiment? Is a "special" scenario more (or less) common than we thought? Do we have to experiment some more to explain the outliers in the data? (Probably.) One of the really important ideas about how science is done is that it doesn't end here. When scientists have a conclusion, they do not pack up and go home.

This lesson can't possibly go into depth on the entire scientific method, or even all of the steps in one of the usual formulations. Here, we choose to focus on hypotheses—generating them, testing them, and building on theories based on the results of those tests. Hypotheses are essential to the scientific method; they are the bridge between pure curiosity and science.

Communication is a very, very important part of science. When scientists make a conclusion, they share it with other scientists. This may not be done after every experiment. Scientists often will wait until they have finished a group of experiments that collectively help answer a question or tell a story about how something in the world works. Scientists share their findings in many different ways. They informally share results with those who work closely with them over coffee, in the hallway, or in a setting called a lab meeting. They also share more formally by writing papers (including a summary of their question, what was known before about the topic, their experiments, results, and the conclusions they drew from these results) that are published in scientific journals or by giving presentations at conferences. In all of these settings, other scientists ask lots of questions about the results and about how the experiments were done, and will often challenge one another about what conclusions can be made from these experiments. This process helps ensure that scientists' interpretations of the results are based on evidence rather than bias, and helps rule out alternative explanations for the results. All of this—although a lot of work—is an important part of the scientific process.

Based on the results from one experiment or a group of experiments, scientists will often revise their hypothesis, which usually leads to more questions and more experiments. This process keeps going and going. As a result, answering one scientific question can lead to many more questions and ultimately a much deeper understanding of the topic that the scientists set out to investigate. The other very cool and exciting thing about this is that there is always something left to discover.

Textbooks often present scientific knowledge as a list of facts, leading students to believe that everything in science has been discovered. In reality, the opposite is true. Every individual discovery that we make opens the doors to many other questions and ultimately more possible discoveries. The sum of these discoveries together builds scientific knowledge.

STEM@HOME: THE BLACK BOX OF SCIENCE

Scientists of all disciplines (biology, physics, astronomy, chemistry, and so on) study how the world around us works, which often requires investigating things they cannot see. Tricky, right? It is, but there are some ways around this problem. In some cases, scientists can use tools that extend their senses—for example, to help them see very small things. A microscope is one such tool. Often, though, a microscope is still not enough. We cannot directly see the atoms that make up all the "stuff" (scientists call this stuff **matter**) in our universe or the proteins that do important jobs in our cells to keep us alive. When this happens, scientists have to rely on indirect information.

Were you ever dying to figure out what was in a wrapped present with your name on it? Did you shake the box? This is an example of an experiment that gave you indirect information. From shaking it, you could get an idea of whether there was one large piece or lots of small pieces. Perhaps you could tell what the pieces were made of based on the sounds they made. From these sounds, you made a prediction about what was inside. At some point, you probably got to open the box.

Scientists almost never get to open the box to look inside and see if their "guess" was correct. When scientists are figuring out how something that they cannot see works, they do an experiment, and the results of this experiment help them construct a model of what is happening. With that information, they will design another experiment. Sometimes this second experiment will confirm their first idea. Other times it will give them clues that they are on the wrong track. And so, over time, with lots and lots of experiments, scientists can develop a good explanation for a phenomenon. They are also always aware that as they gather more information by doing more experiments, they will probably have to revise their explanation.

Make Your Own Black Box!

Test your family members or friends to see how good they are at figuring out something they cannot see by building your own black box of science.

Materials

- ☐ A small box (a shoe box, cereal box, or other package box)
- ☐ A small ball (a bouncy ball or Ping-Pong ball)
- ☐ Tape or glue
- ☐ Distractions (extra pieces of cardboard, cotton balls, a piece of old hose, a funnel, or anything else you can think of that will make figuring out what the inside of your box looks like more challenging)

Devise a Plan

Your goal is to build a mystery box that you'll give to someone else (mother, father, brother, sister, friend). That person will try to figure out the "landscape" of the inside of the box—without looking inside.

(continued)

STEM@HOME: THE BLACK BOX OF SCIENCE (continued)

There are lots of ways to build your box. For instance, you could just put the ball in the box and seal it. Chances are, though, that your family member or friend will guess pretty quickly that there is a ball in the box. So, make it more interesting. This is where the distractions come in:

- What if you glued or taped a cardboard wall inside, essentially making the box smaller? What do you think would happen when someone shook the box gently? What would he or she notice?

- What if you put a hole somewhere in that wall? What if you put a funnel in the hole?

- What if you covered the walls of the box with cotton balls? Would the ball roll quickly or slowly?

- What if there was a maze for the ball to follow inside the box?

There are endless possibilities for your box. See what else you can think of and start building!

Have Someone Test Your Box

Give your box to a friend or family member and challenge him or her to figure out what the inside looks like *without peeking*!

Let this person do a couple of experiments with the box, then ask him or her what he or she is thinking. Does this person have any guesses about what the inside of the box is like?

Give this person the box again, so that he or she can conduct a few more tests. Ask this person whether the information from these new tests helped him or her build a better picture of what is inside.

Give the box to someone else and repeat.

If more than one family member or friend has investigated the box, ask them to share their information (this is very similar to how scientists work). What do they think, and why? By sharing their information, are they able to come up with a better idea of what the inside of the box is like?

Clear, concise communication is one of the most important—and difficult—skills you can master. It requires concentration, dedication, and just plain hard work. How often do you think to yourself, Please just say what you mean! when hearing someone chatter endlessly? How often do you miss the sense of the paragraph you just read, and have to reread it until what the author so desperately wanted to say comes through? Not everyone writes well or deftly, but writing perfection is worth striving for every day.

Assume for a moment that you are an engineer. You have designed a special clip to hold two parts of a spacecraft together. Those two parts must work, or the craft will fail, and in failing might cause harm. You therefore study the best way to explain how that clip must be installed. How do you go about doing that explaining?

First, never write down to your audience. It insults them and demeans you. Second, put yourself in your reader's place. Assume the person wants to do a good job, is eager to learn, but might not have your specific knowledge or abilities. In general, everyone wants to do a good job. You feel better when someone says, "Well done!" than you do when someone says, "Whose fault is this?" You should therefore approach the explanation of how that clip should be installed in a spirit of cooperation and helpfulness.

Think about how you would install it. Does it need a special tool? How is that tool held? Does it need two hands, or one? Is it in an awkward location? Will it need extra light to be seen or someone limber enough to get into the hatchway to install it? Will it need regular maintenance? You must consider the people who will come after you have left for another job, who must work from your directions and who cannot ask you a question if the instructions are unclear.

Be thoughtful, not arrogant. Be creative but not obscure. Be helpful, not obstructive. As a friend of mine says, eschew obfuscation. In other words: be clear, be concise, and be appreciated!

Loretta "Aleta" Jackson

Loretta "Aleta" Jackson has worked for most of her professional life in the aerospace industry, from her first job building parts for the Gemini Program to her work at XCOR Aerospace, which she co-founded in 1999. Along the way she has been an editor, a horse trainer, a technical writer, an airport line boy, and an electronics research technician; she also served in the U.S. Air Force. Her diverse background helps her understand the many ways people communicate.

TECHNICALLY SPEAKING

BASED ON THE ORIGINAL WORKSHOP BY MAI LE

2 SESSIONS, 90 MINUTES EACH
STEM DISCIPLINES: *Engineering, technology, geometry*
WRITING ACTIVITIES: *Technical writing, creative writing*

IN THIS LESSON, STUDENTS WILL LEARN the basics of engineering and technical writing, incredibly useful skills for STEM professionals. They will also learn that despite its crushingly boring name, technical writing can be interesting and fun. It's also hugely important. In the STEM fields, collaboration requires communication, and technical writing is a big part of that. Clear technical writing means that complex, critical procedures are followed correctly; bad technical writing can lead to messes of all kinds. Just think of what happens in the kitchen when a recipe goes awry!

Technical writing is especially important in engineering, where instructions must be followed closely. In this low-stakes scenario, students will discover how readers may interpret their writing differently from how it was intended, and will learn to write clearly and concisely through trial and error. All the while, students will learn what's at the heart and soul of engineering by playing with a common object—the paper airplane. (Yes, we said play. For many of the best scientists and engineers, their work is all brilliant fun.) As a bonus, students will get to reinforce geometry concepts.

Most students have a mental image of what scientists are and what they do, even if it's not

MATERIALS

☐ Copies of "bad" instructions for making a paper airplane (use the example provided in the lesson or write your own)

☐ Sample paper airplanes to show the class

☐ Paper airplane templates (see Handy Lesson Links in the appendix for sources)

☐ Paper airplane-making supplies (paper, of course [varying weights are good], plus rulers, paper clips, scissors, tape, or whatever you think might help make good fliers)

☐ Tape measures (as many as possible, to allow for multiple tests)

☐ Copies of the "Similarity Scoring!" handout (for this

(continued)

and all other handouts, you'll need one per student) (included with other handouts at the end of this lesson)

- ☐ Yardsticks (optional)
- ☐ Masking tape (optional)
- ☐ String (optional)
- ☐ Stopwatches or other timers (optional)
- ☐ Copies of the "Flight Trials" handout
- ☐ Copies of the "Paper Airplane Calculations: Sample Spreadsheet" handout (optional, for bonus activity)
- ☐ Computers (optional)
- ☐ Copies of the "Measure Your Planform" handout
- ☐ Prizes (optional; origami foil paper works well)

entirely accurate and based on stereotypes. Like many people, students imagine a "mad scientist" with crazy hair and a lab coat who's up to no good, creating doomsday devices or monsters through gene splicing. But when you ask them to imagine an engineer, they come up empty. So, what is an engineer? How is an engineer different from a scientist? And why do good engineers also need to know how to write? (For a broad overview of STEM disciplines, see "How to Use This Book.")

This may be simplifying it a bit, but in short, scientists seek knowledge about the way the world works, and engineers seek solutions to problems. (The word "scientist" comes from the Latin word meaning "to know," and "engineer" comes from the Latin for "to produce or bring forth.") There's a lot of overlap between the two fields. Scientists try to uncover knowledge that can then be translated to solving problems, and sometimes they design the apparatuses that will help them do that. Engineers design solutions (whether a new bridge, a piece of software, or a medical device) using well-established scientific principles, and they sometimes make discoveries while engineering those solutions.

If your students are still having trouble picturing what an engineer does, tell them to think of Iron Man Tony Stark, who earned two master's degrees in engineering from MIT and engineers his own equipment. Then remind them that *most* engineers don't battle nefarious villains with jet-packed armor suits, but that their work is still cool and interesting.

Regardless of their primary goals, scientists and engineers go about their work in very similar ways. The practices of science and engineering are both fundamentally processes of feedback and **iteration** (for more on iteration, see the Science-O-Pedia). Engineers try things out, observe results, and use those observations to improve things for next time, not all that differently from how scientists continuously refine hypotheses and theories.

Now, not everyone is interested in the sciences (for example, physics, chemistry, or biology) or engineering fields (for example, electrical engineering, mechanical engineering, chemical engineering, bioengineering, or civil engineering). But the steps scientists and engineers use are helpful to all. Whether they are building a rocket or painting a starry night, people try things out, make observations, and attempt to do things better next time. As Nobel Prize–winning playwright Samuel Beckett wrote, "Ever tried. Ever failed. No matter. Try again. Fail again. Fail better." Engineer Henry Petrovski of Duke University said it a little differently in the title of one of his books: *To Engineer Is Human*.

Session 1: Engineering Airplanes

There's a lot more to paper airplanes than just paper. Here, students explore the engineering behind them. They also practice their technical writing skills by learning to write clear, concise instructions.

Introduction (10 minutes or less)

Give the students a set of bad paper airplane instructions, and have them attempt to follow the instructions. Come up with your own, or use this one:

HOW TO MAKE A PAPER AIRPLANE You will turn the paper and fold it in half. Take the side corners and fold them in to make a point. You should fold the top half in half again and do the same for the bottom half. Now you should paper clip the back of the paper together, but only halfway.

At about the five-minute mark, have your students share what they were able to build based on the instructions, while you display the actual (intended) paper plane. Ideally many attempts don't look like paper planes at all, and laughs are had.

What's Engineering? (10 minutes)

Ask students why their planes don't look like planes, and they're likely to say that the instructions were bad in some way. Let the students know that today they'll have a chance to do better, by writing like good engineers.

Of course, they'll be doing some engineering as well. So ask them what they think engineering is, and see if the group can come to a consensus. You may want to share a very basic definition: engineers create things to solve problems, using scientific principles. If students have shared things that engineers do, you can situate these examples in that framework. For instance, a civil engineer builds bridges to let us get across water. Or a computer engineer designs microchips to draw billions of triangles every second (the foundation of modern three-dimensional imagery).

Once that's straightened out, briefly introduce the task. Students aren't going to engineer actual airplanes. Instead, they're going to engineer paper airplanes that fly as far as they can possibly make them go. They'll also write instructions for reproducing these airplanes so that someone else can fold them. Finally, they'll be testing both the originals and the reproductions to see how the technical writing influenced the quality of each plane.

Let's Engineer! Building Paper Airplanes (20 minutes)

Now task the students with building their *own* airplane. This airplane will serve as the model for which they'll write instructions later. Have paper airplane templates available (see "Handy Lesson Links" in the appendix for Web-based templates) for the students to modify if they like; they can also design their own from scratch. The focus here should not be on trying out as many models as possible, so you may want to restrict the number of choices for the base design to just one or two.

The focus, instead, should be on improving their starter design while doing informal testing. (Hallways work really well for this.) About halfway through this segment, have students do some hands-on engineering to help their plane fly better. Explain to students the option to fold fins, adjust elevators (rear wing flaps), and add weight (have some paper clips available). It's helpful to share some models of paper planes that you've tweaked. Ask questions that point at deficiencies in students' planes and suggest experiments:

◇ Why do you think your plane nose-dives?

◇ What would help your plane fly straight?

◇ Why do you think real planes have fins and tails?

◇ Have you ever seen wing elevators move during a plane flight? During what parts of the flight did they move, and how, and why?

Let students know that taking notes will be helpful in designing and analyzing their plane. Here are a few simple suggestions:

◇ Students can draw and label diagrams.

◇ Students can record plane measurements (for example, length, distance from nose to paper clip).

◇ They can make a T-chart that documents changes to their plane and the results of those changes.

At the end of this segment, students should have finalized their plane design, which they'll use for the next segment. (For the rest of this lesson, we'll refer to this plane as the "engineered plane.")

What's Technical Writing? (15 minutes)

Bring the students back together and ask them to recall the bad instructions at the beginning of the workshop. Can they think of any ways to make them better? Consider writing their suggestions on the board, chart paper, or a projector—or have a version of the instructions on display, and edit them as a class. Ask questions like these:

◇ What about the first set of instructions was confusing? Unclear?

◇ How could the instructions have been better?

◇ Were there steps missing, or in the wrong order?

◇ What information should be included for someone who has never built a plane?

◇ What terms were you unfamiliar with?

After the students have generated ideas and suggestions, explain that the instructions they followed were a type of technical writing. (For that matter, so were the notes taken during the previous segment.) There are a few important characteristics that help make for strong technical writing, but you should choose to focus on the ones that you, as an instructor, feel are most appropriate to address with your students. The following are some guidelines for generating good technical writing:

1. **Use clear, straightforward vocabulary.**

   ▷ If common words are just as clear as big words that sound smart, use the common ones! For example, "Fold the paper in half lengthwise" is clearer than "Bisect the paper along the vertical axis."

   ▷ Only use technical terms when you know your readers understand them, and when they really do make things clearer. For example, "When adding that paper clip, make sure it is parallel to the wings, not perpendicular" is clearer than "When adding that paper clip, make sure it is at a 0- or 180-degree angle to the wing, not a 90-degree angle."

2. Don't assume your readers know things they might not.

▷ Define any specific terminology (for example, "nose," "wing").

▷ Avoid jargon—insider terms not everyone may understand.

▷ Pretend they have never done this before, have never seen a paper airplane, and so on.

3. Remember that when writing instructions, it's always a good idea to . . .

▷ Use imperative sentences.

▷ List steps in a logical order.

▷ Make use of diagrams; drawings; and varied font formatting (different colors, underlining, and so on).

During this discussion, it may also be helpful to introduce geometry terms.

GEOMETRY TERMS If time permits, go over these geometry terms with your students so they'll have the vocabulary to describe what they're seeing.

▸ **VERTEX:** A corner or point where two lines meet.

▸ **EDGE:** A line where two sides of a geometric solid (like a cube or a pyramid) meet.

▸ **INTERSECTION:** A point where two lines cross or meet.

▸ **MIDPOINT:** The halfway point on a line segment.

▸ **PERPENDICULAR:** Meeting at a right (90-degree) angle.

Let's Technically Write! Writing Instructions (35 minutes)

It's time to get writing. Give your students fifteen minutes to write instructions for their engineered plane. (Fifteen minutes might feel fast, but this is okay. Things will be less than perfect, which will help strengthen the revision portions later.) If they used a Web-based template, make sure they don't have the original instructions they used to build their model. Their instructions should assume that the folder starts with a blank piece of paper with no markings at all (as opposed to the templates students may have had earlier in the lesson).

Once that's done, pair the students up, and have them exchange instructions. Give them ten minutes to make their partner's plane using only the written instructions. (We'll call this one the "rough plane.")

After students have had a chance to work through their partner's instructions, there will probably be at least a little confusion. Student A may have written, for instance, "The wing should be folded back until it touches the center line." Student B might be unsure whether the wing should be folded over or under the plane.

Take five minutes (or maybe a little more, if your students finish writing and/or folding quickly) to solicit observations from your students on examples from the instructions they used that were easy to follow, and examples that weren't. This will help everyone understand elements of good instructions. Emphasize that this is not the time for the direction writers to clarify what they meant! That will come during the next session.

Finally, for the last five minutes, have your students write down any clarification questions they may have for the author of the instructions they followed. Students should save this list of questions, plus the engineered planes and their instructions; they'll need them for the next session.

Session 2: Make It Better

All engineering requires reengineering. Here, students use their newfound knowledge to improve their planes and their instructions.

Plane Re-Reconstruction (25 minutes)

At the beginning of this session, make sure students have the instructions they wrote, the rough plane based on those instructions, and the questions from their partner. Take just five minutes and have your students share what they recall about your earlier discussion about technical writing and instructions, then give them about ten minutes to revise and amend their original instructions. They should definitely respond to their partner's questions, but should also take into account mistakes in the rough plane that they see but that their partner didn't realize were there. Once they're done (many will be done before the ten-minute mark; a few may need maybe five more minutes), they should hand the updated instructions to their partner, who will attempt to fold the plane again in about ten minutes. (This plane will be the "final plane.")

Judging Similarity (5 minutes)

Once all the final planes are finished (some students will be able to start early), they should be given to the respective instruction authors. In turn, authors should go around with the engineered plane, the final plane, and the "Similarity Scoring!" handout. With the handout, the authors will ask their peers (and any adults in the room) to score the similarity of the planes. Were the folding instructions so clear that the planes turned out identical? They should aim to get as many scores as possible, and then average them. If possible, record the results (just the averages) on the board or chart paper. Note roughly what the high and low scores were, and which instructions got them—this'll benefit the discussion later.

Flight Testing (45 minutes)

And now, it's time for flight testing of both the engineered and the final planes. Students will get to see how their planes perform, and how the quality of the instructions led to differences in planes (and performance).

Note that although forty-five minutes seems like a long time, more may actually be required. If multiple planes can be tested at a time (which requires a good amount of space and multiple tape measures), that'll help keep this segment manageable. If you aren't able to test multiple planes at the same time, you could test each plane just once or twice—but this will severely affect the quality of the data.

Students will try to throw the planes as far as possible. Emphasize the importance of controlling for as many variables as is feasible, meaning they should make sure that each launch is as consistent as possible with the prior test. (For more on variables and testing, see the Science-O-Pedia.) Have students throw the planes as perfectly horizontally as they can, ideally releasing from the same height. You can use a yardstick or a large piece of masking tape on a wall as a reference. Also, note that launch speed is very likely to be nowhere near constant. Ask your students to think of other variables that should be controlled for, and ideally they'll come up with launch speed and several others. If they can think of ways to control for these variables, put them in action! (For instance, launch angle can be somewhat standardized by asking students to throw their planes from a given mark and through a target made of tape or string.)

Have students collect data by measuring the distance flown from launch to landing point. (A tape measure works best.) You may want to have students work with a partner so they can also measure the flight duration (time in seconds) using a stopwatch or other timer. Students should then find the average distance and duration (remind students to use metric units) of at least three throws (ideally) using the "Flight Trials" handout, for both the engineered plane and the final plane folded by their classmate. Finding the average over multiple trials gets at another important part of science: reproducibility. The length (in distance and duration) of each flight is likely to be different from that of the others because it is impossible to launch the plane in exactly the same manner each time. Taking the average flight length is the scientifically right way to correct for these differences—eliminating the effects of students' personal bias and the tendency to only use the "best" data.

Data Analysis (10 minutes)

Have students use the "Measure Your Planform" handout to estimate the area of their planform for their engineered plane. (Essentially, they'll trace an outline of the flat wing surface onto a square centimeter grid, then count, as best as possible, the number of squares taken up by the silhouette. This is the area.) Then, if you like, you can have them enter their flight results into the online spreadsheet described in the Optional Extension directions, which will calculate lift and drag coefficients for the plane. When students are aware of the connections among form, lift, and drag, it'll allow a richer conversation at the end of the lesson.

Wrap-Up (10 minutes)

At this point, after you have assessed the students' written instructions and the planes, make sure to highlight examples of outstanding instructions (what specific descriptions, phrases, or directions were clearest) and engineering (in terms of either flight duration and length or, if your students completed the extension, lift-to-drag ratio, lift coefficient, or drag coefficient). You should have the opportunity to connect unclear directions with pairs of planes that were very dissimilar. The final plane in some of these pairs may fly worse, but sometimes it may fly better—and you should ask why this is. More important, ask how students would preserve the improvements in the plane for next time. (Here's a hint: technical writing.)

You shouldn't be speaking solo here; make sure to give your students space to contribute their thoughts and observations about writing and engineering. Prizes are optional. (It could be fun, for instance, to have origami foil paper of different colors that can be made by and/or for the winners into planes that double as trophies.)

To end, ask students to share what they would change about their instructions and paper airplane design. And recap what they have discovered!

OPTIONAL EXTENSION WITH A MORE IN-DEPTH COMPUTATIONAL CONNECTION

In this lesson, we're interested in basic technical writing—how to write good instructions—and basic engineering—how to create paper airplanes that fly farther and stay in the air longer. The full picture of aeronautical engineering is significantly more complicated; there's much more to consider. If you have access to computers, you and your students can take a closer look.

Ask your students what keeps a plane in the air, and what brings it down to the ground. See what they say, and have them talk it through. Obvious answers include gravity (which brings down a plane) and an engine (which pushes a plane up and forward).

As it turns out, those two answers are maybe the least important things when considering how to make a paper plane. A plane's **weight** (the downward force of gravity acting on it) isn't something students can reduce significantly with a paper plane. And as for **thrust** (the forward force provided by an engine, or someone's arm)—once a paper plane is launched, there's no more thrust, so it's a moot point.

Students may bring up friction or wind resistance—now they're getting somewhere! Ask students if they've ever felt these forces while running or biking, and most will tell you how hard it is to move into the wind, or even just that they feel more air when moving faster. You might also ask what happens when you stop kicking and stroking while swimming. All of these factors contribute to **drag**—the backward force that a gas or fluid (like air or water) exerts on something moving through it. Drag is really important with paper planes.

Students might not bring up **lift**—the upward force exerted by a fluid. In the likely case that they don't, ask your students if they've ever stuck their arm out of the window while riding in a car. (They should first ask the driver for permission.) Among those who have, many have probably tilted their hand up or down. Tilting their hand up caused it to move upward as it traveled through the air. You can also demonstrate something called **Bernoulli's principle** (and have your students join in) with strips of paper, about 1.5 to 2 inches wide. Have them hold the end of the paper under their lower lip and let the paper droop down. Then they should blow—the paper will rise up slowly. Bernoulli's principle is complicated, and it's only a part of what creates lift (which is even more complicated), but this'll at least show students that airflow can be responsible for more than a simple directional push.

Once they're clear on the existence of lift and drag, let them know that those are the two most important forces to consider for a paper plane (more generally, for gliders), and that the spreadsheet they're going to fill out will tell them how good their planes are at generating lift and minimizing drag.

Simplified Lift and Drag Spreadsheet[1]

We've prepared a spreadsheet, available online, if you want to get really fancy with the data (see Handy Lesson Links in the appendix). It does some basic calculations to figure out the lift coefficient and drag coefficient of a paper airplane. (See a print example of the spreadsheet at the end of this lesson. You can

---

1. The spreadsheet is adapted from Feng, N. B, Mei, K. Q., Yin, P. Y., & Schlüter, J. U. (2009). On the aerodynamics of paper airplanes. Paper presented at the 27th American Institute of Aeronautics and Astronotics (AIAA) Applied Aerodynamics Conference, San Antonio, TX.

(continued)

OPTIONAL EXTENSION (continued)

use the print version if you don't have online access, although then you'll have to do your own calculations.) A brief refresher: the coefficient is the number that you multiply a variable by. In this case, the variable is the area of the plane's wings, so the lift and drag coefficients indicate, respectively, how much lift and drag a plane generates, relative to the size of its wings. The following formulas will be handy:

Mass of plane (grams) = (# of sheets of paper $\times$ 5 grams per sheet of paper)
+ (# of paper clips $\times$ 2 grams per paper clip)

$$\text{Airspeed (meters per second)} = \frac{\text{Distance traveled horizontally (meters)}}{\text{Duration of flight (seconds)}}$$

$$\text{Lift-to-drag ratio} = \frac{\text{Distance traveled horizontally (meters)}}{\text{Height of launch (meters)}}$$

Lift force (Newtons) = Mass of plane (kilograms) $\times$ Gravity of Earth

(Gravity of Earth $\approx$ 9.8 meters per second^2)

$$\text{Drag force (Newtons)} = \frac{\text{Lift force (Newtons)}}{\text{Lift-to-drag ratio}}$$

$$\text{Lift coefficient} = \frac{\text{Lift force} \times 2}{\text{Density of air} \times \text{Airspeed}^2 \times \text{Planform area (meters}^2)}$$

(Density of air = 0.001275 kilograms per meters^3 near Earth's surface)

$$\text{Drag coefficient} = \frac{\text{Lift coefficient}}{\text{Lift-to-drag ratio}}$$

Plane engineer/instruction writer:_____

Final plane folder/instruction follower:_____

Fold over for secrecy!

. . . .

SIMILARITY SCORING!

How similar are the engineered plane (folded by you) and the final plane (folded by your classmate following your instructions)? Let the people decide!

SCORING KEY

0 = Not at all similar

1 = Not very similar

2 = Somewhat similar

3 = Identical

Judge: _____ Score: _____

Judge: _____ Score: _____

Judge: _____ Score: _____

Judge: _____ Score: _____

Judge: _____ Score: _____

Judge: _____ Score: _____

Judge: _____ Score: _____

Judge: _____ Score: _____

Judge: _____ Score: _____

Judge: _____ Score: _____

# of judges: _____ Total score: _____

Average (total score divided by # of judges): _____

FLIGHT TRIALS

WHICH PLANE? (CIRCLE ONE):

ORIGINAL ENGINEERED PLANE   **FINAL PLANE**

Flight #: _____ Distance: _____ Duration: _____

Notes:

Flight #: _____ Distance: _____ Duration: _____

Notes:

Flight #: _____ Distance: _____ Duration: _____

Notes:

Flight #: _____ Distance: _____ Duration: _____

Notes:

Flight #: _____ Distance: _____ Duration: _____

Notes:

# of flights: _____ Total distance: _____

Average (total distance divided by # of flights): _____

PAPER AIRPLANE CALCULATIONS: SAMPLE SPREADSHEET

DATA — Columns B through H should be populated with students' data.

INTERMEDIATE CALCULATIONS — In the online spreadsheet, calculations will be done automatically. (Each header cell has a note that details the calculation.) You should copy the formulas here into subsequent rows as many times as you need to.

FINAL RESULTS — Calculations will again be done automatically after you copy and paste the formulas here. (The headers also have notes with more details.)

	Trial #	Distance Traveled Horizontally (m)	Planform area (cm²)	Duration of Flight (s)	Height of Launch (m)	How Many Sheets of Paper?	How Many Paper Clips?	Mass of Plane (g)	Airspeed (m/s)	Lift-to-Drag Ratio	Lift Force (N)	Drag Force (N)	Lift Coefficient	Drag Coefficient
Example	1	5.6	69	1.1	1	1	0	5	1.553	1.708	0.0490	0.029	4.62	2.71
	2	6.6	158	1.8	0.8	1	0	5	3.667	8.250	0.0490	0.006	0.36	0.04
	3	9.3	120	2.8	0.8	1	0	5	3.321	11.625	0.0490	0.004	0.58	0.05

MEASURE YOUR PLANFORM

Using the blank grid on the next page, estimate the area of your **planform** (the area of the wings). Lay the wings of your paper airplane flat on the grid and trace the outline. Count, as best as you can, the number of squares taken up by the silhouette. Make sure to include fractions! This number is the planform in square centimeters.

Example:

(14 * 7) / 2 = 49 sq. cm.

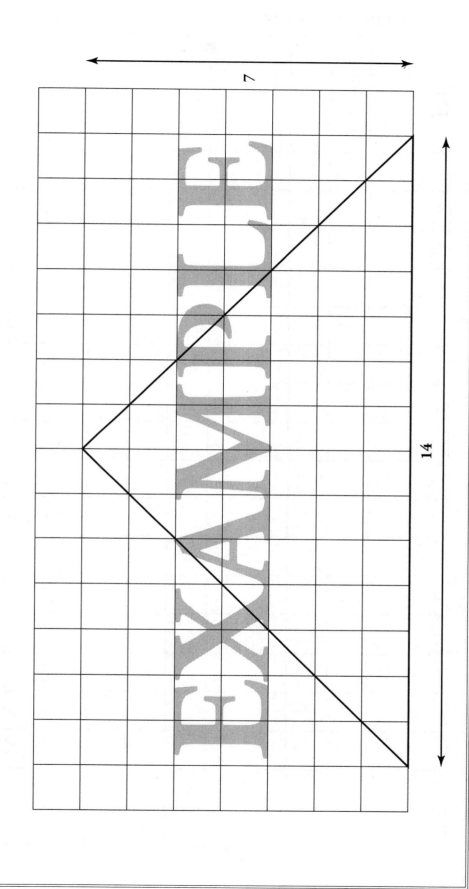

Now, trace your own platform here.

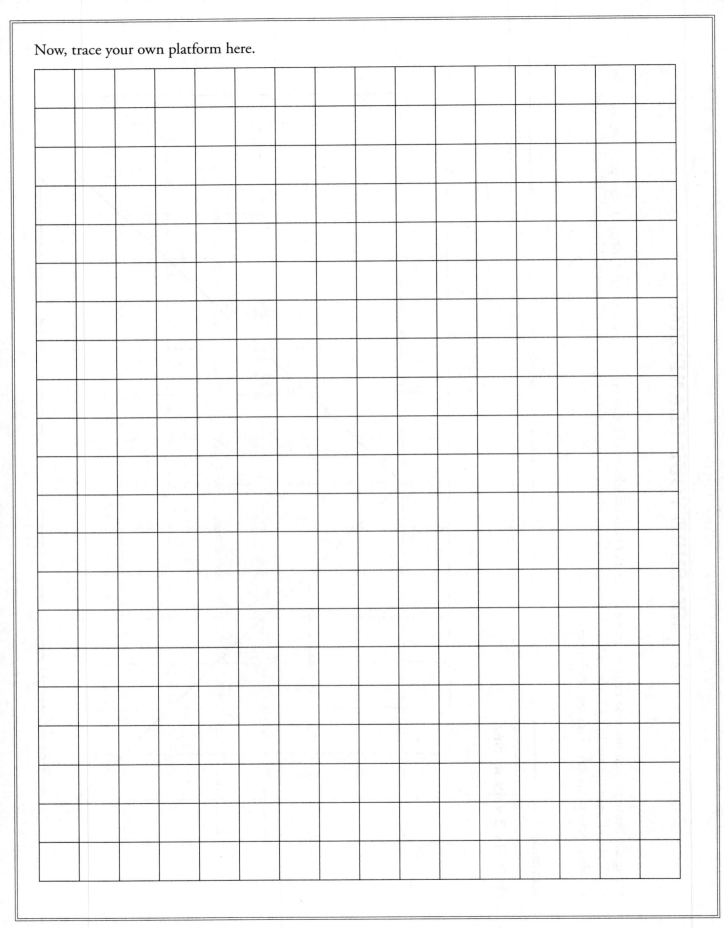

Science is about appreciating every single aspect of the incredible world and universe! There is no subject too small and no item of dessert too insignificant to explore as a scientist. One of the most incredible gifts of being a scientist is having the skill set and the wisdom to want to examine the world in new ways. Every single thing in the universe has the potential to amaze us, teach us, and inspire us. What's especially fun about being a scientist, and what this lesson series will demonstrate, is that once your brain is open to the possibility of learning and exploring and analyzing, the sky is the limit. One set of inquiries inevitably leads to another, and before you know it, you've gone from ice cream to the outer edges of the universe. That's what being a scientist is all about!

Mayim Bialik

Mayim Bialik plays neurobiologist Amy Farrah Fowler on CBS's The Big Bang Theory, *and has received three consecutive Emmy nominations and a Screen Actors Guild nomination for her role. In 2007 she completed her PhD in neuroscience at the University of California, Los Angeles. Her doctoral work looked at the role oxytocin and vasopressin play in obsessive-compulsive disorder in adolescents with Prader-Willi syndrome.*

IT'S (PARTIALLY) ROCKET SCIENCE AND (MOSTLY) ICE CREAM

BASED ON THE ORIGINAL WORKSHOP BY JULIUS DIAZ PANORIÑGAN

2 SESSIONS, 2 HOURS EACH
STEM DISCIPLINES: *Physical sciences, earth and space sciences, life sciences, chemistry, engineering*
WRITING ACTIVITIES: *Technical writing, creative writing, narrative writing*

ACROSS THESE TWO SESSIONS, STUDENTS will do very little actual rocket science (that is, aerospace engineering). They will, however, cover related fields; they'll act as physicists, chemists, and engineers exploring some of the universe's deepest mysteries (such as, How do you make ice cream?!), documenting their findings along the way. Just as important, in each session students will dispel some misconceptions and learn more about the nature and practices of science.

Session 1: Ice Cream

From a scientific perspective, ice cream is pretty interesting: it's a liquid that becomes a solid. From an eating perspective, it's delicious. In this session, we investigate the science behind these highly compelling qualities.

Introduction (15 minutes)

Start at a large shared writing space, such as a chalkboard, a dry-erase board, or chart paper, on which the following prompt is written:

> What do scientists do? Please write down a couple of sentences, and draw pictures, too.

MATERIALS

SESSION 1

Note: Quantities are listed per student per batch. You'll need to double these amounts to permit students to make two batches each (recommended). We highly recommend that you buy more than you think you'll need to account for spills and other mishaps and to let students experiment in groups once they've made their own batches. We've also called for cups and spoons for students to measure their own ingredients, but if you want things to move faster, you can prepare premeasured ingredients in paper cups to use instead.

☐ A small zipper-style ziplock bag

(continued)

□ A gallon zipper-style ziplock bag

□ ½ cup milk

□ 1 tablespoon sugar

□ ½ teaspoon vanilla extract or other flavoring

□ 4 tablespoons kosher rock salt

□ 2+ cups ice cubes

□ A liquid measuring cup

□ Measuring spoons

□ Cups or scoopers for scooping ice to cover the milk

□ Paper towels

□ Copies of the "What Do You Know About Ice Cream?" handout (included with other handouts at the end of this lesson)

□ Copies of the "Let's Experiment with Ice Cream!" handout

□ A cooler large enough to hold the ice and keep the milk cold at the beginning of the session

□ Hand towels for students to wrap around their ziplock bag in case of spilling (alternately, you can ask students to bring their own)

□ Plastic spoons, for taste-testing

SESSION 2

□ Ice cubes (one per student)

□ Aluminum foil

□ Copies of the "Let's Save the Ice!" handout

(continued)

Give the students a few minutes to write down answers of their own. Then have them share, and write their responses on the board. The idea, before jumping into the next phase—making ice cream!—is to at least start to break the "lab coat stereotype." Yes, *some* scientists concoct chemical formulas and shoot lasers/particle beams/death rays in laboratories, but they do tons of other cool stuff. A lot of it happens outside of laboratories. Here, work with students to come up with a list of things scientists do—the more out there and/or the more relevant to everyday life, the better. For example:

◇ Scientists are trying to figure out how to save honeybees and polar bears!

◇ Scientists have used zombies as a model to figure out how to stop the spread of disease!

◇ Scientists are designing robots for all kinds of things, and one day there may be a robot that can do your chores!

◇ Scientists are discovering new, faraway planets and stars as we speak!

◇ Scientists are smashing particles together to learn more about the most fundamental forces in nature!

◇ Scientists designed a suit to simulate how older people experience the world!

◇ Scientists are also designing suits to help augment people's strength!

Thematically, everything you and your students come up with will suggest that scientists are trying to find answers to questions. Today's big question: How do we make some awesome ice cream?

Ice Cream Inquiry[1] (25 minutes)

Before getting started, conduct a very scientific ice cream inquiry. This can either be a written exercise, using the "What Do You Know About Ice Cream?" handout, or a discussion, or both. Ask:

---

1. This lesson is based on "Science Club: Ice Cream!" by Elaine M. Palucki, in 826 National. (2011). *Don't Forget to Write for the Elementary Grades: Fifty Enthralling and Effective Writing Lessons.* J. Traig, Ed. San Francisco, CA: Jossey-Bass.

◇ What's everyone's favorite kind of ice cream?

◇ What ingredients go into ice cream?

Students usually name sugar and milk or cream pretty quickly, and as they do, you can hold up these ingredients to show them they're right. But they almost always forget the salt. Hold that ingredient up next, but don't reveal what it does. You can ask students what they think salt is for, but be prepared for some silence. Use the silence for good effect— suspense or time for new hypotheses. A good question to ask next is, Is each ingredient a liquid, a solid, or a gas?

Ask the students what happens when we put any one of the solid ingredients (salt, sugar, and ice) into a liquid like milk. They usually know that it dissolves into the liquid. Which brings you to your next question: So how is it that, when we make ice cream, we start with a liquid, and end up with a solid?

Have the students brainstorm on how this transition might happen. The discussion can be started with the help of some silly suggestions: Do we use mysterious chemicals? Meteorological forces? Queen Elsa–style magical freezing powers? Or . . . science? They're about to find out.

□ Cooler construction materials, like corrugated cardboard, more foil, construction paper, waxed paper, newspaper, Bubble Wrap, plastic wrap, paper towels, masking tape, Scotch tape, rubber bands, staplers, or whatever seems useful

□ Single-serve cups of ice cream (one per student)

□ Plastic spoons if not included with ice cream cups

□ A cooler large enough to hold the ice cream cups until needed

Making Ice Cream (50 minutes)

It's finally ice cream time. At each table station, set up the ingredients, measuring cups, measuring spoons, scoopers, and paper towels, and distribute the "Let's Experiment with Ice Cream!" handout. You may want to give the students extras, so they can record the results of more than one batch. Take a moment to walk through the handout and the steps. Explain that they should write down what actually happens, as opposed to what's supposed to happen. A lot of things don't go exactly according to plan in experiments, and noting these things helps scientists and engineers answer questions. There should be enough time for two rounds of ice cream making. For the first run, it may also be helpful to have all the students start and stop shaking at the same time. After the first batch is done, taste test! Of course, there's room to record observations on the handout.

Round 2! This time around, ask every student to make one change to the recipe (to be recorded, like everything else, on the handout). Most will decide to triple the sugar or something along those lines, but a few will also play with the shaking time, or try eliminating salt—this will result in some of the most important discussion later. To make sure that students attempt changes that aren't just built around taste, you can challenge each group to make sure that each member tries out a different thing. It may be prudent to have students do half-size batches on their own, especially if supplies are running low.

Rounds 3 and beyond! If supplies remain, students can keep on modifying the recipe and trying out new experiments until the time runs out, always recording any changes they may have made, like using more milk, or less sugar, and varying the shaking time. There are always students who firmly believe more flavor and more sugar will make their ice cream *more delicious*. Wrong!—but everyone needs to learn this for themselves.

Ice Cream, Explained (30 minutes)

Now it's time for the students to sample their work and present their findings. As they eat, ask students to share what happened when they followed the protocol and what happened when they varied it, having them show the results of their experimentation. Then ask the million-dollar question: How did the ice cream freeze? How did we start with a liquid and end up with a solid?

To answer that question, the class will need to revisit the subject of states of matter. The ice absorbs energy (this is what makes it melt), changing the water from a solid to a liquid. Ask students where this energy comes from. (It comes from anything that is touching the ice, like our own hands, the ice cream ingredients, and even the air.)

To make ice cream, and stop this melting process, we need our magic ingredient: salt. Salt lowers the freezing point of the ice, making the ice "colder" than it was before, and changing the temperature at which the ice will melt. This lets the milk freeze while the bag is being shaken.

We all know that water will freeze when the temperature is below 32 degrees Fahrenheit. But if we add salt to the water to make a 10 percent salt solution, the water won't freeze until the temperature is below 20 degrees Fahrenheit. If we add more salt, making a 20 percent salt solution, the water won't freeze until 2 degrees Fahrenheit. By adding salt to the ice in the bag and lowering the temperature at which ice is frozen, we create an environment cold enough to freeze milk and make ice cream.

A complete explanation requires chemistry and physics concepts often not encountered until high school, or even college. It's important to note that an exact explanation, with correct terms like "specific heat capacity" or "enthalpy of fusion," isn't the point. For most students, it's the wow factor that's important. The thrill of discovery, and curiosity about phenomena like this, is what will spur them on to become thermodynamic whiz kids.

Students wrap up by working on a final writing prompt:

> Using the notes you took during the ice cream–making procedure, create your perfect ice cream recipe.

Encourage them to bring their recipe home, and to report back next week if they test it out.

FOR YOU TO KNOW (AND YOUR STUDENTS TO DISCOVER)

It can be confusing for students and adults alike to think that adding salt to ice helps make ice cream freeze. Students from climates with snow and ice during the winter see both their parents and snowplows spreading salt on roads, driveways, and sidewalks to *melt* any accumulated frozen stuff. Why, then, will adding salt to the ice help the ice cream *freeze*? The answer is really cool chemistry (pun intended), and is largely about heat (or energy) flows.

At the molecular level, a single water molecule looks something like mouse ears, with two hydrogen atoms bound to one oxygen atom. In any liquid, including water, the individual water molecules are continuously moving around. As they move around, the molecules "shake hands" with other water molecules,  forming weak bonds called **hydrogen bonds.** These bonds break and reform easily, as the water molecules bump against and jostle one another.[2] The presence of these transient bonds explains why raindrops hold together in a drop shape, why you can slightly overfill a cup of water before it spills, and why a water strider can skim the surface of the water.

Temperature, it turns out, is a measure of the amount of motion (kinetic energy) in a system. If something—a glass of water or the air around you—is hot, that means that the molecules in the system are moving around quickly. A decrease in the temperature of water indicates that the motion in the system has slowed—that there is less kinetic energy in the system. As water molecules move more and more slowly, they behave as if they are sticky. Like other liquids, water actually becomes measurably more viscous (or "thick"; think maple syrup) as its temperature decreases, although with water it can be hard to see this difference using just your senses. With the decrease in temperature, the water molecules are transitioning from shaking to holding hands. Just above the freezing point, there is an equilibrium between the number of water molecules that grab hands and the number that release hands. Water starts to freeze when more molecules grab hands than release them—as it freezes the number of molecules that are connected to one another continues to grow. This freezing process eventually results in the formation of an ice crystal. An ice crystal is well ordered: the water molecules are aligned in neat rows and columns, with each molecule linked by hydrogen bonds to other water molecules.

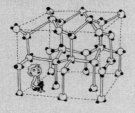

Where does the salt come in? Table salt (sodium chloride, NaCl) is made of one positively charged atom of sodium (Na$^+$) and one negatively charged atom of chloride (Cl$^-$). Sodium chloride is only held together weakly by the attraction of a negative charge to a positive charge, sort of like two magnets. (This bond is still stronger than a hydrogen bond.) When NaCl is added to water, it dissolves, meaning that the sodium and chloride atoms come apart and are separated

---

2. Note that the bonds that hold an individual water molecule together (that connect the two hydrogen "ears" to the oxygen "head") are covalent bonds, which are a kind of strong chemical bond.

(continued)

by water molecules. Although most of the time we use the word "salt" to mean table salt (sodium chloride), salts can be made of other combinations of atoms, such as magnesium chloride, calcium chloride, and potassium chloride. Like sodium chloride, all salts are held together by the attraction between positively and negatively charged atoms (these are called **ionic bonds**), and when these salts dissolve in water, the atoms separate and are spread out among the water molecules.

When the individual salt atoms (for example, Na^+ and Cl^-) are mixed in with water molecules in liquid water, the water molecules have more things to bump against, and as a result it becomes harder for water molecules to find other water molecules with which to form hydrogen bonds. It is sort of like if you were in a ball pit (like the kind they have for toddlers to play in). If red balls stuck to red balls (and there were only red balls in the pit), the pit would

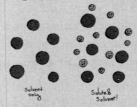

pretty quickly become a solid—all the red balls would stick together. If someone threw in a bag of yellow balls, it would take much longer for the pit to solidify, because many of the times that balls bumped against other balls, the interactions would not be productive—the red balls would be bumping into yellow balls. As a result of this mixing, water must be colder (as cold as –18 degrees Celsius) to form its stable ice lattice (to freeze). This phenomenon is called freezing point depression.

Why, then, does salt melt ice on roads? At its freezing point (0 degrees Celsius), water is in a state of equilibrium—with freezing and thawing happening at the same rate—so a puddle of ice on the sidewalk will stay the same size. If heat energy is added to the system (the temperature goes up), the equilibrium will shift, and more water molecules will break away from the ice lattice than will rejoin it. This results in melting. Salt also can shift this equilibrium. When salt is added to ice, it slowly dissolves among the water molecules that break free of the ice lattice (remember that without the salt, these molecules would, in short order, rejoin the lattice, and others would break free, and on and on), and now these liquid water molecules, instead of only bumping into other water molecules, also bump into Na^+ and Cl^- atoms—reducing the chance that they will find a water molecule in the ice lattice to bind to. More and more water molecules break free of the lattice, and these molecules continue to bump into Na^+ and Cl^- atoms. This will continue unless the outside temperature gets very, very low—low enough to overcome the effect of the salt and shift the equilibrium back toward freezing.

And, when the ice does melt, it actually does take energy (absorb heat) from the outside environment, causing the surroundings to get colder. The directions for making ice cream ask students to mix the salt with the ice that is in a bag surrounding the ice cream mix. This cools the salt-ice mixture to a temperature of –10 degrees Celsius, which is sufficiently low to cool the ice cream mix in the inner bag to its freezing point—resulting in ice cream.

Session 2: Staying Cool

In this activity, students embark on an engineering task that isn't all that difficult: they'll build simple coolers. (Note that there are many suggestions throughout this part of the lesson plan for making things harder, should you be working with students who could use an extra challenge.)

Some students will be pretty successful the first time around, when they build a cooler for an ice cube, and some would probably be pretty successful if they continued to work solo to build a cooler for ice cream. However, the point we're driving home is that STEM professionals collaborate all the time and are more successful because of it.

DIY Coolers (20 minutes)

Before students come in, have ice cubes at the ready, as well as sheets of aluminum foil on which to put them. If possible, keep the class area warm rather than cool. At the start of class, on the dot—even if still waiting for students—bring single ice cubes out on sheets of aluminum foil and place them where the students will be sitting. Distribute the "Let's Save the Ice!" handout. Following the first prompt on the handout, let students choose two square feet of any one "cooler construction material" (or randomly give them two square feet), and tell them that they each have to build their own cooler (using only the one cooler construction material), transfer the ice cube to it when done, and then leave their ice alone for thirty minutes. Set the coolers aside and move on to the next activity while waiting for the thirty minutes to elapse.

Packing a Suitcase (20 minutes)

As students finish building their respective coolers, have them draw them as instructed on "Let's Save the Ice!" handout, then get them started on the following writing prompt:

> Imagine that your crazy uncle comes into town and says he's taking you on vacation. (Your parents are fine with this.) Oh, also, you two have to be at the airport in an hour. He tells you the places where you're going: Alaska, Hawaii, Greenland, Costa Rica, Russia, Tanzania—all very hot or very cold destinations. You have to pack really, really fast. Out of all the clothes at home that you have, what do you pack to stay cool or warm as appropriate?

Thematically, this workshop is all about heat transfer. When students are trying to prevent an ice cube from melting, what they're trying to do is keep heat from transferring to it. This writing prompt gets them to think about heat transfer in a different context. Most students will intuitively wrap their ice cube in something to keep it cool. Yet some of those same students will opt for a swimsuit as stay-cool attire on a hot day. Why don't they choose to wrap themselves in something, as they did the ice cube? Should time permit while reporting out in the next segment, some of these apparent contradictions are great things to discuss.

Reporting Out (20 minutes)

At the forty-minute mark of the class, have students spend ten minutes finishing their writing, unpacking their ice cube, and recording how it looks on the "Let's Save the Ice!" handout.

Then, for the next ten minutes, have individual students report out what they observed. What materials did or didn't work? What combinations did or didn't work? What effects did different shapes and sizes of the materials have? It's best if these results can be recorded on a chalkboard, a dry-erase board, chart paper, or a projector screen for everyone to see and refer to.

Near the end of the big group report-out, you can take the opportunity to mention that this is what scientists and engineers do all the time. They share findings at conferences (as well as with the people in their workplace, and in giant discussion groups over the Internet); and the knowledge they share helps advance what everyone does.

The Ice Cream Test (20 minutes)

After you've shared your findings, it's time to bring out the ice cream. Put students into groups, and let them know that their task is almost exactly the same (but tastier): to save the ice cream from melting! This time around, each group can have access to whatever cooler construction materials they want.

Observation, and Writing About Space Shelters (25 minutes)

In all probability, students will have picked up some tips for better cooling in the report-out, which they're likely to have employed in their second-generation cooler. Once they've got their coolers built, have the students draw and describe their coolers as directed on the "Let's Save the Ice!" handout.

Once that's done, it's time for a little writing. The following writing prompt is a recontextualized version of the first one, and students ideally will take what they've learned via experimentation and collaboration to inform their response:

> You are an interplanetary explorer and thrill seeker, and you never know what kind of planet you're going to land on next. Some freeze, and some burn, and some have a difference of a thousand degrees between day and night. What kind of equipment do you need to be prepared for these extreme climates? What are your space suits and shelters made out of? (Ever crafty, you make them all yourself.)

Students should take occasional breaks in writing to observe their ice cream.

Sharing and Eating (15 minutes)

Have the students open their cooler and record their final results on the "Let's Save the Ice!" handout. Discuss briefly as a large group what strategies were successful, and see if the group can come to conclusions about what works well. As they may notice, the best coolers probably have multiple layers. At least one layer is probably relatively light (as in not dense): corrugated cardboard, Bubble Wrap, or just newspaper loosely packed around the ice cream; another layer is probably shiny (like aluminum foil). Once that's done, they can eat their (hopefully still-cold) ice cream!

FOR YOU TO KNOW (AND YOUR STUDENTS TO DISCOVER)

In a very loose sense, the entire universe "wants" to be the same temperature, and so energy in the form of heat transfers from warmer things to cooler things. Classically, there are three methods of heat transfer: **conduction** (direct heat transfer between things that are touching); **convection** (heat transfer when a fluid moves around—think boiling water in a pot, and why you have to stir your spaghetti when it cooks); and **radiation** (from visible light, UV rays, microwaves, and so on). To prevent surrounding heat from getting to the ice cube or ice cream, we probably want a material that reflects radiation (like foil), some space between layers or layers that aren't dense (to prevent direct heat conduction), and a structure that doesn't allow air to flow between the inside and the outside (to prevent convection).

WHAT DO YOU KNOW ABOUT ICE CREAM?

1. What is your favorite flavor of ice cream?

2. What ingredients do you think you need to make ice cream?

3. For every ingredient just listed, write whether you think this is a solid, a liquid, or a gas.

4. How do you think we will turn these ingredients into ice cream? (Will we run with them? Stir them? Put them in the refrigerator?)

LET'S EXPERIMENT WITH ICE CREAM!

Record your ice cream-making findings here.

1. Get a small ziplock bag and label it with your name, then add ½ cup of milk.

2. Add a flavoring to your ice cream (such as ½ teaspoon of vanilla). Add 1 tablespoon of sugar. Seal your ziplock bag, leaving as little air as possible on the inside.

3. Place your first bag with flavoring, milk, and sugar in a gallon ziplock bag. Cover the smaller bag with **ice**, filling your gallon bag. Add 4 tablespoons of salt to the top of your ice. Get all the extra air out of your bag, then wrap your ziplock bag in a towel.

4. Shake, roll, or move your bag for 8 minutes total. Make sure that the ice continues to cover the milk mixture bag as you shake.

Trial # _____: What happened? Did you vary the recipe? (Record what you changed.) Did you observe anything that was interesting or different or unexpected?

Trial # _____: What happened? Did you vary the recipe? (Record what you changed.) Did you observe anything that was interesting or different or unexpected?

Trial # _____: What happened? Did you vary the recipe? (Record what you changed.) Did you observe anything that was interesting or different or unexpected?

Trial # _____: What happened? Did you vary the recipe? (Record what you changed.) Did you observe anything that was interesting or different or unexpected?

Describe your ice cream, using as many of your senses as possible. How is your ice cream similar to or different from store-bought ice cream? If you made more than one batch, how did the batches taste, feel, and look different? Why do you think that is?

LET'S SAVE THE ICE!

1. Quickly! You don't have much time! Get two feet of something—waxed paper, paper towels, aluminum foil, and so on—and build something that will prevent your ice cube from melting. Once it's built and your ice cube is secure, draw and describe your ice-saving device.

2. Now we're building a cooler for something more precious: ice cream. Draw and describe your cooler creation here.

Observation time 2:
Describe the ice cream.

3. Don't forget to record your observations! Even while building your cooler and writing, keep an eye on your experiment.

What time did you get your ice cream? _____

Observation time 1: _____
Describe the ice cream.

Observation time 3: _____
Describe the ice cream.

Observation time 4 (final): _____
Describe the ice cream. How successful was your cooler?

Science matters.

Any child born after the year 2000 has been born into a world in which humans live in outer space. Like a work of science fiction made real, in a single lifetime we've gone from the dawn of flight to traveling beyond our planet, seeing the break of day crest from the far side of the moon. This growth is not attributable to a single decision, and it was not the work of one high-profile individual. It was not the brainchild of a small, localized group, or due to the machinations of a powerful government. It stemmed from the dedicated effort of generations of individuals, building vast pyramids of knowledge from which we could move farther and farther toward the stars.

None of these advances were guaranteed. Research is unpredictable—it can see great leaps forward, and equally great leaps back. It is often slow, complex, and esoteric, unable to be made into an easy headline.

If we, as a species, are to continue growing our knowledge, not only do we need to be productive in our time, but also we must inspire others to continue on in our stead. We need to learn the unique language of the sciences, and we must also be prepared to translate it for those who have yet to understand.

Science matters. We once looked to the heavens. Now we walk among them. It is up to all of us to continue to help build on our knowledge, and to spread our passion to others. Each step we take as individuals is another step forward for us all.

Col. Chris Hadfield

Canadian astronaut Colonel Chris Hadfield is a man of many firsts. He was the first Canadian to operate the Canadarm, walk in space, and command the International Space Station. He's even been known to strum a tune once in a while. In An Astronaut's Guide to Life on Earth, *Col. Hadfield writes about his years of training and space exploration to show how to make the impossible possible.*

PLANET OOBLECK

BASED ON THE ORIGINAL WORKSHOP BY JULIUS DIAZ PANORIŃGAN

2 SESSIONS, 2 HOURS EACH
STEM DISCIPLINES: *Physical sciences, earth and space sciences, life sciences, engineering*
WRITING ACTIVITIES: *Technical writing, creative writing, narrative writing*

THERE ARE THREE THINGS JUST ABOUT ALL students enjoy: (1) animals; (2) spaceships; and (3) ooey-gooey, shape-shifting Oobleck.[1] This lesson uses all three to help students explore astronomy, zoology, and the amazing features of our Milky Way neighborhood, including its unbelievable wildlife. It builds on a lot of the skills learned in "It's (Partially) Rocket Science and (Mostly) Ice Cream," and makes a great follow-up to that.

Session 1: Oobleck

In this session, students must directly consider what wonders might be out there in the universe around us, and are presented with a (seemingly) out-of-this-world challenge.

MATERIALS

SESSION 1

☐ Copies of the planet handouts (1 per group; included with other handouts at the end of this lesson)

☐ Images of exoplanets[2] (show these using a computer and digital projector, or print them out and post them)

☐ Computer and digital projector (optional)

☐ Copies of the "What Is This Stuff?" handout

(continued)

---

1. For the origin of oobleck, see Dr. Seuss. (1976). *Bartholomew and the Oobleck.* New York, NY: Random House. (Original work published 1949)

2. There are many links to exoplanet imagery online. Photos featured in the article "Alien Worlds: Exoplanets in Pictures" by Phil Plait are an excellent example, and can be found here: *http://www.slate.com/articles/health _and_science/bad_astronomy/2012/11/exoplanet_pictures_astronomers_have_photos_of_alien_planets.html.*

- Cornstarch (2 or 3 16-ounce boxes per group)

- Water (4–5 cups, maybe more, per group)

- Food coloring (optional)

- Paper bowls, plates, or cups

- 1 large bowl for each group (enough to hold 6–8 cups of Oobleck)

- A large assortment of items to experiment with, like egg cartons, paper clips, aluminum foil, drinking straws, plastic knives, craft sticks, packing foam pieces, Bubble Wrap, and small paper or plastic cups

- String or a paper clip chain

- Masking tape, cut into small squares

- Construction paper

- Disposable vinyl tablecloths

- Corrugated cardboard

- Plastic wrap

- Scissors

- Key ring (optional)

- Yardstick (optional)

- A few paper airplanes (optional)

SESSION 2

- Copies of the "It's Alive! (Or Is It?)" handout

- Things that may or may not be alive, like a heat pack;

(*continued*)

Preparation

To keep things under control, divide the students into work groups of four or five. Before the students arrive, place the planet handouts on the table for each group, highlighting each of the planets in our solar system. These handouts consist of the following:

◇ A high-resolution picture of the featured planet

◇ A brief description of the atmosphere and/or surface (for example, information about how Earth's surface is mostly water)

◇ A brief fun fact about the planet (for example, the existence of Jupiter's Great Red Spot)

As a bonus, it's fun to include Pluto, our dwarf planet, and Enceladus and Europa, two potentially life-bearing moons.

Introduction: What Are Other Planets Like? (20 minutes)

As class begins, have the students look over the planet handouts. Also have direct images of exoplanets—planets outside our solar system—up on the projector (or printed out and posted). (Note that the images are very, very fuzzy, for two reasons. First, they are very, very, very far away. Second, most of the exoplanets we've found so far are relatively close to stars, and things that are that bright will of course result in poor image quality.)

Now it's time for a writing warm-up. Ask the students to imagine what a mysterious exoplanet is like by responding to the following prompt:

Write about what things are like on the planet's surface, being as detailed as possible.

Is the surface solid (rocky, dusty, soil covered, icy, metallic, crystalline, or something else); liquid (water, lava, or a different liquid); or maybe even gas?

Is there air on your planet? If there is, can humans breathe it, or is it poisonous?

Is it bright on your planet's surface, or is it shadowy?

Incidentally, astronomers do something very similar to this writing exercise. There's a lot to glean from a picture. Using a process called spectroscopy, scientists are able to determine what chemical compounds are present in stars and planets, all based on the color of the celestial body.

An Intro to Oobleck (20 minutes)

Everyone already knows that Earth is full of crazy physical phenomena. Imagine how many more crazy physical phenomena there are out in space! Here, you will present one of the Milky Way's finest features: Oobleck.

Introduce Oobleck as a substance forming the surface of a mythical planet. Then make some. If you don't have much time, and want to keep things a little cleaner, the Oobleck can be made beforehand. If at all possible, however, have each group of students make their own. It's much more engaging (make some Oobleck yourself if you don't believe us). We think that kinesthetic learning is a learning modality that is underused, but that lots of people respond to. Also, Oobleck is messy—which will encourage students to collaborate to keep the mess under control. Finally, the constant testing and refinement that go into making Oobleck mirror elements of both the scientific method and the writing process.

To make the Oobleck, you simply combine the cornstarch and water in a large bowl, adding more of each as necessary, until you get a mixture that becomes a solid when you grab a handful of it and a liquid when you release it into the bowl. Such is the magic of Oobleck. Food coloring can be added now or later, if desired.

a candle; a compass; or a toy car (bonus points for a remote-control car); a perpetual motion toy;[3] something moldy (cheese, bread, leftovers); live mushrooms; bugs (garden bugs; such as worms or roly-polys; or pet bugs); a pet fish; a potato; or an onion with roots and/or sprouts; a cut flower in a vase; moss; lichen; bark; seeds; a carrot; a pinecone; a guinea pig; a toy robot; or a Roomba

☐ Phylo cards (See "Preparation" in session 2.)

☐ Images of animals or plants that have adapted to their environment, like certain dog species and insects (you can project these from a computer, or simply print them out and pass them around)

Plan on up to twenty minutes max for the mixing of the Oobleck—if mixing goes quickly, any extra time can be well spent on experimentation or writing later in the session. It's easiest to mix one big batch per group, which can be divvied up afterward to individual students. To get everyone in on the action, assign roles as follows: one student in charge of cornstarch, one student in charge of water, one student in charge of mixing, and one student in charge of testing consistency. Roles are flexible depending on the size of each group. Groups should share a big bowl of Oobleck, and can use paper plates, cups, or bowls for their individual experiments.

Testing and Observation of the Oobleck (10 minutes)

After all the Oobleck has been distributed, it's time for students to plan some small experiments they'd like to do with the Oobleck, using their "What Is This Stuff?" handout. These mini-experiments should give them a better idea of how the Oobleck affects, and is affected by, various materials, which they'll need to know when designing Oobleck-proof spacecraft in the next segment.

---

3. These are great if you can get hold of one: *http://en.wikipedia.org/wiki/Drinking_bird*.

The mini-experiments might explore what happens when they pour Oobleck from a cup, drop a paper clip in it, poke it with a pencil, or smear it on paper. Ideally, one experiment will lead to the next. After students poke it with a pencil, they might investigate what happens when they poke it with something sharper, or blunter, poking it harder, or softer. What happens when they put paper on the Oobleck versus Oobleck on the paper? Does it interact with crumpled paper differently than with smooth?

If you can, review the planned mini-experiments—or have an adult helper do so—before each student starts to experiment. You can also ask to see their results before they move on to the next activity.

Spacecrafting (15 minutes)

Now that they've explored the mysteries of Oobleck's surface, it's time for students to create a space-craft. Working individually and in conversation with lab group members, students grab materials on hand: string, paper clips, construction paper, disposable vinyl tablecloths, corrugated cardboard, plastic wrap, and scissors. Their task, should they choose to accept it, is to design a craft that can both take off from and land on Oobleck—without sinking! If the clock is ticking, you can limit anything extremely intricate or time consuming by imposing a size maximum on the spacecraft constructions—for example, six inches max in any dimension. (*Note:* Because giant strips of masking tape may result in high-indestructible spacecraft, it's best to cut tape into squares as directed in the materials list.)

Landing Tests, Takeoff Tests, and Retests (15 minutes)

Before beginning testing, make sure each group has a pretty full bowl of Oobleck. If not, they should return some of their individual test Oobleck to the group bowl. It's okay if there's junk in the gunk—we're guessing that any planet out there with a surface remotely like Oobleck probably has some irregularities.

The proof of the pudding is on Oobleck's crust. Depending on the students' and/or your propensity for mayhem, you can define landing and taking off in any way you like. Landing is often easier: drop the spacecraft from one or two or five or ten feet. Or toss the craft onto the Oobleck, slide it off some sort of ramp at a 45-degree angle, and so on. A short drop is easy to execute, but making a landing at an angle is less so. Taking off is probably harder. You can tie a piece of string to a spacecraft or use a paper clip chain, then yank. Or you can create a skyhook—affix a key ring or paper clip to the upper portion of the craft, and attach a hook to the end of a yardstick, which can be swung gently so that it catches the ring. Ideally, the craft (1) survives the stress, and (2) successfully separates from the Oobleck surface.

Optional: To further liven up the testing section, you can chuck paper planes into Oobleck to demonstrate *disastrous* landings. Planes might bounce. Planes might get stuck. (Planes will probably not be in good enough shape to fly again.)

Writing and Reflection (40 minutes)

With a few minutes' warning, announce that Oobleck time is ending. It's tempting to experiment with Oobleck for hours (believe us, we've been there!), but make sure everyone stops—there's more stuff to go through!

Give students ten minutes to take notes about how their spacecraft fared. Then give them another twenty minutes to answer the following prompt, using their recent findings:

Imagine that you are part of the crew in the spacecraft you built. Write an action-packed story about your landing and/or takeoff, either on the Oobleck planet or the planet you wrote about earlier. What problems were there? How did you (and your crew, if you had one) ingeniously fix things?

In the final ten minutes of the session, ask students to discuss their Oobleck findings. It's useful to note here how Oobleck works like quicksand. Left on its own, it's a gooey liquid. When you apply force, it acts like a solid! (Science is crazy and leaves room for infinite discovery; who knows what's out there in the universe?)

FOR YOU TO KNOW (AND YOUR STUDENTS TO DISCOVER)

Oobleck is so much fun because (in addition to being messy) it doesn't behave as we would expect it to. Sometimes, when it is sitting in a bowl or you are letting it drip between the fingers of your cupped hand, it seems to be a liquid. Other times, though, it acts like a solid—if you squeeze your cupped hand, or slap or hit the liquid in the container, it seems to suddenly solidify. Weird.

Water, which is our reference for a normal fluid because it is the one we use most, doesn't behave this way. Water molecules flow past one another. If we want to make them flow faster, we have to apply more force. For example, if you put a hole in a balloon filled with water, the water will begin to drip out. Squeeze the balloon lightly, and the water will flow out more quickly. Squeeze it hard, and the speed of the water increases yet again. If you could quantify the pressure of your squeeze (the amount of force) and the rate of the water flow, you would find that to double the rate of the water flow, you would have to double the force you applied to the balloon. Isaac Newton, the amazing physicist, figured this out (along with many, many other important discoveries).

Oobleck is a non-Newtonian fluid, meaning that it doesn't behave according to the rules that Newton discovered. A non-Newtonian fluid does not have constant **viscosity**—depending on what's happening to the liquid, it becomes more or less likely to flow. **Shear** is a type of force, and when Oobleck experiences that force, the molecules in the liquid rearrange themselves in such a way that the fluid thickens.

With a fluid like Oobleck, applying a force increases the friction between the molecules, making them resist flowing (appear more thick, or in science-speak, viscous). The more force you apply, the more resistance there is—and the more solid-like the "liquid" appears—until the force is released.

Oobleck isn't the only non-Newtonian fluid, or even the only *type* of non-Newtonian fluid. Other fluids behave very differently—ketchup, for instance. In what ways does ketchup behave differently from water or Oobleck?

Session 2: Is It Alive?

In this session, students first will attempt to define what life is, and then they will use everything they've learned to hypothesize what life out there in the universe might be like, if it exists.

Preparation

For this session, you'll need some Phylo cards (see following). Students will also need some examples of life to examine, so before class begins, set up exhibits of potential life forms around the classroom, like a candle, a carrot, a pinecone, and so on.

> Before class, you'll need to get some Phylo cards, which you can either purchase or print yourself from *http://phylogame.org*. A few sets should be enough for the whole class. Phylo founder David Ng explains the game:
>
> > The Phylo Project is a biodiversity trading card game inspired by research that showed that children were more familiar with Pokémon characters than with real plants and animals. This inspiration has led to a crowdsourced effort where a flexible biodiversity game platform has been created. Here, cards (and decks) are freely accessible for easy selection, downloading, and printing; whereby the cards can also be used to play a variety of existing games, as well as be used to create new and novel game systems. The Phylo Project also allows interested individuals to make their own DIY cards and decks. Due to the project's popularity, a number of educational hosts (research labs, museums, teacher classrooms) have taken it upon themselves to produce high-quality Phylo card decks, many of which can be purchased locally or online.

What Is Life?[4] (40 minutes)

At the start of class, distribute the "It's Alive! (Or Is It?)" handout and instruct students to walk around and examine, ponder, and record whether they think things are or are not alive. Students should continue exploring and recording until the fifteen-minute mark; they may or may not have assessed everything, but that's okay.

For the next segment of this activity (about fifteen minutes), bring the group together for discussion. For every item, ask who thinks it's alive, and who thinks it's not alive. Students may indicate their answer by raising their hand, calling out, or—to keep things active—moving to one side of the room or the other. For items that are controversial or perplexing, ask students to share reasons why the item might be alive or why it might not be, preferably drawing out one point of view from each side. Record reasons on a large writing surface in front of the class.

To lead out, mention that scientists disagree on things! It's cool! Sometimes scientists ask really hard questions (like, What is life?), and they have to learn new things to find better answers.

In the final ten minutes of this activity, ask students the really hard question: What is life? Let them come up with characteristics, a definition, whatever works best for them, using the notes on

---

4. This activity is adapted from "What Is Life," *http://seplessons.org/node/94*.

the chalkboard or other surface as food for thought. (It might be useful for students to answer in the negative, saying what life *isn't*.) Also, students may decide to work in groups; or, if the previous discussion has a lot of good momentum, feel free to change things up so the entire class works together to create a definition.

Adaptation Presentation (15 minutes)

Ideally, you've just blown students' minds with a giant question, and now you want to expand their horizons a little more. You've shown them some ordinary, everyday things that may or may not be alive, and now you'll show them some less ordinary things that we generally can agree are alive: animals and plants. Animals and plants adapt to their environment. A great example can be found by comparing the Chaco tortoise (a species from mainland South America that is closely related to the ancestor of the Galápagos tortoise) with two different Galápagos subspecies. Even though all three tortoises come from the same plodding pedigree, the two Galápagos subspecies have developed different shells from the Chaco tortoise, that help them reach available food sources in different ways. It's not obvious, but the shell shapes let them flex their back and neck in different ways to enable them to grab higher or lower food. Show some images of animals and plants that have adapted to their environment—like sloths, leaf insects, bee orchids, and metalmark moths. And close out with some extremophiles—deep sea creatures that survive pressure that would crush most submarines, for instance.

You have now come to one of the session's key ideas: *How do animals' (physical) characteristics help them in their environment?* As a group, brainstorm a list of ways that various animals have adapted to their environment. Camels and polar bears are an easy place to start, and then discussion can move on to less obvious adaptations. This is a fantastic place to adapt the lesson to fit the interests of your students. You could even do a lesson built entirely around dog breeds.

There are far more organisms here than you have time for, so pick your favorites from the brainstorm list, or those you think will be most interesting to the group. Select a few, explain adaptations, and open things up for discussion and hypotheses.[5]

Adaptation Activity with Phylo Cards (25 minutes)

Give students a selection of Phylo cards and the following writing prompt:

> In the future, bioengineering has made huge advances. Humanity can now easily produce chimeras—combinations of two or more organisms. Unfortunately, "easily" is a relative term—it still takes a vast amount of resources to do this. Despite the amount of resources the process takes, however, it has been determined that a chimera lab is important for flexibility in space exploration. You can take the genetic code from five and only five different organisms into space, and use these organisms to create chimeras that you may need on each planet. Look through your Phylo deck and determine which five organisms you will bring, and briefly explain why. (For example, you can choose to bring a chameleon if you want to make chimeras with adaptable camouflage.)

---

5. Various organisms' info, with accompanying slides if you'd like more visuals, can be found here: *http://www.bbc.co.uk/nature/adaptations*.

Organisms in Space (40 minutes)

Now that students have chosen their organisms, have them each select a planet (or planet-like body) of their choice—a planet in our solar system, planet Oobleck, or the exoplanet they wrote about in session 1. Using this planet as their intergalactic home base, students now explore the final writing prompt:

> Hello, explorer! Your adventures have taken you to this planet. Write about the chimera(s) you would create from your genetic bank to help you and humanity survive, settle, and thrive here. Focus on some of the difficulties your new planetary home poses, and write a story about how you, your chimera(s), and your fellow explorers tackle the problems and make a new home.

Students may want to consider some of the essentials of life on Earth, and whether or not they're present on this new planet. For example: Is there sufficient water, and in a form that people can use (that is, not all frozen under the ground)? Can regular Earth plants grow in the soil on this planet, if there's soil at all? What is the atmosphere like—can animals or plants breathe in it? Are there major atmospheric disturbances, like Jupiter's Great Red Spot?

If students finish early, ask them to consider, as a bonus prompt, how native life on their planet may have evolved, and to create a catalog of some of the life forms. Students can even draw these life forms, labeling the elements that are specific adaptations to the planet's conditions.

And now you're done, and you've done *a lot*. By this point, students have covered a number of different topics (thermodynamics, geology, and adaptation) that could be considered the domains of different types of scientists (physicists, geologists, and biologists, respectively). The reality is, though, that many of these fields blend into each other, and all of these disciplines are necessary to consider while we as a civilization think about going to Mars and beyond. The hope is that students start to decompartmentalize their scientific thinking, which will help them think both analytically and creatively—having a lot of messy, Ooblecky fun along the way.

FOR YOU TO KNOW (AND YOUR STUDENTS TO DISCOVER)

Biologists generally agree that all living things share some common characteristics. For example, all living things **grow; reproduce; respire** (harvest energy from food); **obtain energy** (nutrition—plants make their own through photosynthesis, whereas animals eat to obtain energy); **excrete** (remove) waste products from their cells; and **sense and respond** to their environment. Most scientists would agree that **movement**—but not necessarily the kind you can see—is also a characteristic of living things: living things, whether made of one cell or trillions, need to be able to move things (nutrients, water, waste, cellular components, and so on) in and/or between cells. Finally, scientists agree that all living things are **made of one or more cells.** Beyond these characteristics, though, it is hard to find absolute agreement on definitive criteria.

This list raises interesting questions—dilemmas about life. For instance, is a cut flower alive? We generally don't think of cut flowers as dead until they are brown or start to lose petals. Yet, even though a cut flower may continue to photosynthesize (obtain energy) and transport water up its stem, it is no longer growing or capable of reproduction. What about a potato or a tulip bulb lying dormant, doing few of these actions as it is waiting to be planted? Both the potato and the tulip bulb have the potential for life, but are they alive?

Viruses are yet another gray area. Even among scientists, there is some debate as to whether or not viruses are alive. Viruses cause diseases, such as the common cold. They are not made of cells; rather, they are much simpler—just genetic material surrounded by a protein coat. Viruses cannot reproduce on their own—they have to infect a host cell (and there is some really cool movement that happens in this process). Once inside, they subvert the cellular machinery to reproduce. Thus, viruses present a conundrum by exhibiting some but not all of the characteristics of living things. Most scientists would state that viruses are not living things, but it is possible that as our understanding of both viruses and the range of living things grows, our ideas will change.

Students bring a lot of prior experiences to any discussion about what "makes" something alive. Sometimes their prior knowledge can lead them to jump to conclusions without really thinking through whether or not they have direct evidence that something is alive. For example, if presented with a flickering candle, students using their prior knowledge will say that it is not alive. A flame is a really interesting item, however, precisely because it exhibits many of the characteristics of a living thing. It moves, it can reproduce, it requires an energy (fuel) source, it can grow, and we can see the formation of waste products (smoke and soot). Similarly, students may very quickly say that a potted plant is alive. But they are unlikely to see it move, reproduce, make (photosynthesize) and use energy, grow, or excrete waste. We like to encourage students to pretend that they are visitors from another planet, encountering these items for the first time—and collecting evidence based on what they can observe for whether or not the specimens are alive.

MERCURY

Mercury's surface is rocky and covered with craters, like that of Earth's moon.

Mercury has next to no atmosphere because radiation from the sun pushes its atmosphere into space.

EARTH

Earth is where we live!

Earth's surface is almost 70 percent water.

VENUS

Venus is the hottest planet in the solar system (up to 880 degrees Fahrenheit), in large part because it has a dense atmosphere of carbon dioxide, a greenhouse gas.

Venus has lightning from clouds of sulfuric acid.

MARS

Mars has the biggest mountain of any planet in the solar system, Olympus Mons. (It's a volcano.)

NASA's *Curiosity* rover landed on Mars in 2012 to look for signs of life, among other things.

JUPITER

Jupiter is made mostly of gas, but it's more massive than all the other planets in the solar system put together.

Jupiter's Great Red Spot is a giant storm (bigger than Earth) that has been observed for over three hundred years.

SATURN

Saturn's winds can be five times as fast as the strongest hurricanes on Earth.

Saturn is very large (the biggest planet after Jupiter), but it's relatively light (it's made mostly of gas), and it would float in a big enough pool of water.

EUROPA

Europa, one of Jupiter's moons, has a surface mostly made of ice.

Scientists believe that under the ice there may be water and volcanoes, which may support life.

ENCELADUS

Enceladus, one of Saturn's moons, has shown evidence of both water (mostly ice) and toasty temperatures (from volcanoes).

Some scientists think it's the place (other than Earth) in our solar system that is most likely to be able to support life.

URANUS

Uranus was the first planet found with the aid of a telescope (in 1781).

Uranus is a so-called ice giant (so is Neptune), with a core made of icy materials (similar to those on Earth), but the "ice" is actually a very hot, thick liquid.

NEPTUNE

Neptune was the first planet found via mathematical predictions (in 1846).

Neptune (like Uranus and Jupiter) has a giant storm, called the Great Dark Spot.

In the photo shown here, Pluto is the larger dot in the middle. The smaller dot to the right is Charon, Pluto's largest moon.

PLUTO

Pluto used to be considered a planet, but isn't anymore.

Pluto is very rocky and icy, and it's even smaller than Earth's moon!

PLANET OOBLECK

How do you imagine this mysterious planet? Draw it in the space above.

WHAT IS THIS STUFF?

STEP 1:

What are your mini-experiments?

Describe what you intend to do with the Oobleck.

Experiment #1:

Experiment #2:

STEP 2:

What do you think will happen?

Describe how the Oobleck will react to the mini-experiment.

Hypothesis #1:

Hypothesis #2:

STEP 3:

How did things turn out?

What actually happened to the Oobleck?

Result #1:

Result #2:

WHAT IS THIS STUFF? (continued)

STEP 1:

What are your mini-experiments?

Describe what you intend to do with the Oobleck.

Experiment #3:

Experiment #4:

STEP 2:

What do you think will happen?

Describe how the Oobleck will react to the mini-experiment.

Hypothesis #3:

Hypothesis #4:

STEP 3:

How did things turn out?

What actually happened to the Oobleck?

Result #3:

Result #4:

WHAT IS THIS STUFF? (continued)

STEP 1:

What are your mini-experiments?

Describe what you intend to do with the Oobleck.

Experiment #5:

Experiment #6:

STEP 2:

What do you think will happen?

Describe how the Oobleck will react to the mini-experiment.

Hypothesis #5:

Hypothesis #6:

STEP 3:

How did things turn out?

What actually happened to the Oobleck?

Result #5:

Result #6:

WHAT IS THIS STUFF? (continued)

STEP 1:

What are your mini-experiments?

Describe what you intend to do with the Oobleck.

Experiment # ____:

Experiment # ____:

STEP 2:

What do you think will happen?

Describe how the Oobleck will react to the mini-experiment.

Hypothesis # ____:

Hypothesis # ____:

STEP 3:

How did things turn out?

What actually happened to the Oobleck?

Result # ____:

Result # ____:

WHAT IS THIS STUFF? (continued)

LET'S LAND ON THIS STUFF.

STEP 4:

Oobleck, meet spaceship.

Now that you're more familiar with the physical properties of Oobleck, design and build a spaceship that will land on and take off from a planet made of it. Draw and describe that spaceship here.

WHAT IS THIS STUFF? (continued)

STEP 5:

Did you get there okay?

Describe what happened when your spacecraft landed on the Oobleck surface. Diagrams may be helpful.

STEP 6:

Can you make it back home?

Describe what happened during your attempted take-off from the Oobleck surface. Diagrams may be helpful.

IT'S ALIVE! (OR IS IT?)

Examine the specimens, and determine: What is that thing? Is it alive? Why or why not? Make sure to describe important characteristics or behavior.

Specimen 1:

Is it alive? Circle one: Yes   No

Why or why not? Describe:

Specimen 2:

Is it alive? Circle one: Yes   No

Why or why not? Describe:

Specimen 3:

Is it alive? Circle one: Yes   No

Why or why not? Describe:

Specimen 4:

Is it alive? Circle one: Yes   No

Why or why not? Describe:

Specimen 5:

Is it alive? Circle one: Yes   No

Why or why not? Describe:

Specimen 6:

Is it alive? Circle one: Yes   No

Why or why not? Describe:

The best science fiction writers don't just cram a bunch of futuristic inventions and alien weapons and crazy mutations into a story and say, "Finished!" Good sci-fi explores characters who live in strange and wonderful worlds—and by doing so tells us a little bit about our own place in the crazy, wonderful world we live in. Before I wrote books—including a couple of science fiction picture books—I used to run an 826 center in Los Angeles. 826LA used to be housed in a building with very old plumbing, and, for some bizarre reason, one of our students loved flushing great reams of paper towels down the toilet. One day I walked into the bathroom to find this little guy up to his ankles in (clean!) water. The whole place was flooded. He looked at me, shrugged, and said, "Sorry." Then he left to do his homework. It was a pretty casual reaction to the complete disaster he'd caused. This episode inspired *Oh No! Or How My Science Project Destroyed the World*, about a girl who builds a rampaging robot and doesn't seem nearly alarmed enough about the damage her creation causes. Laser eyes, huge claws, giant toads—all the nutso sci-fi stuff in that book helps us get to know a very specific kind of character.

Mac Barnett

Mac Barnett is the author of over fifteen books for children, including Oh No! Or How My Science Project Destroyed the World *and* Oh No! Not Again! (Or How I Built a Time Machine to Save History) (Or at Least My History Grade), *both of which won the Golden Duck Award for the best science fiction picture book for children. He's also the former executive director of 826LA, and founded the Echo Park Time Travel Mart.*

HOW TO WRITE SCIENCE FICTION

BASED ON THE ORIGINAL WORKSHOP BY CORY DOCTOROW

4 SESSIONS, 60 MINUTES EACH
STEM DISCIPLINE: *Technology (science, technology, and society)*
WRITING ACTIVITIES: *Narrative writing, creative writing*

WRITING A SCIENCE FICTION STORY IS LIKE BUILDING A MACHINE WITH TWO gears: a big one (the world you're creating) and a little one (the characters in it). The little gear turns the big one around. The big wheel doesn't have a lot of torque; what it has is a lot of stuff. The characters, meanwhile, don't have a lot of stuff, but they've got the emotions that keep things happening in the big world and keep readers interested. In this lesson, students will explore technology by creating a big world and a small group of characters, and then bringing them together to form the beginnings of a science fiction story.

This lesson is a little different from the others in this book, with more creative writing and less hands-on STEM. You're going to ask your students some big questions: Where have we gone with technology? Where might we go next?

These are central questions in the interdisciplinary field of science, technology, and society (STS), which is concerned with how science and technology affect human society, and vice versa. This lesson introduces students to STS thinking through the lens of science fiction. Ray Bradbury once said, "Science fiction is really sociological studies of the future, things that the writer believes are going to happen by putting two and two together." (For a great interview with Bradbury, see "Handy Lesson Links" in the appendix.) The best science fiction isn't about lasers and robots and time travel; it's about what happens to humans and humanity because of lasers and robots and time travel. This lesson helps students break down the elements of science fiction, examine what makes the genre go, and explore STS all along the way.

Session 1: Exploring Technology

Before students build the parts of a science fiction story, help them contemplate one of the drivers of science fiction: technology. A lot of the best sci-fi explores the implications of technological change, so you'll start by having students explore the technologies that have shaped our world.

Technology Brainstorming and Discussion (25 minutes)

Start by asking students what they think is the most important invention ever, and write their responses on the board. After you have a few good suggestions, turn each example into a bubble diagram as a class, listing the things that rely on that invention, then all the things that rely on *those* inventions, as far as you can go. For example, if someone suggested the wheel, you could write down cars, gears, conveyor belts, and more. Students could then extend that—the conveyor belt could lead to tank treads and factory assembly lines, and factory assembly lines could lead to just about anything, from tennis shoes to Twinkies.

When things have slowed down a bit, ask: "What would happen if we, today, lacked technology X? Did the importance of any particular invention surprise you?"

The Story of the Wheel (5 minutes)

Presumably, someone suggested the wheel (or some related technology, such as transportation) during the first segment. If, somehow, nobody did, bring it up with the class. Go through all the things that the wheel makes possible, focusing on the less obvious possibilities. (As already noted, wheels enable mass production of such important things as clothing.) Crazy, right? Then share the history of the wheel. Researchers think it likely that the wheel as we know it was only invented once—possibly in Sumeria, or in what is now Ukraine—and that its use spread from culture to culture like wildfire because it was so amazing. A version of the wheel was invented in Central America, but it was never used for complex machines or hard labor—just for little trinkets and toys. The moral of the story is that not everyone necessarily gets a given piece of technology.

Let There Be No Light (30 minutes)

This activity works best if you can split up the students into two groups, and can turn off the lights in just one part of the room. If you can't split into two, that's okay; everyone will just go through the experience of having no electricity.

For one group (or the whole class, if you can't split them up), let students know that they'll be completing the writing task they are about to be assigned without the use of anything that requires electricity. Shut off the lights, bar the use of phones, computing devices, and so on. Students may point out that, say, pencils were sharpened electrically, or produced in a factory that used electricity. Should that happen, acknowledge that they're right, and say that pencils aren't allowed either. In that case, they'll probably have to compose their assignment in their heads, memorize it as best they can, and deliver it orally.

The other group will have access to everything the first group doesn't. Then ask students to respond to either of the following two writing prompts they prefer:

> Write about what a life without electricity would be like. How would you live, day after day? What are the things you would have to do to survive? What are the things you would do for entertainment? If you could have one (and only one) thing that used electricity, what would it be? What would be better about a life without electricity? What would be worse?

and

> Write about what a life with electricity would be like. How would you live, day after day? What are the things you would have to do to survive? What are the things you would do for entertainment? If you had to get rid of one (and only one) thing that used electricity, what would it be? What would be better about a life with electricity? What would be worse?

For the group that has electricity, you can either hand out copies or share the prompts electronically (via e-mail, or Edmodo, or a class dashboard, if students are on computers). For the students that don't—really, there'll only be handwritten copies available, and there will be just a few, because you can't have used a copying machine to mass produce a copy for every student.

Having students live the experience for a little while, with a normally menial task, should drive home a point: technology changes everything. Students don't even necessarily need to complete their assigned prompt—before too long, the frustration from one half of the room (or everyone) with not having the usual helpful technologies will facilitate a transition into a valuable discussion about the experience. Students are likely to dwell, at first, on the inconvenience of not having electricity. But you can hope that a few will come up with pros, and others will realize that there are just different ways of doing things, not necessarily good or bad.

At the end of this segment, share with students the very true fact that large portions of the world do not have regular access to electricity.

Session 2: Imagine a World . . .

Every story has to happen somewhere, but it's very common, when you're a new writer, to start in a white room. That's because even *you* don't know what's there yet. But the more that's there, the more it's going to feel like the story is really happening, which is going to help your readers care about what's going on. One way to make a story believable is to make this world somewhere you really know. It can be an imaginary place you've thought a lot about, or it can be somewhere real. We tend to think of science fiction as always happening in outer space, but lots of science fiction stories take place in actual cities.

You want to have some kind of premise, whether real or imaginary—some problem or question your story is going to explore. In *Little Brother,* the premise that author Cory Doctorow started with came from wanting to write a story in which the technology actually worked. He'd seen innumerable thrillers where the computers were treated as narrative conveniences, without regard for how computers actually function (which is too bad, because real-life computers can do some really amazing stuff). So he started brainstorming scenarios in which computers can help with exciting things: cat-and-mouse games, kids hiding from schools, individuals hiding from authorities and from criminals. From there the story followed naturally.

Once you've got an idea of what your world will be like, you can start to populate it with things, structures, infrastructures, and so on, all of which usually emerge organically from your premise. The world just starts to spin itself out. Whenever something new has to appear, you ask yourself what the material would look like. Some detail you draw from real life, and some you imagine.

For this session, have your students each come up with a premise for a story about an imagined world. First, ask them to imagine a technology that is changing their fictional world. Then, have them write up a detailed description of the world they'll be writing about, and how changing technology affects it. Invite them to draw it; map it; and describe its landscape, its climate, its sky, its streets (if it has streets), and its dwellings (ditto). They should think about time, too: Is this in the future, the present, or the past?

They should also think about the society. Is it a totalitarian regime, or an anarchic utopia? Remind them that, as in the real world, some people will have access to different technologies, and others won't. Ask, "How are things similar or different between these groups of people? How does technological access relate to the structure of a society?"

Session 3: Create the Character(s)

When you stop and think about it, caring about fictional people is really weird. Why do we care about Charlie Brown, who's not much more sophisticated than a crosswalk figure? The answer is that, to some extent, your brain believes that Charlie Brown is a real person, so he matters to you.

That's the writer's job. You're trying to trick someone else's brain into thinking a fictional character is a real person, so that that individual will care about him or her. How do you do that? There's no one true way, but in general it's a good idea to figure out who your main character is, and what he or she knows and doesn't know—and really stick to that consistently.

Part of what makes dramatic tension is what one character knows and another doesn't, and one way to blow it is to have characters act like they know something they don't, like when a character expresses a certainty about how another character is feeling. "I walked into the room, Janet was waiting for me, she'd been there for hours, she was internally furious." How do you know that? It starts feeling too made-up.

For this session, have your students each imagine a person who, for a reason that's entirely plausible, showcases the most interesting aspects of the world they'll be writing about. This is the person who'll be taking the reader through the tour of the imagined world. Students should describe this person in concrete detail. What does he look like? What gets her excited? What makes him afraid? What's her best trait, and her worst? How does he respond to authority? What other people are in her life, and how do they relate to her? What's his biggest problem, his greatest wish? Does the character have access to the world-changing technology? Has the character seen the different parts of the world, and been in different parts of its society? If so, what were those experiences like? If not, what does the character think he knows about the rest of the world? Is he mostly right or mostly wrong?

Session 4: Bring Your World and Your Characters Together

Now students will bring the elements together to start their story. The basis of pretty much every story is a person and a place with a problem, and things are getting worse. Technology may be part of the problem, part of the solution, or both—but students don't need to get hung up on the details just yet. Ask them to start with one scene, and see where it leads them.

Make sure to set aside some time, maybe ten minutes, at the end of this last session so that your students have time to share their writing!

STEM@HOME: WAY BACK WHEN

Technology changes our lives. As we're reminded firsthand in this lesson, electricity has changed almost every aspect of what we do and how we do it, from allowing us to stay up after dark reading or watching TV, to enabling us to keep food fresh in refrigerators, to . . . you name it.

There are lots of other technologies that are continuing to change how we live. Can you imagine life before cell phones? The Internet? Computers? How has the combination of cell phones or smartphones and computers changed the way we communicate with one another?

Your parents probably remember life before cell phones and computers. Your grandparents (or an elderly neighbor) most certainly do. What was life like for them at your age? How did technology (or its absence) affect them?

Oral History

Perhaps one of the best ways to learn about what life was like in the past is to hear stories from people who actually lived it. These stories are filled with intimate details of memories and events recalled by those who participated in them—and when those people are your relatives, their stories help you develop a rich narrative of your own family background and experiences.

Oral history is the collection and study of the experiences of people, whether famous politicians, popular culture figures, or your own family members. Oral historians often approach subjects with a list of interview questions that help them prompt those subjects to share information about a topic of interest.

Find a time to interview a parent and/or one of your grandparents or older friends or relatives. You can conduct the interview in person or using technology (on the phone or via Skype or FaceTime).

Following are a few interview questions to get you started. Look them over, and then add others that are meaningful to you. Don't forget that you can always ask a follow-up question if you want to learn more about a particular topic.

1. How old were you when you got your first cell phone?

2. How did you communicate with your friends before cell phones, texting, and online messaging?

    a. How did you communicate in the evenings (after school)?

    b. How did you communicate during school (and during class)?

    c. How did you figure out how, when, and where to meet up with friends?

    d. If you were already out, how did you find and catch up with your friends?

(continued)

STEM@HOME: WAY BACK WHEN (continued)

3. Did you spend a lot of time talking on the phone? Where were you when you were on the phone?

4. Was it expensive to use the phone?

5. How many phones and extensions were in the house? Did you have your own phone number?

6. Did your parents limit how much time you spent on the phone? Why?

7. How did you remember or find phone numbers?

8. How could you call someone if you were not home? What if you did not have any money with you?

Here are some additional questions for a grandparent, older friend, or older relative:

1. Do you remember when your family got a phone for the first time?

2. What did you do before you had a phone?

3. What was the phone used for? Were you allowed to use it?

4. What is a party line? Did your family have one?

5. How did having a phone change your life, and your family's life?

6. What is a telegram? Did you ever send or receive one? Why?

Fun Telephone Facts[1]

▸ The first telephone call was made in March 1876 by Alexander Graham Bell.

▸ The push-button (touch-tone) phone was introduced in 1963. Before that, phones had rotary dials (and many people still used rotary phones for many years).

▸ The idea for mobile phones originated in 1888, but the technology did not exist until nearly a hundred years later.

---

1. The facts are derived from the following sources: "Telephone History," *http://www.telephonymuseum.com/ telephone%20history.htm*; "Telephone," *http://www.ideafinder.com/history/inventions/telephone.htm*; Motorola DynaTAC (n.d.). In *Wikipedia,* from *http://en.wikipedia.org/wiki/Motorola_DynaTAC.*

(continued)

STEM@HOME: WAY BACK WHEN (continued)

- To make a phone call when phones were first introduced, you would call the operator and tell her (although the first phone operators were men, they were quickly replaced by women, who were found to be "more gracious and polite") the name of the person you were trying to reach. It wasn't until later that phone numbers were introduced.

- In 1970 the first Picturephone system made its debut, but people hated it, and the idea did not catch on (until Skype and FaceTime).

- The first cell phone call was made in 1973—but it took ten more years for the first commercial system to be set up in the United States.

- The first cell phones weighed nearly two pounds, with batteries that were the size of a brick (and a charge only lasted about an hour).

- The first mobile phone cost almost $9,500 in today's dollars.

- Actress Hedy Lamarr and composer George Antheil coinvented something in 1941 that is now called frequency-hopping spread spectrum (FHSS). (Back then, in U.S. Patent 2,292,387, they called it "Secret Communication System.") FHSS is a core technology for things like cell phones and Wi-Fi!

MAKING WAVES

BASED ON THE ORIGINAL WORKSHOP BY A. REID

1 SESSION, 2 HOURS
STEM DISCIPLINES: *Physical sciences, engineering, mathematics*
WRITING ACTIVITIES: *Technical writing, creative writing, narrative writing, songwriting*

ANYONE WHO'S SPENT TIME WITH KIDS knows they're *really* good at making noise. In this lesson, they'll learn the science behind it. Through their explorations, students will also begin to investigate the elegant relationship between music and math. The lesson concludes with students putting their new science insights into lyrics they can share with the group, accompanied by simple melodies played on homemade instruments.

"Music is just math in its best dress," wrote Aimee Bender. At 826, we often set writing to music: students are inspired by music, they write lyrics to it, and more. We have fewer opportunities to explore the math behind music, which is a shame, because there's a lot of it. Musical beats and rhythms connect to counting and series and fractions; and pitch and volume connect to more advanced math—inverse relationships and trigonometric functions, even Fourier transforms. In this lesson, we start to check out those connections.

MATERIALS

- ☐ Musical instrument, such as a drum, guitar, or harmonica (optional)
- ☐ Rubber bands
- ☐ Unsharpened pencils or other sticks
- ☐ Semisturdy containers (such as Tupperware, shoe boxes, or tissue boxes)
- ☐ Cups
- ☐ Bottles
- ☐ Paper towel or toilet paper rolls
- ☐ Straws
- ☐ Metal hangers

(continued)

- ☐ Anything else that might make an interesting sound

- ☐ Copies of the "Sound Exploration" handout (optional; included with the other handout at the end of this lesson)

- ☐ Pictures of musical instruments (optional)

- ☐ Slinky (optional)

- ☐ Bowl filled with water (optional)

- ☐ Clean, empty can (optional)

- ☐ Rubber band (optional)

- ☐ Copies of the "Musical Instrument Building" handout

- ☐ Tape (Scotch or masking)

- ☐ String

Introduction (15 minutes)

First, you'll explore what your students know about sound. To start the session, have students, on their own, write responses to questions like the following:

◇ What's the quietest sound you hear every day? What's the quietest sound you've ever heard?

◇ What's the loudest sound you hear every day? What's the loudest sound you've ever heard?

◇ What do you think was the loudest sound ever heard on Earth?

◇ What's the loudest sound you can make?

If you know your students are familiar with basic wave concepts, you can ask tougher questions:

◇ How are sounds different when you're underwater, or when you have your ear against a solid surface? Are there any things that are easier or harder to hear?

◇ How do microphones, speakers, and telephones work? How about sound recording and playback?

◇ Have you ever felt a sound? How is this possible?

When students have answered most of the questions (either basic or advanced, depending on your group), ask them to share their responses. If you're in an appropriate setting, have them demonstrate the sounds they can make. (Some students might scream; others might stomp. Some might whistle; and maybe someone will pull out a banjo.)

Ask students how sounds can be different, besides being quiet or loud. Having a musical instrument on hand and questions that will elicit specific details will help them come up with answers. (You could say, for example, "What's the difference between a monkey's scream and a gorilla's grunt? Both are pretty loud.") We want students eventually to get at **pitch**, shrill sounds versus deep sounds. Past that, other distinguishing sound characteristics, like **timbre** (see the "Timbre" sidebar), are much harder to describe and analyze. If your students understand wave concepts in relation to sound, they'll probably quickly (and reasonably accurately) bring up volume, pitch, and maybe more. For these students, move right into discussing their thoughts on the advanced sound prompts.

After students have shared their observations, ask why, why, why? Why are certain materials better conductors of certain sounds? (Follow-up questions: Can anything conduct all sounds? Or no sounds?) If you can feel things you hear, why can't you always hear things you feel? Why can't you hear everything, for that matter? You can ask "how" questions to get students thinking even harder: If sound is a physical wave, how is it stored in an MP3 player with no moving parts? How does sound travel from cell phone to cell phone, from radio tower to radio?

Before moving on, ask your students to write down what they know (or think they know) about what makes sounds different, and what they want to know about how different sounds are made. Having them brainstorm in small groups here may be helpful. Let them know that their knowledge and questions shared now will become part of an educational song later! (Some educators may recognize this as the *K* and *W* of KWL. In KWL, students first indicate the things they think they **K**now, then decide what they **W**ant to know. At the end of the inquiry, students will record and reflect on what they've **L**earned. The *L* will form the most important portion of their eventual song. KWL lines up pretty nicely with the scientific method, actually, corresponding to the research, hypothesis, and conclusions in some step-based formulations.)

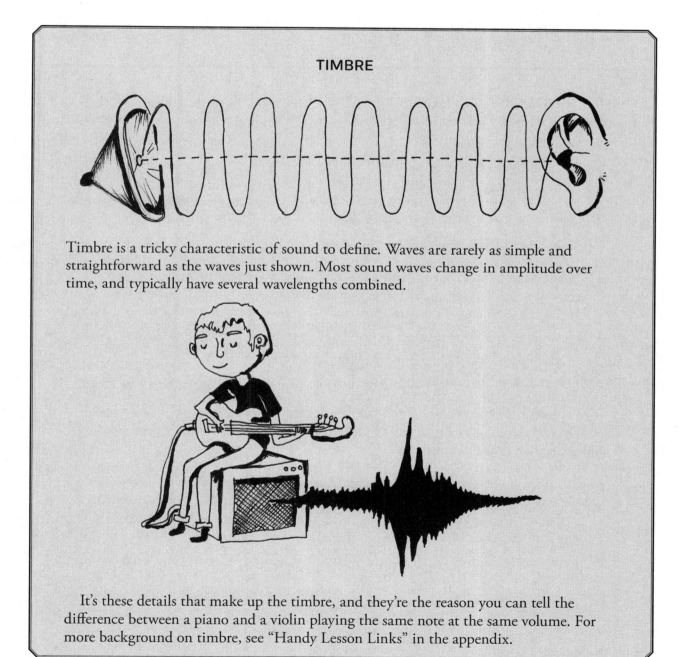

TIMBRE

Timbre is a tricky characteristic of sound to define. Waves are rarely as simple and straightforward as the waves just shown. Most sound waves change in amplitude over time, and typically have several wavelengths combined.

It's these details that make up the timbre, and they're the reason you can tell the difference between a piano and a violin playing the same note at the same volume. For more background on timbre, see "Handy Lesson Links" in the appendix.

What Makes a Sound? Sound Exploration (15 minutes)

For this activity you want to have materials on hand that the students can make sounds with, but not musical instruments. The list at the beginning of this lesson is *not* exhaustive; feel free to add things like Bubble Wrap, crinkly aluminum foil, or a box of pasta. Bring them out and let the students experiment.

Now that you've differentiated between quiet and loud, low and high, challenge students to create those types of sounds with various materials, thereby giving them a chance to discover how different kinds of sounds are made. At this stage, let them explore.

Before too long, students will probably discover that a given material is likely to make a certain kind of sound (why?); at this point, challenge them to make a high and a low sound, a loud and a quiet sound, with the exact same material.

Students should document their findings as they explore. Younger students may want to use the "Sound Exploration" handout, whereas older students can just take notes.

IF THEY'RE STUCK, ASK THEM QUESTIONS As always, asking questions can help students along in their thinking. A number of generic questions can be very useful here:

- ▶ What have you tried?
- ▶ What did you observe or notice?
- ▶ How do you think it works?
- ▶ How do you know that? or Why do you think that?

Of course, domain-specific questions are good too:

- ▶ What types of instruments have you seen before? (General responses and specific responses, such as string instruments and guitars, respectively, are both encouraged. You can have images of instruments ready if necessary to keep the activity moving.)
- ▶ How do we use these instruments to make sounds? (Answers might include plucking a string, blowing into or on something, or striking something.)
- ▶ What are the key parts of these instruments, and can you make something similar?

If your students already have more than a basic familiarity with sound, you can ask them questions to challenge their understanding and spur them on to be inventive in sound generation. For example:

- ▶ What are some examples of similar instruments of different sizes? (Responses might include a violin, viola, cello, and double bass; a bass drum and a snare drum; a guitar and a ukulele; a piccolo and a flute—and some very rare other large flutes.) Are there any similarities or parallels between these instrument families?
- ▶ How does size affect the sound the instrument makes? Why do you think size affects the sound?
- ▶ *Challenge:* Can you make a sound whose pitch is either so high or so low that it is outside the range of human hearing (like the sound of a dog whistle, for example, or part of the range of the hyperbass flute)? How will you be able to tell if you have been successful?

How Does Sound Work? (10 minutes)

Ask students how they think sound works, and have them share their evidence from their explorations earlier in the lesson; take notes on the answers on chart paper or the like.

Then, explain sound waves by first showing the students visualizations of waves of different shapes (by making a string vibrate in different ways, or moving a Slinky around, or creating ripples in a bowl, and so on). Point out that some waves are taller than others (that is, they have different **amplitudes**), and that some waves are longer than others (that is, they have different **wavelengths**). Explain that waves move through the air or other material and eventually reach our eardrum. At that point, our brain translates those vibrations into our perception of sound.

Wavelength and Amplitude Exploration and Discussion (15 minutes or more)

If your students already know a lot about how sound works, you might want to skip this activity and devote the time to musical instrument building instead. Otherwise, take a little time to check students' understanding. Ask how clapping your hands makes sounds, or how a drum works (easier), or how a flute works (harder). Note that students can see the vibrations on a drum head by placing rice or sand on the surface before striking it (you can use a homemade drum made from a clean, empty can with a balloon stretched over one open side and secured with a rubber band, to function as a membrane). Having students visualize what goes on will probably be very useful.

Then, have students revisit their earlier sound exploration and consider what sounds were made by what kinds of waves. (This concept is easiest to visualize with string and percussion instruments.) Did they notice that louder sounds tended to be made by waves with greater amplitudes? Or perhaps that higher-pitched sounds matched up with shorter wavelengths? Probably! (If not, resist the urge to tell them—it's more fun when they figure it out on their own.)

As a class or in small groups (for bonus discussion time!), have students summarize their understanding of sound waves, pitch, wavelength, and amplitude using evidence from their investigation. Give them time to ask each other questions, and challenge them to defend their ideas with evidence (it can be really exciting when students question one another, each drawing on his or her own experiences from his or her own investigation).

Musical Instrument Building (25 minutes)

Distribute the "Musical Instrument Building" handout and the supplies students made noise with earlier (boxes, paper towel rolls, rubber bands, unsharpened pencils, and so on), plus some tape and string. Task the students with each creating an instrument that can play different pitches and/ or at different volumes. (At one time, an instrument that could play at different volumes was actually really revolutionary. The piano [or pianoforte, roughly meaning "soft and strong"] was a game changer—its predecessors excelled at playing many notes, but they could only play at one volume.) Wavelength is the bigger challenge here. See if your students can build instruments that can play very low notes, very high notes, or both! (Any number of smartphone apps can measure both volume and frequency of sound,[1] so you can have contests for lowest note, highest note, and broadest range; see "Handy Lesson Links" in the appendix.)

You have many choices when structuring the instrument-building part of the lesson.

◇ For a relatively easy challenge, you can show the students pictures of sample instruments and/ or describe different instrument families. (In this scenario, make sure to ask students how their instrument is different from the original inspiration(s), and how those differences connect to changes in sound. If a student makes a guitar out of a shoe box and a rubber band, for example, why is the pitch different from that of a standard guitar?)

◇ To be a little less obvious, hold back on the suggestions, and ask students to be inspired by their explorations earlier and/or their prior experience with music. Making an instrument from scratch is a lot harder if you do not provide any guides at all—no visuals, no discussion.

◇ You can provide available materials along with any presentation of sample instruments to help students make connections.

◇ For an increased challenge, restrict the materials that students have on hand. Generally, string and percussion instruments are easier to understand and work with than other types of instruments—so you can drastically limit surfaces to be struck (for example, containers) or strings to be plucked (for example, rubber bands).

------

1. Note that although this lesson focuses on wavelength, you can choose to describe frequency, as wavelength's inverse, as well. You'll have to if you use an app to measure frequency.

◇ Here's a particularly tough one: have students create an instrument that can play a chord—multiple notes simultaneously. The really difficult part is playing simultaneous notes that sound good together. (If you feel like this is too hard, you can provide your students with one hint: fractions. Wavelengths that are whole-number fractions of each other—produced by strings whose lengths are whole-number fractions of each other, for example, 1/2, 1/3, 3/4—tend to produce harmonious notes.)

◇ The big one(s): have your students collaborate to make a scaled series of instruments that span as much of the human hearing range as possible. For even more of a challenge, the class can try to tune all these instruments to play in harmony.

Documentation, as always, is important. Students should use the "Musical Instrument Building" handout to catalog their successes and failures: these will form a lot of the content for the songs to be written at the end of the session. And to keep things light (and to help transition into writing in a bit), also have them record onomatopoetic words (real or made-up words that sound exactly or almost exactly like the thing that they represent, like "twang" or "thud" or "whine") that describe the sounds their instrument makes. Should students so choose, they can come up with their own name for their new instrument.

Wavy Songwriting (25 minutes)

At this point, students ideally will have done and learned a lot. In all likelihood, they'll want to keep going—but it's time to move on to a different task, songwriting.

To ensure that students have enough material for songwriting, ask them to stop building and to make sure that they've written notes about their sound explorations and musical instrument. Also have them refer to their earlier notes from way back when, reviewing what they knew and wanted to know about making different sounds. Make sure they've already written down anything they've discovered, and ask them to clear away any unused materials while they're at it.

Finally, it's time: have students write a shortish ditty about how sound works. Encourage them to form bands (ideally with two students, and definitely with no more than four). Their song should aim to explain sound and instruments to someone their age or younger, and they should draw from their notes about what they knew earlier, what they wanted to learn, and what they discovered (and how well that meshed with their earlier knowledge). They'll probably be using the session's science terminology—"wave," "amplitude," "wavelength." Encourage them to connect the sounds they make with instruments (including the ones they've built themselves) to illustrate the concepts they're trying to get across (for example, banging on a makeshift drum while describing waves with large amplitude).

A great example to present, if you have extra time for the lesson, is a pair of songs from *Here Comes Science* by They Might Be Giants: "Why Does the Sun Shine?" and "Why Does the Sun Really Shine?" The second song, in an appropriately different musical style from that of the first, reflects updated knowledge concerning the nature of the sun and admits at the end, "That [old] thesis has been rendered invalid." (This concept is a very important part of science.)

Your students have a few options for their songwriting:

◇ Like They Might Be Giants, students can write a simple two-verse song. The first verse can talk about an incorrect guess about sound, and the second can talk about the truth that students discovered.

◇ They can write a back-and-forth debate, with alternating verses, between two scientists (that is, students) with competing hypotheses on sound.

◇ Here's another alternating-verse idea: one verse can pose a question about sound, and the next can answer the question.

◇ Or, very simply, students can write verses about musical experiments (that is, instruments) that did work, and ones that didn't.

◇ And all of the preceding ideas can be combined into an epic sonic/scientific discourse (see the "Epic Sonic/Scientific Discourse" sidebar).

Ask students to consider the different parts to their song, and how sounds of different wavelengths and amplitudes can highlight the differences between those parts. (You probably won't have time to play, say, Queen's "Bohemian Rhapsody," but it's a great example of a song with movements that shift back and forth between high pitches and low pitches, loud sounds and quiet sounds. These aren't the only ways that the music changes, however. In some sections, certain instruments dominate, and in others, vocals take center stage. Some sections are faster, and some sections are slower.)

SONG STRUCTURE At 826, we often teach a pretty basic song structure: chorus, verses, bridge.[2]

The chorus generally states the main message of the song, or an overview of the problem or plot. Also, the chorus usually contains the hook—the catchiest, most energetic or emotional part of the song. The chorus is usually repeated after every verse, and maybe repeats an extra time or two at the song's end.

Verses can explain different aspects of a theme, or can tell different parts of a story. Verses tend to be very similar musically, often sharing the same melody.

The bridge often falls close to the end of the song, frequently before the final verse. We tell kids that the bridge is their chance to do something crazy and deviate musically from the rest of the song.

For this lesson, most of our song suggestions are built around two verses, or alternating pairs of verses. A chorus between verses and at the end can hit home the students' main scientific message. If they have anything extra to say, they can do so in a bridge!

_____
2. Listen to an example song at *http://826la.org/battleofthebands/2009/songs.html#boring*.

EPIC SONIC/SCIENTIFIC DISCOURSE It's not so hard to write a song about scientific principles. In fact, a song can mirror the general narrative of science. Here's how a song like this might be structured:

1. The first part would introduce the question (for example, How do we make sounds?)—science starts with questions, after all.

2. The next segment would be a back-and-forth debate about students' varying hypotheses.

(continued)

3. Experiments follow hypotheses, so students would next write about their observations from the experiments—that is, what worked and what didn't work.

4. *Optional:* The song can have another debate over different interpretations of the observations.

5. The song would finish with a final discovery—the true answer, as students have determined it, to their original question. (If they're left with more questions, those can become more songs!)

STEM Concert! (15 minutes or more)

Have your students perform their songs! Afterward, in sort of a backstage interview experience, lead your students in a reflection discussion about what they learned, what questions they still have, and what it was like setting everything to music.

FOR YOU TO KNOW (AND YOUR STUDENTS TO DISCOVER)

Sound is created when an object vibrates. The vibration of the object pushes against neighboring air molecules, causing these molecules to begin to vibrate and creating a chain reaction. These molecules then push against those next to them, and so on. These "pushes" create waves of air pressure that travel to your ear. Your ear detects these changes in air pressure, and you perceive them as sound. (Dropping a stone into a puddle creates a visual example of this phenomenon. The initial impact or push of the stone on the water pushes the water molecules out of the way. These molecules then push on the molecules next to them, creating the waves of ripples you see in the water.)

Air Molecules

(continued)

Sound can travel through lots of different materials. For example, sound can travel through water (ever have someone talk to you underwater?) and through solid objects (try knocking or drumming on a desk, and have someone put his or her ear on the surface at the other end). In these cases, the sound vibrations are not moving air molecules, but are pushing against the neighboring molecules (for example, water molecules when you talk underwater or wood molecules when you drum on a desk). Because outer space is essentially empty—there are neither air molecules nor any other matter in the space between celestial objects—there are no molecules to push against each other, so sound does not travel.

Sound waves can be represented with drawings. The height of the wave is called the **amplitude.** The amplitude is measured from either the peak to the axis or the trough to the axis.

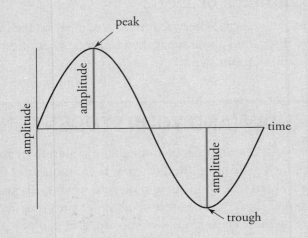

The human brain can perceive the amplitude of a wave. Louder sounds have a greater amplitude. Quieter sounds have a smaller amplitude.

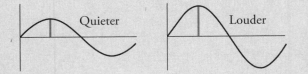

The distance between the peaks of the waves is called the **wavelength.**

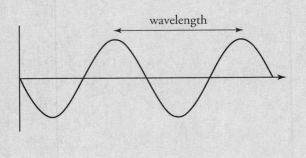

Our brain can also perceive differences in the wavelengths of waves. The image that follows shows waves of three different wavelengths. The wave with the longest wavelength will have the lowest **pitch;** that with the shortest wavelength will have the highest pitch.

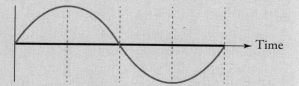

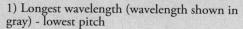

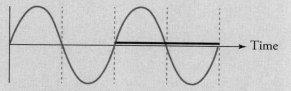

1) Longest wavelength (wavelength shown in gray) - lowest pitch

2) Intermediate length wavelength - pitch will be higher than that shown in 1, but lower than sound from 3, below.

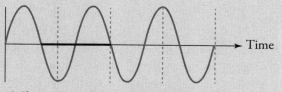

3) Shortest wavelength - highest pitch

"Pitch" is the term that musicians and scientists both use to describe how low or high a sound is. Long wavelength equals low pitch; short wavelength equals high pitch. The shorter the wavelength, the greater the number of cycles of the sound wave that reach our ear in a unit of time. The number of cycles is called the **frequency.** It's often more convenient (mathematically, for instance) to refer to a wave's frequency rather than its wavelength. For example, most sound analysis software, including smartphone apps, will measure frequency. Our brain perceives these more frequent pushes by a sound wave as a higher pitch. Examples of sounds with a low pitch include the rumble of trucks as they drive by, a dog's growl, and the sounds of a string bass. Examples of sounds with a high pitch include a microwave's beep, the sounds made by an instrument like a piccolo, and many bird chirps.

SOUND EXPLORATION

Use the space here to describe or draw the different materials you used to make sounds.

What did you notice?

How could you make the sound change?

On a scale from 1 to 10 (with 1 being very quiet and 10 being very loud), how loud were the sounds you made?

Sound 1:   Sound 3:

Sound 2:   Sound 4:

What was one thing you discovered or were surprised by during your exploration?

MUSICAL INSTRUMENT BUILDING

How did your building go? Did you try some things that worked? Things that didn't? Scientists document both their successes and their failures (that way, they can remember what they should and should not do in the future). Use the space here to describe some of your failures and your ideas that ultimately worked:

Use the space that follows to draw the instrument you built. Be sure to label the different parts of the instrument.

Onomatopoeia is when a word sounds like the thing it describes: bang, plop, whoosh, splat. Describe the sounds your instrument makes using onomatopoetic words:

Describe how you were able to change the sounds your instrument made. Try to include scientific sound words in your description (for example, "wave," "amplitude," "wavelength," "frequency," and "pitch")!

STEM@HOME: THE SOUND OF SCIENCE

There are lots of ways to continue exploring the science of sound at home. When you attempt either of the activities that follow, try to come up with an explanation for what you think is going on, based on your new understanding of sound waves.

Robot Voice Modulator

This activity is easiest to do in hot weather (when you have fans out around the house).

MATERIALS

☐ A fan

☐ Musical instrument (optional)

☐ Something that plays music, like a radio or a smartphone (optional)

☐ Your face

1. Turn on a fan, and then stand in front of it with your face near the fan cage. **(Don't stand so close that your hair can get caught in it.)**

2. Talk into the fan in a normal voice.

   What do you notice?

   ▶ What happens if you increase the speed of the fan? What happens if you slow it down? How does changing the speed of the fan change the sound of your voice? Does the fan also change the sound of an instrument? What about the sound of speech or music coming from a radio or a smartphone?

   ▶ What do you think is going on? How might the fan be affecting the sound waves?

▸ What are other ways that you can change the way your voice sounds? What happens when you're making a constant sound (such as "Aaaaaaaaaaaaaaaaaaaaaaaaaaaaa"), and somebody pats you on the back repeatedly? Or when you're making the same constant sound as you travel over a bumpy road?

Cup Phones

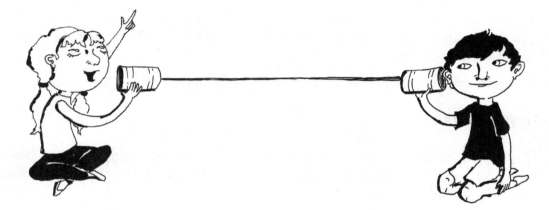

This phone is so low-tech it's almost no-tech, but it works!

MATERIALS

☐ 2 paper, Styrofoam, or plastic cups

☐ String (butcher's twine works well)

1. Poke a hole in the bottom of each cup. A sharp pencil makes a good poker.

2. Cut a length of string about 5 feet long.

3. Thread the string through the bottom of one of the cups, tying a knot in the string to secure it. Note that you want the cup portion (the part that holds liquid) to be facing away from the length of string.

4. Repeat with the second cup on the opposite end of the string.

5. Grab a friend, sibling, parent, aunt, uncle, or cousin, or anyone else who likes doing experiments with you. Have this person hold one cup to his or her ear, while you speak into the other cup. Then switch roles. *Note:* You and your partner should be considerate of one another's ears—do not YELL into the cups!

(continued)

What do you notice?

▸ Can you hear your experiment partner when he or she talks through the cup?

▸ Do your cup phones work better when you and your partner are close together, or when you make the string taut (taut means "stretched" or "pulled tight")?

▸ What do you feel through the cup when your partner talks?

▸ Do you notice any movement in the string when you or your partner is talking? What happens if you change the pitch of your voice? What happens if you change how loud you are speaking? (Remember not to yell.)

▸ Can you explain your observations in terms of sound waves?

Fun Sound Facts

▸ The loudest sound ever heard on Earth (in recorded history) was the cataclysmic explosion of the volcano Krakatoa near Indonesia in 1883. The sound from the explosion was heard clearly 3,000 miles awway.

▸ Different animals can hear sounds of different pitches. Many mammals can hear sounds with a higher pitch than what humans can hear. This is why a dog will respond to a training whistle that you cannot hear.

▸ Human sensitivity to sound changes with age, too! As people grow older, they lose the ability to hear higher-pitched sounds.

▸ If an astronaut on a spacewalk were to drop a wrench onto the surface of the International Space Station (ISS), the astronaut would not hear the clank of the metal-metal impact. Any astronauts inside the ISS, however, would hear the sound. (Can you think of an explanation for this?)

▸ The speed of sound, in air, is 768 miles per hour.

▸ Sound travels more than four times faster in water than it does in air (because water molecules are closer together than air molecules).

The power of one is incredibly important. As a naturalist and biologist who cares about our planet and its conservation, I think the greatest and most dangerous challenge to conservation is when someone feels that their choices are insignificant. When that happens, it's all too easy to think, "What does it matter?" or "I don't matter." Well, you do matter. You have the potential to matter in the most positive way and the most negative way. We each leave behind a footprint and cause a ripple effect by what we do.

Every day, each of us has a tremendous power to make an impact on the planet. You can make a huge impact through the products you buy, through the amount of non-biodegradable waste you create, and through what you ask your local and global leaders to do to take care of the environment. We all have power economically, politically, and civically within the community. And we all have individual responsibilities in the choices we make. The truth is, you are extremely powerful, and you can exercise your power *positively*.

In writing, you use your imagination to come up with new ideas and make sure no two narratives are the same. Imagination is just as valuable in exploration and conservation, as nature can often surprise us. We are also constantly faced with critical choices that affect the environment. As you apply your imagination on and off the page, remember that the greatest support to conservation is an understanding that you do matter, and that your choices do make a difference.

Jeff Corwin

A biologist, environmental conservationist, and Emmy-winning TV host, Jeff Corwin has shared his love of nature on shows like ABC's triple Emmy-winning series Ocean Mysteries with Jeff Corwin *and Animal Planet's* The Jeff Corwin Experience *and* Corwin's Quest. *Jeff frequently lectures on ecology and conservation, and works to inspire the next generation of environmental stewards by connecting kids to our planet and its species. You can connect with Jeff at www.facebook.com/jeffcorwinconnect and learn about his newest project for kids at www.juniorexplorers.com.*

THERE MAY BE BONES

BASED ON THE ORIGINAL WORKSHOP BY DANIEL JOHNSON

3 SESSIONS, 90 MINUTES EACH
STEM DISCIPLINE: *Life sciences*
WRITING ACTIVITIES: *Technical writing, creative writing, narrative writing*

SHHHHH . . . IT'S A SECRET. THIS LESSON focuses on how science deals with the unknown.

In this lesson, students assume the roles of both biologist and detective as they dissect a mysterious object (an owl pellet), attempt to reconstruct the specimens found within, and determine the nature of the object. Through multiple iterations, each time with more information at hand (from facts gleaned earlier, thoughts shared by colleagues, and better background information), students continually refine their hypotheses about their mystery object. Students will have the opportunity to do some fiction writing, in addition to technical lab journal writing.

We used to call this lesson "Owl Pellets." Then we changed it to "Birds and Bones." And then we changed it again. We don't want, even inadvertently, to give students a chance to learn any information about the mysterious objects that this lesson explores (that is, the owl pellets). The less the students know up front, the better they'll be able to experience how gathering more direct evidence and conducting research to gain more background knowledge help scientists draw better conclusions.

Throughout this lesson, students will make increasingly better guesses as to what their object (an owl pellet) is as they learn more about what's inside and where those contents come from. The lesson

MATERIALS

SESSION 1

- ☐ Owl pellets (The bigger these are, the better [some vendors sell them in different sizes!]. One per student is ideal, but students can share in groups of two or even four. Be sure to remove any skeleton charts that shipped with the pellets, and save them to give to students during session 3.)

- ☐ Lab journals (optional)

- ☐ Forceps or tweezers (one per table)

- ☐ Magnifying glasses (one per table)

- ☐ Cotton swabs (one or two for every student)

- ☐ Toothpicks (one or two for every student)

(continued)

- ☐ Bowls of water (one per table)
- ☐ Medicine droppers (one per table)
- ☐ Paper towels
- ☐ Scissors (one per table)
- ☐ Glue dots or Scotch tape
- ☐ 8-by-10 mat board (Card-stock or construction paper will also work, as will, in a pinch, regular old 8.5-by-11-inch paper. You'll need one sheet per owl pellet.)
- ☐ Index cards (one per student)
- ☐ Rulers (one per table)
- ☐ Specimen bags (Gallon-size ziplock bags will do. You'll need one bag for every owl pellet.)
- ☐ Dissection trays (Aluminum lasagna pans or disposable plastic takeout containers work well, though you need to put a piece of white paper on the bottom of black containers. You'll need one tray for every owl pellet.)
- ☐ Digital camera (optional)
- ☐ Digital projector (optional)
- ☐ Hand sanitizer (if sinks to wash up afterward are not accessible)[1]
- ☐ A bell or timer
- ☐ Skeleton charts if not given with owl pellets (one per student; see Handy Lesson Links in the appendix)

therefore provides an opportunity for students to become immersed in the practices of science. They will ask questions; analyze their data; and use this information to construct, refine, and revise their explanations. Students will have to engage in argument based on evidence, and obtain, evaluate, and communicate information. They will also have to synthesize information from their own observations as well as from prior knowledge and outside sources. And they will do these things constantly—not in a linear order, but in an ongoing and iterative way—just like practicing scientists! (For more on iteration, see the Science-O-Pedia.)

If you would like an example of this process, consider the dinosaur. Before the word "dinosaur" was even used, people all over the planet found many large bones. The ancient Chinese considered them to be from mythical dragons, and Europeans thought they came from (human) giants. More fossils were discovered, and tenuous connections came with them. In 1842 Richard Owen grouped the megalosaurus, iguanodon, and hylaeosaurus together as the *dinosauria*—meaning "terrible lizard," roughly, in Greek.

The whole "terrible lizard" idea eventually fell apart, however. After more fossil discoveries, we learned how un-lizard-like dinosaurs are. Scientists are more convinced than ever that most dinosaurs were warm blooded, whereas lizards are cold blooded. Dinosaurs' legs tend to be more vertical than those of lizards, too. As for "terrible," which referred as much as anything to dinosaurs' large size—that also turned out to be wrong, as many fossils have been found that are as small as a house cat or a pigeon.

The pigeon, by the way, is a dinosaur. Further fossil evidence (including, among other things, lots of dinosaurs with feathers) has shown that the ancestors of modern birds are a group of dinosaurs called the maniraptorans. If one so desired, one could include a pigeon, ostrich, penguin, or falcon under the umbrella term of "dinosaur." (The term "bird" is still more precise, as is "avian dinosaur.")

In short, learning more helps us continue to learn, and it's part of the scientific process to make the most informed guesses we can at the time. Part of that learning involves making mistakes. In this lesson, you're not giving students a lot of information, either about the object

---

1. Owl pellets are not poop (see this lesson's "For You to Know" section). That said, they are still a digestive waste product. Even though most commercially purchased owl pellets are sterilized before being sold, students should wash their hands thoroughly after exploring their pellet and/or use hand sanitizer.

they're studying or about how to study it. Encourage students to try different things, to continuously consider their approach and thinking, and to change things based on what is or isn't working. (For more on "mistakes" in science, see "'Mistakes' Are Normal" in "How to Use This Book.")

We're going for mystery here. But if the students know or find out what the objects are, this lesson isn't over. At some point, a student with prior knowledge may, in a fit of excitement, yell out what the objects are. Alternately, students may decide they know what the objects are and declare that they're done. All is not lost! Remind students that during these activities, the focus is on direct evidence— what they have before them, and any information you choose to share later.

More important, this emphasis on evidence allows for a subtle shift in the lesson. Let students know that it's essential for a good scientific theory to stand up to challenges. From this point on, future note-taking and discussion will revolve around the evidence, how it supports or contradicts hypotheses, and how valid certain hypotheses seem to be in light of the evidence. (For our purposes here, hypotheses include both the accepted owl regurgitation hypothesis and whatever hypotheses students put forward. See the Science-O-Pedia for more on hypotheses and evidence).

Session 1: Excavation

Throughout the entire lesson, be careful about presenting assumptions as the truth. This lesson is called "There May Be Bones," but you should not tell students that they will find bones (though they almost certainly will). If, during pellet excavations or discussions, people start referring to bones as bones, don't accept that! Ask students how they know those objects are bones. Similarly, later in the lesson, do not tell students they're reassembling a creature, or an animal. If students refer to an assembled skeleton as an animal, again, ask them how they know that it is an animal.

Preparation

To save time during class, you may want to set up the dissection stations beforehand. If your classroom has shared tables, one dissection station at each table should be sufficient. Every dissection station will need forceps or tweezers, a magnifying glass, cotton swabs, toothpicks, a bowl of water, a medicine dropper, paper towels, glue dots or Scotch tape, mat board, index cards, scissors, a ruler, and specimen bags.

How Do You Solve Mysteries? How Do Scientists Solve Mysteries? (15 minutes)

Have your students respond in writing to the following prompt:[2]

What would you do if you found a mysterious package outside your door?

What if you heard the package make noise?

Write down each step of what you would do. Be very specific. For example, "First, I would _____. Then, I might _____ or _____, and would be sure to _____ . . ."

How is your process similar to or different from the ways scientists solve mysteries?

---

2. Note the similarity of this prompt to the STEM@Home activity "The Black Box of Science," from the lesson "The Science of Saving Daylight." Feel free to have your students do that activity on their own!

Briefly discuss as a class some of the ideas students came up with. Write as many of them on the board as possible! It may be helpful to use a T-chart, where one side lists student ideas, and the other compares and contrasts those ideas with what students know about how scientists answer scientific questions and solve scientific mysteries.

Excavating This Particular Mysterious Object (15 minutes)

Let your students know that the point of this sequence of activities is to see how scientists try to answer questions. You're going to show the students an object, and they're going to work—sometimes individually, sometimes collaboratively—to unearth the mystery behind it. Inform them that if some of them know (or even think they know) what the object is right away, they should pretend like they don't, and that their contributions to the class should be limited to what a person unfamiliar with the object would say. That means no leading statements or questions, and definitely no sharing what the object is.

If students in your class are the type to blurt out answers, remind them beforehand to raise their hand silently. Hold up an owl pellet and ask students if anyone knows what it is. If some do, recognize that knowledge, and remind them that sharing even a little bit can hurt the process of learning for the whole class.

Talk about how such biological samples are often delicate; how great care needs to be taken; and how in similar scenarios (fossil or archaeological excavations) it can be even easier to break fossils and artifacts, and to disturb their location. Location can be an important clue in figuring out what fossils and other objects are!

Modeling is, as always, important, especially in this first session. Have students gather around and watch you start excavation on a pellet. (You can also use a digital camera and projector setup if you have one.) Definitely try this yourself before doing it in front of the class! The more familiar you are with the pellets, the better equipped you'll be to demonstrate points about documentation and mistakes in the next few minutes.

Delicately take apart the owl pellet using the supplies at the dissection station. As you retrieve pieces from the pellet, use glue dots or Scotch tape to mount each piece to mat board, explaining to the students what you're doing. (Glue dots or Scotch tape allow for a temporary mount, which is what we want; students will likely move these pieces a few times as they try to figure out what they are.) You'll also want to emphasize the importance of not losing anything.

Make sure you're recording every step of your process on the board or on an overhead projector so the students can see your notes. (You may wish to have a TA or student assistant help you out.) Here's an example:

I used water. What happened?

Next, I tried to take the specimen apart with _____. What happened?

More than anything else, emphasize the necessity of documentation in science. In scientific fields, reproducibility of experiments and processes is essential for the validation and acceptance of results. When things don't go according to plan (and even when things do), recording exactly what happened and how enables scientists to communicate, collaborate, and improve further research.

This is a really good time to demonstrate what happens when a mistake is made, or something goes wrong. There's still something to be learned from this, so write down an observation like:

I used a forceps to try and pull something out. I was way too rough, though, and I broke it and maybe some other things. Now I know to be more gentle, and I need to be aware that some of the pieces in here are broken. Maybe I can figure out what they are, and put them together again.

You want to normalize mistakes as part of the scientific process. Let students know that mistakes will be made in this lesson, and that it's up to students to learn from them, just like professional scientists.

Taking the Mysterious Object Apart (40 minutes)

Next, distribute the owl pellets on the dissection trays. Be sure not to include those skeleton charts and don't tell them what the mysterious object is! Instruct the students to carefully take the object apart, using the supplies at the dissection station. As they go, they should mount any pieces they excavate onto mat board using glue dots or Scotch tape. Remind them to carefully document their procedures and results in their lab journals, if using. Let students know that the best documentation will include drawings of the process. (As a bonus, if you have access to digital cameras, or if your students have camera phones, allow them to use those! This works exceptionally well in pairs, whereby students can trade off picture-taking responsibilities. Note that even if students can take pictures, drawing will work best for noting interesting things they find.)

In the likely scenario (at several points during this lesson) that students become frustrated by not having a name for something, encourage them to make up their own. This is more than okay; it's how scientists do things.

SCIENTIFIC NAME GAME When Jaci Thomas at 826 Boston piloted this lesson with students, she hit upon the idea of giving students license to name what they found in their mystery object (owl pellet). Not only does this mirror what happens in science, but it's also exciting for students and brings us back to the idea of discovery. When a student (young or old) discovers something new independently, it's thrilling. Allowing the students to name their discoveries helps fully immerse them in the process of discovery and validates the importance of the work they are doing.

When a scientist discovers something new—a creature (or a new part of a creature), a phenomenon, or even a scientific technique—that scientist will give it a name. At first, that name will only have meaning to the scientist who gave the name. It is not until the scientist communicates his discovery—and the new name—to others in the field that it becomes an accepted part of the scientific language.

Paleontologists provide a great example of how this works, literally, in the field. If a paleontologist discovers a fossil of what is, to the best of her knowledge, a new type of dinosaur, she can name it. The name chosen usually has some meaning. Sometimes fossils are named after the place where they were found (for example, Denversaurus was the name given to a dinosaur fossil stored at the Denver Museum of Natural History), and sometimes they are named after the person who found them (or someone that person really respects—for example, Lambeosaurus was so named to honor the paleontologist Lawrence Lambe). Most of the time, however, they are named after a physical feature the new dinosaur seemingly possesses. A great example of this is the triceratops (meaning "three-horned head").

Sometime later (after getting home, unpacking the fossil, and so on), the paleontologist will share her discovery with others in the field. She will probably invite experts who have worked on similar animals to come study her fossil. This process helps confirm that the discovery is indeed a new type of dinosaur (in the case of the Denversaurus, paleontologists discovered that it was, in fact, an example of an ankylosaurus, and so the name did not stick). In most cases, once the discovery is confirmed, the name still needs to be reviewed and approved by a group of scientists, who then make the name official.

Putting the Mystery Together (20 minutes)

With the whole group, ask your students to share a couple of guesses (really, just a few) about their object's origin, nature, and contents. At this point, anything goes. Keep this bit to five minutes.

If it hasn't already been brought up, introduce the possibility that students' objects did not always exist in their current configuration. Let that settle for a bit, and then introduce the session's final activity: to imagine how the mysterious fragments they've excavated might best fit together, using glue dots or Scotch tape to rearrange them on the mat board. (Students should take pictures, if possible!) Should your students have time, have them write, in their lab journal, what they think the object is and/or was. They can and should also illustrate! Make sure they note what evidence leads them to think the way they do, as well as the questions they still have.

At the end of this session, students should carefully place their mounted specimens in the specimen bags. But before they do, ask them to set aside one fragment that they're particularly curious about, and use a glue dot or Scotch tape to mount it on an index card labeled with their name(s). Collect the index cards; you'll display them in the next session.

Session 2: Hypotheses

Preparation

If you have time before this session, take the index cards with the one interesting bit of material that each student or group set aside last time, and arrange these pieces around the room as observation stations (you can fold the cards in half so they stand upright). Otherwise, you can set up the cards after the introduction, when students are writing.

Putting on Your Scientist Hat (5 minutes)

Have your students retrieve their pellet and initial reconstruction as well as their notes, if necessary. Give them a few minutes to review and get back into the mind-set of a curious scientist.

Telling the Tale of What It Was (25 minutes)

Before you get started, remind students not to share if they have prior knowledge about the mystery object. You can preface your discussion-guiding questions and comments with something like, "Can someone who's never handled one of these before tell us . . ." or "If you don't know what these are . . ."

Ask your students to imagine and then write about what this thing (the pellet with its contents) was like before it became their mystery object. What could it be? How did it come to be? What does all this mean?

Here, the line between creative writing and science writing is pretty blurry. The writing must rely on a little bit of fact, on the evidence they have compiled from the pellet. The contents of the pellet will not tell the whole story, however, and the writer must make guesses—some of which will be more or less informed than others. At this point, drawing from both the facts before them and their imagination, students can describe whatever they like—eggs with embryos inside; anthropomorphic monsters of some sort; a three-headed rat that shoots bugs out of its mouths, inspired by the remains of multiple animals?! All are great for now, as you're saving questions about the probability that these guesses are correct for (a few minutes) later.

If students are in a very factual mind-set, this is a good opportunity to spark their imagination with questions about things they almost certainly don't know at this point. Scientists have to make guesses, and sometimes out-of-the-box guesses are important for scientific discourse (and at times, those guesses are right). Alternately, if students are writing a story that is more fictional, great! Don't tell them that they're wrong (because they're not), but do ask them questions about the specimen before them to help them connect their imagination with the facts. For example, you can prompt, "You're not writing about this one thing you found in the object. What do you think it is, and can you work it in?"

Learning What Makes a Good Hypothesis (15 minutes)

Invite some students to share their narrative. After a couple of narratives are shared (and not necessarily in their entirety), ask students, "Who thinks his or her story makes a good hypothesis?" Now is the time to introduce the term, if you haven't already. Students will soon be thinking about the content of their narrative, and what evidence from their excavation could possibly support that narrative. Get a rough feel for which students think their story is a good hypothesis and which don't, and use that to transition to a discussion about what makes a good hypothesis, or guess. A key question to ask is, How would we prove or disprove that hypothesis?

Here, note that students are not speculating on how likely it is that a guess is correct. They should just be concerned with whether or not it's a good hypothesis—that is, whether or not the guess is testable and falsifiable. Those are the requirements for a usable hypothesis, among other things, like simplicity. (For more on hypotheses, see the Science-O-Pedia.)

Taking a Closer Look at the Mysterious Object's Contents (25 minutes)

Now it's time to take a closer look at some of the objects found within the pellets that have been displayed on index cards. Have students visit each station, making drawings and observations, and ultimately guessing what each object is (and justifying that guess, of course, with their observational evidence). It may be helpful to have a bell or timer to pace things, at around two minutes per station (give or take—this depends on your students, of course).

Lab Meeting: Debating Hypotheses (20 minutes)

Lead a discussion of the merits of varying hypotheses (guesses about the objects, or any of their parts or contents) proposed by the students, trying to mix things up between different objects that are more agreed on or less agreed on. Make sure to revisit the key question from earlier: How would we prove or disprove that? Your students ideally will have generated testable and falsifiable guesses. If not, remind them that these characteristics are essential for good hypotheses, and have them amend their guesses accordingly. Once that's all set, shift the focus to testing and verifying or falsifying hypotheses. Ask students these questions:

◇ What evidence supports this hypothesis?

◇ What evidence might contradict this hypothesis?

◇ What other possible explanations are there?

Note that the students are likely to transition, on their own, from hypotheses on various pieces in the pellets to hypotheses on the nature of the pellets themselves.

Questions might lead to answers that lead to more questions. Sometimes it'll happen without that answer step in the middle. Reassure your students that this is okay—it is part of scientific practice.

In the likely scenario that students become frustrated by not having a name for something, remind them that they can make up a name for temporary use. When they name something during the discussion, make sure they make clear to their fellow scientists what it is they have named and introduce the new name.

Should students say that they wished they'd had this discussion earlier, let them know that that's exactly right—good scientists make use of as much information as possible, including information from debate and discussion with colleagues, before jumping into a task.

If they say nothing of the sort, bring it up anyway. Let the students know that during the final session, they'll be leveraging far more information and evidence, and will finally get at the truth behind the mystery.

Session 3: A Closer Look

The tasks in this session are remarkably similar to tasks in the earlier sessions (recall the earlier comments on iteration). Remember that the point of this lesson is for your students to see how scientists discover more information, step by step. The final session makes this process abundantly clear.

Like all science, this lesson can be a little difficult and repetitive at times. But if all's been going according to plan, your students will still be curious and very motivated. Recognize all that your students have done, remind them that they shared ideas and gathered new ideas from their fellow scientists in the previous session, and emphasize that this information can inform this next phase. Cheer them on to the finish!

This session is the time to bring out the skeleton and bone charts that you probably took out of the owl pellet packages. If your pellets did not come with charts, see "Handy Lesson Links" in the appendix to access example PDFs of such charts. The charts will help the students identify the mysterious bits—that is, bones—that they've dissected from the owl pellets, as they finally arrive at the answer to the puzzle.

Moment of Truth (10 minutes)

Ask your students whether they feel like they've been getting closer to the mystery's solution, and let them know that you have more clues to share with them. Tell the students that these objects (the owl pellets) were most likely found in forests and on farms, probably next to trees, though possibly in a barn or something. You can even let students know that the objects are called pellets.

Then let them discuss. Woodland creatures will come to mind, probably birds or rodents because of the mention of trees (they may already have been brought up before). At the appropriate time, ask students if it would be helpful to have a diagram of, say, a rat skeleton, or a squirrel skeleton, or a sparrow skeleton, or even an owl skeleton. At this point, hand over the skeleton charts you either removed from the owl pellet packets or printed yourself. (If you have a choice, it is highly preferable to hand students a complete skeleton diagram, as opposed to a bone comparison chart. Because a skeleton chart is not likely to exactly match the bones your students have excavated, your students will be left with questions, and will be motivated to continue investigating.)

AN OWL PELLET BY ANY OTHER NAME . . . You can also share some non-English names for owl pellets. In Spanish, an owl pellet is *egagrópila,* with *-pila* perhaps suggesting *pelota* ("ball") or *pelo* ("hair"), either of which is appropriate. In French, it's *pelote de réjection* or *boulette de régurgitation*—"rejection ball" or "barf pellet," roughly, the former being more mysterious than the latter. These names are evocative, yet still withhold the key detail: that the pellets come from owls.

Putting the Mysterious Object Back Together . . . Again (40 minutes)

Task students with taking the information they've gathered and revising their skeletal mount and sketches. (At this point, they can return the fragment they'd set aside to display on an index card to its place on the mat board.) How do they think the fragments best fit together now? Some things will probably not match up with any of the diagrams students may have; make sure they note these discrepancies to themselves in writing. Students are likely to discover that there are plenty of pieces missing from what they think is a skeleton, and in this scenario, they should do more digging through their pellet contents to come up with a more complete picture.

Process Reflection Discussion: How Does Knowledge Help Us Discover Knowledge? (10 minutes)

Ask your students how the same basic task of mounting their findings was different the second time around, with the additional information and with improved communication. Did their guesses (hypotheses) change? You can ask, simply, what was the most helpful to them in reconstructing this object, and how it was helpful. Some students might say discussions were most helpful; others, skeleton charts; still others, where the pellets were found. Most students will probably think that all of these things were very helpful.

Really, What Was That Thing? (20 minutes)

Once students have collectively determined what the mysterious objects actually are (owl pellets!), have them describe in writing what the owl pellet was and how it got to be this way, this time specifically referring to both evidence from the pellet (for example, which bones or other parts in particular helped solve this mystery) and evidence from outside sources (for example, how a diagram, location clue, or other bit of information helped them figure things out).

Reinforce that it's great (not just okay, great!) if they still have questions—that's how science works! They should definitely write them down.

Note that they're essentially answering the same question they did during "Telling the Tale of What It Was" in session 2. The line between creative writing and science writing will still be a bit blurry. Students have more evidence, but they'll still have blanks to fill in—and quite possibly new blanks, if they have more questions (that is, if they're more aware of things they don't know). As with everything else in this lesson, this is part of the scientific process. They're revisiting earlier ideas and updating them with better information and more questions. One can view science as a never-ending series of iterative revisions.

If students are in a particularly creative mood, ask them to pretend that they are researchers who've found the notebook of a previous explorer (that is, the notes they themselves have written throughout this lesson), which includes, of course, a tentative explanation of the mystery object and its contents, and notes on further investigations. Given all this information, they can take a creative approach to the situation by writing about their new hypothesis as if it's the plot twist in a mystery. Science is about solving mysteries, after all, and finding mind-blowing new evidence is not unlike reading a mind-blowing revelation in a mystery novel.

Coming to Finalish Conclusions (10 minutes)

Invite students to share both their most complete answers so far and any questions they have. Congratulate them on uncovering large portions of a mystery, and, just as important, help them think of ways they can continue to investigate!

If they really want to know, you can tell them that the object is called an owl pellet. But leave it at that! They can and should be excited to do more research on their own.

FOR YOU TO KNOW (AND YOUR STUDENTS TO DISCOVER)[3]

Birds are cool; owls particularly so. Why are birds cool? Because they are different from us—and from mammals in general. We can learn a lot from how they do things differently than we do.

For example, birds don't chew their food. Most birds swallow their food whole—though some large birds of prey (eagles, for instance) will peck and pull smaller pieces off of a particularly large catch. Many birds (though not owls) have a specialized food storage structure called a crop, a pouch next to the throat that is a part of their esophagus and is unique to birds.

Owls are birds of prey. They hunt, largely at night. Just as there is a wide range in the size of owls (elf owls are less than six inches tall, whereas great horned owls can be over seventeen

---

3. Information is derived from the following sources: "All About Owl Pellets," *http://www.carolina.com/teacher-resources/Interactive/basic-information-on-owl-pellets/tr11103.tr*; Deane Lewis, "Digestion in Owls," from *http://www.owlpages.com/articles.php?section=Owl+Physiology&title=Digestion*.

(continued)

inches tall), the size of their prey varies greatly. Great horned owls will swallow their smaller prey (rodents, small rabbits) whole, but will pick apart their larger prey (raccoons, swans, young alligators). The smallest owls primarily eat insects, but medium-size owls eat small mammals (rodents), birds, and reptiles in addition to insects.

Nearly all birds' stomachs have two parts, each with a different function. Because owls do not have a crop, food passes directly from the esophagus into the stomach. Food first passes into the glandular stomach, also called the proventriculus, which produces enzymes and acids that begin the process of digestion. Food then moves into the muscular stomach, also called the ventriculus or gizzard. The gizzard is very muscular and is a grinding organ. The motions of the strong muscles, enzymes and acids from the proventriculus, and abrasive action from a little sand or gravel combine to dissolve all of the usable material from the swallowed prey. Material from prey that can be digested and used includes skin, muscles, fat, and internal organs. This dissolved material then passes into the intestines, where nutrients from the food can be absorbed into the bloodstream of the owl.

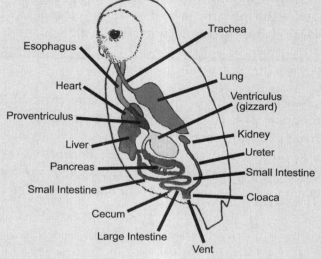

Much of the material that cannot be dissolved in the gizzard—including bones (and teeth) and fur—would be dangerous if it passed into the intestines. But the owl has to have a way to get rid of it—otherwise its gizzard would fill up, and it would not be able to eat again.

So, in owls the gizzard acts as a trash compactor. The owl packs the material that cannot be digested into a tight pellet, which the bird is able to spit out (regurgitate). This pellet will be "ready" a few hours after the owl eats, but an owl may store the pellet in its proventriculus for up to twenty hours before ejecting it. It is important to note that the owl cannot eat again until it has ejected the pellet. Owls usually eject their pellets from their roost or nest.

Owl pellets allow us to study owls and their diets. Ornithologists (bird scientists), ecologists, and conservationists all use owl pellets to study owls and their diets, and to learn about the environments in which owls live. Because owls' digestive process leaves most bones of their prey intact, scientists can examine the pellets to learn about the owls' diets, how they change during the year, and so on. With other animals, such studies often require killing an animal to examine the contents of its stomach.

Owl pellets are not poop! Owls do poop, however—kind of. Owl droppings (and those of other birds) come out of a structure called the vent. Like the droppings of other birds, owl

(continued)

droppings are liquidy and contain both black and white components. The black part contains the waste material left after the digested food passes through an owl's intestines, very similar to mammalian excrement, or poop. Birds, however, don't have a bladder, so their droppings are actually a mixture of urine (waste from the kidneys—the white, mushy part of bird "poop") and waste from the intestines. These materials are stored together in a structure called the cloaca before they are eliminated by the vent.

Note for instructors: This lesson contains two STEM@Home activities that are variations on the same activity—a chicken wing dissection. The first is a fairly directed dissection, with step-by-step instructions and content information accompanying each step. The second is a more open ended take on the same activity that encourages students to learn by exploring. You know your students best. Pick one of the sheets to send home with your students—sending both is likely to cause confusion— based on what you think they will find the most interesting and fulfilling.

STEM@HOME: MODELING A MYSTERY

For hundreds of years, scientists and doctors have been fascinated by the human body. Generations of scientists and doctors have worked to unravel the mysteries of how the human body works.

Solving these mysteries has had the added challenge that it is unethical (unethical means "morally wrong") to experiment on humans. For this reason, biologists frequently rely on **model systems** to help them learn how we as humans work, and how to improve human health and well-being. Model systems are other organisms whose biology is in some way similar to our own. (Other types of models exist—physical scale models, abstract mathematical models, and so on.) Biologists have learned a lot about how human beings develop from a single-celled, fertilized egg (called a zygote in bio-speak) from studying small worms and fruit flies (yes, those annoying flies sitting on bananas in your kitchen). And they have learned a tremendous amount about health and diseases (including how to cure them) from studying rats and mice.

In this lesson, you discovered bones in mysterious pellets and worked to put them together into a skeleton of the creature who might once have relied on those bones. Through your reconstruction, you could get a good idea of where each bone was positioned in the creature you discovered. But how were the bones held together? What holds together the bones in your body? How do your bones and muscles work together to allow your body to move?

MATERIALS

- ☐ A cookie sheet
- ☐ Bamboo skewers or toothpicks
- ☐ A chicken wing (or a combined wing and shoulder)
- ☐ Scissors (Ask a grownup's permission to use these on chicken—and promise to wash them when you are done.)

IMPORTANT SAFETY NOTE: Raw chicken can contain bacteria called salmonella that can make you sick. Keep your hands away from your face during this investigation, and be sure to wash your hands and all implements (the scissors, cookie sheet, and table) with hot, soapy water when you are finished.

We've got our materials, and we're ready to go. Place your chicken wing on your cookie sheet, get your bamboo skewers or toothpicks to poke and prod, and let the dissection begin!

IT'S ALL CONNECTED A chicken's skin (much like your skin) is attached to the underlying structures by **connective tissues** that hold the skin to the muscle. What do you think would happen if you didn't have these tissues? Imagine what might happen when you stood up. Would you need a belt (or suspenders) to keep your skin from slipping down to your feet? Talk about awkward!

(continued)

WHO ARE YOU CALLING CHICKEN?

WHO ARE YOU CALLING CHICKEN? The structure of a chicken wing is very similar to the structure of a human arm. In biology we call such similar structures **homologous structures.**

In humans, chickens, and other animals, muscles work together in pairs (called opposing pairs). One muscle of the pair is on one side of the bone, and the other is on the opposite side. Bend and straighten the chicken wing again. Do you notice that the muscle on one side of the bone is pulled tight (contracts) while the other relaxes? The same thing happens when you bend your arm or your leg.

TENDON LOVING CARE The shiny, white piece of tissue that connects muscle to bone is called a **tendon.**

Move your fingers while looking at the backs of your hands. Do you notice tight "strings" moving? These are really long tendons that connect your finger bones to the muscles in your forearm.

A fairly common sports injury is a tear in the Achilles tendon. The Achilles tendon connects your heel bone to the calf muscle in your leg. A tear or rupture in the Achilles tendon can make it hard to flex your foot or point your toes.

1. Chickens and Humans Both Have Skin

Spend some time exploring the skin.

To do and notice:

- ▶ Can you see where the feathers were attached?
- ▶ What are some similarities between your skin and the chicken skin?
- ▶ How is the skin attached to the structures underneath?
- ▶ What do you think the structures are that you see underneath the skin?

2. Getting Under the Skin

Let's think about muscles.

To do and notice:

- ▶ What do your muscles do when you bend and straighten your own arm? If you had X-ray vision, what would this look like?
- ▶ What do the chicken muscles do when you bend and straighten the chicken wing (arm)?
- ▶ What happens if you pull on one of the wing muscles? Explore pulling on different muscles to see what happens.

3. Digging a Little Deeper

Let's take a closer look at how muscles work.

To do and notice:

- ▶ Spend some time exploring the muscles. Don't be afraid to dig, poke, prod, and cut. What do you notice?
- ▶ Are the muscles connected to the bones? How?
- ▶ What happens if you break the connection between the muscle and the bone?
  - ▷ Can the muscle exert a pulling force on the bone any more?
  - ▷ Does that affect the ability of the bone to move?

(continued)

4. Elbow Bone's Connected to the Arm Bone

Now let's take a look at the bones.

To do and notice:

- Spend some time exploring the bones. Again, don't be afraid to dig, prod, and cut. You may want to remove most of the muscle to get a clear view.

- What do you notice about how the bones are connected to one another?

- What happens if one (or more) of the connections is stretched out of shape or, worse, torn (separated from the bone)?

- Can you think of explanations for why it is important for bones to be connected to one another directly (not just held together by the muscles)?

5. Capping It All Off

Let's see what's at the ends of the bones.

To do and notice:

- Spend some time exploring the ends of the bones. Use your sense of touch here: poke, prod, and disrupt things a bit too.

- How does the material at the end of the bone differ from the bone in both look and feel?

- What job do you think this material plays?

REMEMBER TO CLEAN UP ALL OF YOUR SUPPLIES, WASHING THEM AND YOUR HANDS IN HOT, SOAPY WATER!

IT'S LIGAMENTARY, MY DEAR WATSON The white pieces of tissue that connect bones are called **ligaments.** Injuries to ligaments are also very common in sports. The ulnar collateral ligament is on the inside of the elbow and connects your upper arm to your lower arm—stabilizing your elbow in the process.

BENDY BONE The shiny, white material at the ends of bones is called **cartilage.** Cartilage serves several purposes in our body. For example, our nose is made out of cartilage (as are the structures of our outer ears). It is much softer than bone, and can be bent. The slippery surface of the cartilage allows the bones in our joints to move smoothly relative to one another. Injury or damage to the cartilage can make moving a joint painful.

STEM@HOME: ALIEN DISSECTION

Okay, so it's really a chicken wing, but the idea is the same.

Science fiction is littered with accounts of aliens abducting humans in which the curious aliens try to figure out how our foreign bodies work. And there are just as many accounts of humans coming upon the wreckage of an alien vessel and promptly trying to figure out how the alien bodies are put together. You, too, can get in on the action, but because alien parts are hard to obtain, we suggest that you use a chicken wing, easily available at your local grocery store.

Take a moment to get in the mood. You are a scientist at the top secret Area 51, and someone has just brought in the victims of a recent alien ship crash. You are tasked with coming to understand the anatomy of the alien species. If this scenario seems weird, here's our reasoning. If you know what something is, you make assumptions about it, based on your prior experience and knowledge. If you are dealing with something completely unknown, you are often more likely to approach it with an open mind. There is much to discover if you are the only person who has ever dissected this species of alien.

MATERIALS

- ☐ A cookie sheet or cake pan
- ☐ Bamboo skewers or toothpicks
- ☐ A chicken wing (or a combined wing and shoulder)
- ☐ Scissors (Ask a grown-up's permission to use these on chicken—and promise to wash them when you are done.)

IMPORTANT SAFETY NOTE: Raw chicken can contain bacteria called salmonella that can make you sick. Keep your hands away from your face during this investigation, and be sure to wash your hands and all implements (the scissors, cookie sheet, and table) with hot, soapy water when you are finished.

Place the alien arm on the cookie sheet, get your bamboo skewers or toothpicks to poke and prod, and let the dissection begin! A few tips:

1. The more methodical your dissection, the more you are likely to learn. In medical school, students typically start from the outside and work their way in, which means that before making any cuts, they examine the outside surface (the skin), then proceed to the next layer, and the next layer.

2. Make connections. As you work on your dissection, compare and contrast what you are discovering in the alien arm with observations about your own body. Don't be afraid to move your arm (and the alien's). How are they similar or different? We can learn as much from how things are different as we can from how they are similar.

(continued)

Copyright © 2015 by 826 National

3. Move things, break things. Breaking things often helps confirm our ideas about how they work. Scientists and engineers do this all the time. If you notice something interesting (for example, something holding the alien bones [if it has bones] together), move things around to see how the connection seems to work, then break (cut) the connection and see what happens.

4. Have fun.

5. Clean up after yourself so your family will let you do more STEM@Home explorations.

Don't Read This (Unless You Are Stuck)

Here are a few questions to prompt your thinking and to help your dissection move forward.

Skin

▸ Is there any evidence of there having been something attached to the skin? What might these structures have been? What might they have done?

▸ What are some similarities between your skin and the alien skin?

▸ Is the alien skin attached to the structures underneath?

Muscles

▸ What do your muscles do when you bend and straighten your arm? If you had X-ray vision, what would this look like?

▸ What do the alien muscles do when you bend and straighten the alien arm (wing)?

(continued)

MAKING CONNECTIONS: BACK TO CHICKEN A chicken's skin (much like your skin) is attached to the underlying structures by **connective tissues** that hold the skin to the muscle. What do you think would happen if you didn't have these tissues? Imagine what might happen when you stood up. Would you need a belt (or suspenders) to keep your skin from slipping down to your feet? Talk about awkward!

The structure of a chicken wing is very similar to the structure of a human arm. In biology we call such similar structures **homologous structures.**

In humans, chickens, and other animals, muscles work together in pairs (called opposing pairs). One muscle of the pair is on one side of the bone, and the other is on the opposite side. Bend and straighten the chicken wing again. Do you notice that the muscle on one side of the bone is pulled tight (contracts) while the other relaxes? The same thing happens when you bend your arm or your leg.

(continued)

The shiny, white piece of tissue that connects muscle to bone is called a **tendon.**

Move your fingers while looking at the backs of your hands. Do you notice tight "strings" moving? These are really long tendons that connect your finger bones to the muscles in your forearm.

A fairly common sports injury is a tear in the Achilles tendon. The Achilles tendon connects your heel bone to the calf muscle in your leg. A tear or rupture in the Achilles tendon can make it hard to flex your foot or point your toes.

The white pieces of tissue that connect bones are called **ligaments.** Injuries to ligaments are also very common in sports. The ulnar collateral ligament is on the inside of the elbow and connects your upper arm to your lower arm—stabilizing your elbow in the process.

The shiny, white material at the ends of bones is called **cartilage.** Cartilage serves several purposes in our body. For example, our nose is made out of cartilage (as are the structures of our outer ears). It is much softer than bone, and can be bent. The slippery surface of the cartilage allows the bones in our joints to move smoothly relative to one another. Injury or damage to the cartilage can make moving a joint painful.

▶ What happens if you pull on one of the alien muscles? Explore pulling on different muscles to see what happens.

▶ Are the muscles connected to the bones? How?

▶ What happens if you break the connection between the muscle and the bone?

  ▷ Can the muscle exert a pulling force on the bone any more?

  ▷ Does that affect the ability of the bone to move?

Bones

▶ What do you notice about how the bones are connected to one another?

▶ What happens if one (or more) of the connections is stretched out of shape or, worse, torn (separated from the bone)?

▶ Can you think of explanations for why it is important for bones to be connected to one another directly (not just held together by the muscles)?

▶ How does the material at the ends of a bone differ in both look and feel from the bone?

▶ What role do you think this material plays in helping the system work together?

REMEMBER TO CLEAN UP ALL OF YOUR SUPPLIES, WASHING THEM AND YOUR HANDS IN HOT, SOAPY WATER!

TINFOIL SHIPBUILDING

BASED ON THE ORIGINAL WORKSHOP BY DANIEL JOHNSON

1 SESSION, 2 HOURS
STEM DISCIPLINES: *Physical sciences, engineering*
WRITING ACTIVITIES: *Technical writing, narrative writing, creative writing*

THERE'S SOMETHING ABOUT SHIPS THAT captures the imagination. After all, we call spaceships spaceships, and not spaceplanes or spacetrains. We ship things from one place to another. And we name ships: the *Pequod,* the *Titanic,* the *Argo,* the USS *Arizona, Jenny* . . .

In this workshop, students engage and exercise their imagination by building ships with some very accessible materials. Along the way, they learn about density, a key principle in physics and chemistry and beyond, and the center of one of science's all-time-great aha moments (actually, literally the first Eureka moment—read on!). Then, using their new insight, students write tales of adventure and exploration on ships.

Preparation

In this lesson, students will be building tinfoil boats and testing their seaworthiness by weighting them with load material. Before the lesson, you should try out different load materials and decide which

MATERIALS

☐ Load materials for testing boats (such as laboratory weights, marbles, or pennies)

☐ At least 1 container full of water (like a wading pool, a large plastic bin, a bucket, a cooler, or a sink)

☐ Copies of the "Shipbuilder's Blueprint" handout (included with other handouts at the end of this lesson)

☐ Demonstration items, including the following:

■ Things that float (such as a wine cork, a piece of wood, or a glass baking dish)

(continued)

- Things that sink (such as a piece of metal, a rock, or a solid piece of glass)

- At least 1 dilemma item—something that looks like it should sink, or something that's heavy but will still float (such as a pumice stone or a bag of ice, respectively)

□ Aluminum foil cut into 12-by-12-inch sheets (several for each student, plus extra for demonstration)

□ Copies of the "Captain's Log: Shakedown Cruise" handout

□ Copies of the "Captain's Log: Shakedown, Too" handout

you prefer. Lab weights, marbles, and pennies (twenty to thirty per boat) all make a reasonable weight load. The marbles shift significantly if the waters get rough; pennies will shift less. This shifting can affect boat performance under different conditions.

Note on classroom setup: Although there are multiple ways to set up this lesson, be aware that the ship testing can take time and be somewhat distracting. This time-consuming activity can create a bottleneck, with students waiting to test their own ship and students who have finished testing their own watching other students' tests. You will want to manage traffic flow through the testing station. If you have enough water containers to allow for multiple tests simultaneously, that's ideal. Tubs, buckets, and coolers will all work fine. If you have access to a kiddie pool, or a real pool, even better! Encourage students who have finished their testing to move on to documenting the results of their tests, and then move again to refining their ship design. As written here, we have used a station model to manage the student flow (that is, a testing station, a documentation station, and a refining and rebuilding station).

Introduction (10 minutes)

Using the "Shipbuilder's Blueprint" handout, ask your students to imagine building a ship from any point in history. Have them describe their ship: What does it look like? What is it made of? Who and/or what will go on it? Where will it go, and why? What are some of the challenges it might face on its journey? What are some of the design features of the vessel that make it uniquely suited for this journey? Have students write down a few ideas about their ship and the adventure it is about to embark on. Encourage them to include a lot of detail in their description. Should time permit, they can sketch a quick picture.

Keep This Discussion Afloat (15 minutes)

Ask the students, "What are some things that float? What are some things that don't float?"

At this point it's useful to bring out some materials—some that float and some that don't, as well as some that look like they should sink but actually float, and vice versa. You can ask students to make predictions based on their prior knowledge of the items and/or the items' appearance. Then test the students' predictions in the prepared pool of water.

After testing, ask the students, "What makes something float?" This last question is a tricky one. When the guesses stop, share the story of Archimedes.

ARCHIMEDES AND THE BIG DISCOVERY Two thousand years ago, King Hiero of Syracuse gave a metalsmith gold to create a crown for a temple. The smith produced an intricate crown that weighed what it was supposed to when tested. But Hiero was troubled by a rumor that the smith had replaced some of the precious gold with silver, to keep some gold for himself.

Hiero asked the mathematician and scientist Archimedes to devise a test to see if the crown was, in fact, pure gold. While Archimedes was pondering this, he decided to take a bath. He noticed that the water overflowed when he climbed into the tub, and realized he'd found his solution. He hopped out of the bath and ran through the streets yelling, "Eureka!" (Greek for "I've found it!")

Once he'd dried off, Archimedes tested his theory. He took a piece of silver that weighed as much as the crown, and placed it in a container of water. By doing this, he could determine its volume. Then he did the same with an equal weight of pure gold, discovering that its volume was less than the silver's. Finally, he placed the crown in the water. Its volume was more than that of the piece of pure gold, proving that the crown must contain some silver as suspected. Eureka!

Whoa! How did Archimedes do that?! (Ask your students this; it's okay if the story went a little over their heads for now.) How does this tie into the previous tests of things that float and things that don't? What's more essential to an object's ability to float, its **mass** (the amount of stuff in an object, which, on Earth's surface, is basically its weight) or its **volume** (the space that it takes up)? Ha—that's a trick question! Students may argue back and forth, but really, it's the **density**—how much mass (stuff) is packed into a space of a particular size. It's okay if they don't get to realizing this point—they will later.

To move things along, lead out with the following question: How do ships, which are really, really, really massive, float in water?

Shipbuilding (15 minutes)

For this initial phase, we want students to get their feet wet. (Yes, pun intended.) They've just been introduced to density, and we can hardly expect them to apply that tenuous knowledge without seeing the concept in action.

To begin, ask students to reflect back on the ship they imagined at the start of the workshop. What are common features of ships? What are some special features of particular ships that make them suited for specific tasks? What, exactly, is a ship? (They'll probably come up with a definition like "a thing that floats and carries stuff over the water.")

And now, give them a challenge: to build a ship that can carry weight and does not sink. For dramatic effect, fold a piece of tinfoil over on itself repeatedly (until you cannot fold it any smaller) and drop it into the pool of water, where it will sink. Let them know that they will now be creating a ship out of this material that sinks. Tell students at the outset that they will have time later to refine their design, after testing. Students should be thoughtful about their design, but also attentive to time so that they each have the opportunity to test their ship, refine their design, and test again. Set them loose to get to work!

Station 1: Shakedown Cruise[1]—Testing and Observation (15 minutes)

Students will take different amounts of time to build their respective ships, and that's a good thing; if everyone finished at once, there would be a really long wait to test each ship. As students finish building the first "draft" of their ship, encourage them to move on to the testing station.

Based on the basic definition from earlier, a ship will be a success if it meets the following criteria:

◇ It floats.

◇ It can carry stuff (for example, laboratory weights, marbles, or coins).

For a bonus challenge, students might deem their ship a success if it meets these additional criteria:

◇ It can move. Students can tie a string to the prow of the ship and pull gently (this might not be possible in a confined space).

◇ It can turn while loaded, without capsizing (flipping over or on its side) or taking on water.

Encourage students to move through the testing station quickly so that other students get a chance to test their ship.

Station 2: Captain's Log—Documentation (10 minutes)

After students have completed testing, have them move on to the next station, where they should document their ship's successes and failures using the "Captain's Log: Shakedown Cruise" handout. Emphasize specificity: the more specific your students are now, the better they'll be able to refine their ship design.

Station 3: Shipbuilding, Again! (15 minutes)

Now that students have actually seen density in action, task them with improving their original design. If their ship sank or capsized (flipped over or on its side), how might they prevent this from happening again? If their ship passed the first suite of tests, can they improve it so it can carry more weight, or sail more quickly or smoothly? Some questions that may help your students refine their design include the following:

---

1. This is actually the name for the first test voyage of a ship. Amazing!

◇ Did the density of your ship change during the test (for example, via leaks or hull deformation)?

◇ Are some parts of your ship more or less dense than others? (This variability can cause a ship to lean over and sink.)

◇ Is it possible to change the density of your ship? What about the density of certain parts of your ship?

◇ How does adding cargo affect the density of your ship?

Students should enter this station at different times, depending on when they finished testing their original ship design (and documenting their tests). In addition, they will take different amounts of time to execute their refined ship design, once again spreading out the arrival of students at the testing station.

Shakedown, Too: Testing, Observation, and Documentation . . . Again! (15 minutes)

Via the methods used earlier, possibly subjecting the ships to extra stresses (greater speed, more cargo), have students each test their redesigned ship! Using the "Captain's Log: Shakedown, Too" handout, and again moving through the testing, documentation, and refinement stations, students will document their tests as before; assess their design improvements, comparing their refined design to the original; and propose another round of design changes.

Letters in Bottles (25 minutes)

Now that students have seen ships in action, they should have a better idea of how density works, and of how changes in density affect ships.

Ask them to recall the ship and the adventure they imagined at the beginning of the lesson. Prompt them to think more about the ship's adventures and what they've learned from their experiments—and then to use all of that to write a story. For example, students can write about a scenario in which the density of their ship (defined loosely—they may have imagined a submarine or an airship earlier) changes dangerously and unexpectedly (due to extra cargo, a leak, stowaways, even missing cargo—if a ship isn't dense enough, and it's poorly designed, it can float too high and tip over!). Perhaps their narrator saves the day. Students' stories can take many different forms: a captain's or crew member's log, a letter to a friend or loved one, or a message in a bottle letting its finder know a ship's final fate.

FOR YOU TO KNOW (AND YOUR STUDENTS TO DISCOVER)

What makes something float or sink seems simple on the surface, yet is a fascinating and complex question. Students' understanding of the idea of density develops gradually. As you will see through your group discussion, students, even young ones, can provide examples of things that float or sink. Their experiences with investigating these phenomena will vary greatly, however, as will their understanding of why one object floats and another sinks.

In highly unscientific terms, whether an object will sink or float is related to how much "stuff" is crammed into the "space" that the object takes up. This concept can be relatively easy to visualize: a solid cube of steel will sink, but if you hollow it out, it is a crudely

(continued)

shaped ship and will float. The solid block has more "stuff" (in this case, steel molecules) crammed into the space (or volume).

Students will often say that something is "heavy for its size" or "light for its size," which signifies that they are developing an understanding of a relationship between weight and volume.[2] They will also begin to recognize that objects that are heavy for their size are likely to sink (in water), and those light for their size will probably float.

Getting a little more scientific, scientists tend to call stuff **matter,** and at a microscopic level, matter is made up of atoms or groups of atoms (called molecules). In an object that is heavy for its size, the molecules are more closely packed than they are in an object that is light for its size. Imagine filling two identical bags with balls—the first with baseballs, the second with Wiffle balls. Which bag is lighter? You can think of the baseball "molecules" as more tightly packed: each ball is solid, so there is relatively little air in the bag. The Wiffle ball "molecules," in contrast, are hollow, making room for lots of air. Thus, the Wiffle ball "molecules" are not as tightly packed, and there is a lot of air in the bag.

The scientific term for the amount of space something (a solid, a liquid, or even a gas) takes up is its "volume."

The scientific term "density" refers to how much stuff is in a given amount of space, or volume. Let's go back to the example of the solid steel cube and the hollowed-out cube. Although the dimensions of the cubes are the same (they take up the same amount of space), the hollow cube contains fewer steel molecules in that space, so it's less dense than the solid one.

When developing the concept of density with students, there are a lot of great questions you can pose to challenge their thinking. Most students know that a ship is very heavy (imagine an aircraft carrier!), but that it also floats. Why is this? Here is a great opportunity to get students thinking about the amount of stuff in a given space, or the density of an object. Once again, though, let the students explore. Prompt their thinking with well-placed questions, and then stand back and see where their explorations take them.

Determining the Density of an Object

Different materials all have different densities. Density is a characteristic property of a material, and figuring out something's density is relatively easy (and fun). Moreover, as you will see, you can use density to solve a mystery—to figure out what an object is made of (or if it has been contaminated by other materials).

To figure out the density of an object, you need to know two things: (1) how much stuff you have, and (2) how much space that stuff takes up. Scientists use the term "mass" to describe how much stuff or matter is in an object. For our purposes, on Earth's surface, mass is equivalent to weight. So, to know how much matter you have in an object, you weigh it. (And because this is science, and you want to be able to communicate and share your findings, you should

2. Driver, R., Squires, A., Rushworth, P., & Robinson, V. W. (1994). *Making sense of secondary science: Research into children's ideas.* New York, NY: Routledge Press, p. 78.

measure things the same way that other scientists worldwide do: using a metric scale that reads in grams.)

Determining how much space the object takes up is where this gets fun. Liquids are easy; you just pour them into a measuring cup and read the metric volume (measured in milliliters, or mL for short). But how can you figure out the volume of a solid—how much space the object takes up—in milliliters? As it turns out, it is relatively simple to measure how much space something takes up, in water.

You probably already know something about how to take such a measurement from your everyday life. For example, when you get into a bathtub, the water level of the tub goes up. This is because your body pushes the water out of the way, or **displaces** the water. Your body and the water cannot both occupy the same space at once. One way to measure the volume of an object, then, is to use the volume displacement technique. First fill a measuring cup partway with water (and note the volume of water in the cup—say, 125 mL). Now add an object to the water (a Matchbox car) and note the volume of water in the measuring cup (for example, the volume might now be 150 mL). The difference between the starting volume of water and the volume after you added the Matchbox car is the volume of the car (150 mL – 125 mL = 25 mL, which is approximately two tablespoons). This technique works if you drop any solid (that sinks) into water (a toy car, a steel cube, a penny, a spoon) and is an easy way to calculate the volume of something.

Now, on to density. The formula for density reads:

$$\text{Density} = \text{Mass} \div \text{Volume}$$

Because mass is measured in grams (or g) and volume is measured in milliliters, density is measured in grams per milliliter. The density of liquid water is 1 g/mL. Anything with a density greater than 1 g/mL will sink when placed in water. Objects with a density lower than 1 g/mL will float.

SHIPBUILDER'S BLUEPRINT

Imagine what kind of ship you'd build if you were a shipbuilder. It can be from anywhere and from any time, including the future. It can be tiny, enormous, simple, ornate, practical, ridiculous; an old-timey pirate's galleon, a futuristic submarine, a kayak, a raft, a yacht, a cruise ship—anything you want, as long as it floats (hopefully!).

What does your ship look like? Describe it:

What is your ship made out of?

Who and what will go on your ship?

Where will it sail, and why?

What are some of the challenges it might face on its journey?

What adventures might it encounter?

Now, draw your ship on the back of this sheet!

CAPTAIN'S LOG: SHAKEDOWN CRUISE

In this space, draw your first attempt at floating your ship. Draw it from the front and the side, being as specific as possible about (1) the location of any leaks; (2) the orientation of your ship (that is, how upright it is or how much it leans over); and (3) where the water comes up to on the side of the ship (with measurements if possible). Take lots of notes on what you observe after you've put your ship in the water.

Now, draw your ship under load (that is, with weight). Again, draw it from the front and the side, and be specific about leak locations, your ship's orientation, and the water line.

Finally, draw your ship in motion, while continuing to pay attention to detail.

CAPTAIN'S LOG: SHAKEDOWN, TOO

We hope you were able to improve your ship! Here, document the differences between your original ship and your redesigned ship. Again, record how your redesigned ship performs, making sure as always to be specific about leak locations, ship orientation, and the water line. You'll probably have a number of different diagrams here—make sure to label them all appropriately.

Based on these results, how might you further improve your ship's design?

STEM@HOME: WHAT FLOATS BOATS?

We all know that boats can float. But do you think you can float water . . . on top of water? Lots of experimenting fun ahead!

MATERIALS

☐ Clear glasses or plastic cups

☐ Tap water

☐ Food coloring (Yellow and blue work well.)

☐ A fridge or freezer

☐ Salt

☐ An eyedropper, a medicine cup, or some other object that will help you slowly transfer water from one glass to another

Fill a glass with water. Add several drops of yellow food coloring (until the water is noticeably yellow). Place the glass in the fridge or freezer until it is cold (but not frozen!).

Later, fill another glass half full with hot water from the tap. **Be careful not to burn yourself.** Add blue food coloring.

Next, create a saturated salt water solution. Add salt to water a bit at a time, and stir until the salt dissolves. You're done when you can't dissolve any more salt; at this point, you can add some blue food coloring.

Now, explore and see what you can discover about the properties of water by seeing how these different water preparations interact. A note about technique: when you add one type of water to another, you want to do so slowly and carefully.

▸ Does cold water float on hot water? Does hot water float on cold water?

▸ Does saturated salt water float or sink in tap water? (Be sure to tint the tap water yellow so you can distinguish it from the blue saturated salt water.)

▸ What do you think is going on?

Don't Be Too Dense: A Tale of Greed and the Elegant Engineering That Saved the Day *

Serving on the crew of a merchant ship has always been a dangerous job. Throughout history, ships were frequently lost in shipwrecks due to bad weather or disrepair, and crews had to risk attacks by pirates (and during wars were frequently targeted for attack by enemy military). A ship's crew also faced more mundane dangers, such as injury or death from onboard accidents or disease from lack of freshwater or safe food.

---

*History and facts are derived from the following sources: "Load Lines," *http://www.rmg.co.uk/explore /sea-and-ships/facts/ships-and-seafarers/load-lines*; Roman, "Episode 33: A Cheer for Samuel Plimsoll," *http://99percentinvisible.org/episode/episode-33-a-cheer-for-samuel-plimsoll/*; "A Commercial Ship Is Properly Loaded When the Ship's Waterline Equals the Ship's Plimsoll Line," from *http://oceanservice.noaa.gov/facts /plimsoll-line.html*.

(*continued*)

STEM@HOME: WHAT FLOATS BOATS? (continued)

These jobs became even more dangerous in the 1800s. It was during this time that insurance on ships and their cargos became commonly available to shipowners. Prior to a voyage, a shipowner would pay a fee to an insurance company that was based on the declared value of the ship and its contents. If the ship did not make it to its destination safely, the owner would collect an insurance payout—money equal to the amount the owner *said* the ship and cargo were worth.

Many greedy, dishonest shipowners used this system to their advantage. They would fill out a false declaration, stating that the value of the ship and cargo was very high—higher than what the ship and cargo were truly worth. As a result, a ship was worth more to the owner sunk than afloat. Shipowners would deliberately overload their ships (essentially making them too dense) so that they would sink. They did not care about the lives of their crewmen. This practice became so common that off the coast of Britain in only one year (1873–1874), more than four hundred ships sank, killing over five hundred sailors. It is not a surprise that these vessels were called "coffin ships."

In the 1870s a member of the British Parliament, Samuel Plimsoll, became very concerned about this practice and worked to put in place regulations to protect the lives of the ships' crewmen. His solution was very simple and elegant, and is still in use today. Plimsoll's legislation required that a load line be placed on the outside of every ship. This line, situated on the hull of a boat, shows how full the boat can be filled and still be seaworthy.

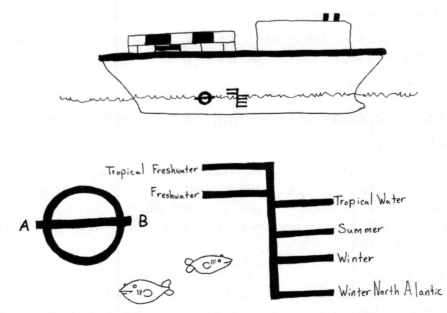

This image shows the load line on a ship in the water. The lines on the left indicate the load level in different types of water. These different lines are necessary because the density of salt water is different from that of freshwater, and the density changes at different temperatures. The line with the circle shows whether the boat has been loaded evenly, and the letters on either side of the circle indicate the registration authority governing the ship.

(*continued*)

STEM@HOME: WHAT FLOATS BOATS? (continued)

For a ship to go to sea, the load line must be visible (above water). As in your experiments, the more cargo added to a ship, the lower the hull rests in the water. The load (or Plimsoll) line allows anyone outside of a ship to determine how much cargo has been loaded, and critically to know if the ship is now too heavy to go to sea safely.

Plimsoll and the line that bears his name became very famous (particularly among sailors—he wasn't so popular among shipowners), and several songs were written about him. Following are the lyrics of one song, "A Cheer for Samuel Plimsoll," written by Fred Albert in 1876.

> So a cheer for Samuel Plimsoll and let your voices blend
> In praise of one who surely has proved the sailors' friend
> Our tars upon the ocean he struggles to defend
> Success to Samuel Plimsoll for he's the sailors' friend.
> There was a time when greed and crime did cruelly prevail
> and rotten ships were sent on trips to founder in the gale
> When worthless cargoes well-insured would to the bottom go.
> And sailors' lives were sacrificed that men might wealthy grow.
> For many a boat that scarce could float was sent to dar the wave
> 'til Plimsoll wrote his book of notes our seamen's lives to save
> His enemies then tried to prove that pictures false he drew
> but with English pluck to his task he stuck, a task he deemed so true.

Fun Density Facts

▸ If we could find a bathtub big enough, the planet Saturn would float.

▸ Would you use concrete to build a canoe? Every year, teams of college students participate in a competition to build (and race) concrete canoes. The winning teams win college scholarships.

▸ The density of materials changes as the materials change their state (between solid, liquid, and gas). Most materials are more dense as solids than they are as liquids.

▸ Water is relatively unique among common substances on Earth: its solid form, ice, is less dense than water. We are really lucky that this is the case; if it weren't, Earth would not be able to sustain life.

▸ Diet cola is less dense than regular cola. (Really, it's true; try it. Place two unopened cans in a sink full of water.) Why do you think this is?

WATER, WATER EVERYWHERE, NOR ANY DROP TO DRINK

BASED ON THE ORIGINAL WORKSHOP
BY CHRIS PECK AND KAREN SAMA

3 SESSIONS, 2 HOURS EACH (**NOTE:** *This workshop works best with at least a couple of days—ideally a week—between sessions.*)
STEM DISCIPLINES: *Physical sciences, earth sciences, engineering*
WRITING ACTIVITIES: *Technical writing, creative writing, narrative writing*

MOST OF US TAKE THE AVAILABILITY OF clean water for granted. Unfortunately, lots of people around the world (including many in the United States) aren't so lucky. And even those of us with reliable sources of water sometimes find ourselves without, after a natural disaster or just on a hike that goes too long.

In these scenarios, it's useful to know how to get clean water, and with this lesson, students will explore exactly that. They'll learn some of the science behind purifying water and will engineer devices that perform part of the process. Along the way, they'll learn about isolating variables and iterative design. At the end, they'll communicate what they've learned to others, sharing scientific knowledge and helping everyone be more prepared. As they proceed through the lesson, students will take what they've learned and use it to write a narrative about the Thirstiest Person in the World—which hopefully ends well.

MATERIALS

SESSION 1

☐ Cabbage juice indicator (See "Handy Lesson Links" in the appendix for instructions.)

☐ Rubber chicken bones (Wing bones are recommended. See "Handy Lesson Links" in the appendix for instructions.)

☐ A naked egg (See "Handy Lesson Links" in the appendix for instructions.)

☐ 2 small, clear containers

☐ Tap water

☐ Salt

(continued)

- ☐ Fruits or vegetables
- ☐ Salty snacks (saltines, pretzels, and so on)
- ☐ pH strips (optional; found in most drugstores and online)
- ☐ An assortment of beverages, preferably on the clearer side (optional)
- ☐ Clear plastic cups (You'll need a lot; about 5 per student, plus more for demonstration.)
- ☐ Teaspoon measures
- ☐ Tablespoon measures
- ☐ Carbonated water
- ☐ Baking soda
- ☐ Vinegar
- ☐ Copies of the "Cabbage Rainbow pHun" handout (included with the other handout at the end of this lesson)
- ☐ Colored pencils (optional)
- ☐ A fresh egg
- ☐ Distilled water (optional)
- ☐ Straws (optional)
- ☐ Disposable gloves (optional but recommended for bonus activity)
- ☐ Goggles (optional but recommended for bonus activity)
- ☐ Plant cuttings (Begonia, philodendron, and coleus cuttings work well, but you can use anything.)

(continued)

Session 1: Contamination

During this session, students begin to explore the effects of not having enough (clean, usable) water. Then they get to have fun contaminating water in very colorful ways, learning about acids and bases as they do.

Preparation

Before class, you'll need to prepare some cabbage juice indicator (which you'll be using in all three sessions), plant cuttings, rubber chicken bones, and a naked egg. They're all pretty simple to make. For the naked egg, you'll need to get started a good twenty-four hours before the lesson. Rubber chicken bones work best when started a full three days beforehand; we recommend wing bones.

You'll also need to dehydrate a fruit or vegetable or two. This procedure is about as easy as preparing a naked egg, and it'll also need to be started a day ahead of time. You should have two small, clear containers, one containing tap water, the other containing a mixture of tap water and salt. (Saltier is better. If it smells like the ocean, great! If you can't add any more salt and it just piles up at the bottom, that's even better.) Place a fruit or vegetable or two in each—both containers should have the same fruit(s) or vegetable(s) inside. (So each container can have a clementine and a jalapeño, but you shouldn't put a clementine in one and a jalapeño in the other.) Note that your mileage may vary. You can try this out with different fruits or vegetables to see which show the most drastic results. (We've had good results with snap peas and strawberries.)

Introduction (15 minutes)

Start with a snack—a sneaky snack. Have saltines and pretzels available for students. (If you're feeling particularly devious, you can have the thermostat cranked up a few degrees higher than usual.) Ask them what it feels like to be thirsty. How does their mouth feel after eating the salty snacks with nothing to wash them down? What are some other times they've felt really, really thirsty? You can have students write down a response, or you can use the chalkboard to record responses from the group.

To focus the activity a little more, you can ask students to write a saltine diary. Have them eat one saltine at a time, then write down how they feel. You're likely to have students around the five-saltine mark declare that they're done, especially if they're eating pretty quickly!

(*A safety note:* Don't crank the thermostat up *too* high. Remind students to eat the saltines one at a time, and not too fast. And have water available in case anyone needs it.)

The Thirstiest Person in the World: I'm So Thirsty (15 minutes)

Have students brainstorm some narrative situations in which someone might be really thirsty: marooned on a desert island, lost on a car race through the Sahara, whatever they can come up with. Then set them loose to start the story of the Thirstiest Person in the World, of how someone unexpectedly finds him- or herself without water. Give them the following prompt:

Where does the story take place?

Who are the characters?

How does the main character become so, so thirsty?

How does the character feel when he or she gets really thirsty? Think back to your own experience with the salty snacks to describe the character's thoughts or senses.

They'll have a chance later to flesh out the story more; right now, they should just focus on the setting and exposition.

The Importance of Water (10 minutes)

Ask students how important water is. The answer: *very!* You can share some fun water facts (for example: the human body is 50 to 70 percent water;[1] Earth's surface is 70 percent water, but less than 1 percent of that is drinkable; human beings can survive for perhaps three weeks without food, but only for maybe three days without water; and so on).

Follow that up with the more important question, What makes water safe or unsafe to drink? Collect answers and put them up on the board to share. Students may at first bring up things like dirt and animal waste, which are both definitely dangerous. But why is that? It actually has more to do with microorganisms than the disgusting stuff we can see (and smell). You'll tell students this later on.

SESSION 2

☐ Salt tester (See "Handy Lesson Links" in the appendix for instructions.)

☐ 2 clear containers

☐ Potting soil or garden-variety dirt

☐ Distilled water

☐ Alum

☐ Plant cuttings in solutions from the previous session

☐ Tap water

☐ Carbonated water

☐ Salt

☐ Baking soda

☐ Vinegar

☐ Clear plastic cups (about 2 per student, or 4 per student if making additional solutions to experiment with the salt tester)

☐ Printouts of Centers for Disease Control and Prevention (CDC) info on waterborne diseases and contaminants (See "Handy Lesson Links" in the appendix.)

☐ Empty 1- or 2-liter soda bottles, cut crosswise to give you a top and a bottom half (1 bottle per student plus one for demonstration)

(*continued*)

---

1. The percentage varies among people (by age, gender, fitness, and so on), and between body parts of an individual (your skin has less water than your muscles).

- ☐ 2-by-2-inch squares of cheesecloth (5 per student plus extra for demonstration)

- ☐ Filter materials: soil, sand, pebbles or rocks, cotton balls, and charcoal or activated carbon (Activated carbon is much, much better than charcoal, and can be found in pet stores, with the aquarium supplies.)

- ☐ Cabbage juice indicator

SESSION 3

- ☐ Potting soil or garden-variety dirt

- ☐ Tap water

- ☐ Baking soda

- ☐ Salt

- ☐ Copies of the "Purification Challenge" handout

- ☐ Soda bottles from the previous session

- ☐ Cheesecloth squares from the previous session

- ☐ Filter materials (soil, pebbles, charcoal, and so on) from the previous session (Restock if supplies are low.)

- ☐ Clear plastic cups (about 2 per student)

- ☐ Orange juice

- ☐ Cabbage juice indicator

- ☐ Salt tester

- ☐ Colored pencils (optional)

- ☐ Empty soda bottles or food storage containers (optional)

Direct the conversation to invisible additives. Salt water is a good discussion point. What's bad about salt? We put it on our food, right? But salt water will suck a lot of water out of your body. This is why shipwrecked sailors can die of thirst in their lifeboat, surrounded by (salty) water. At this point, bring out your dehydrated fruit(s) or vegetable(s) to show what salt water can do, and let the oohs and aahs commence.

Testing Water (35 minutes)

Before we clean water, we're going to contaminate it, and we're going to do it with **acids** and **bases.** Ask students if they know what these are. Most students will have heard of acids, and they will probably "know" that acids burn (or burn through) things. They're much less likely to have heard of bases. If they have, it will probably have been in the context of acids, as in "bases are the opposite of acids." If this comment comes up, get them to clarify! Ask students if they've ever eaten anything acidic. They have—citrus fruits and tomatoes, for instance. Students might not realize that these items are acidic, however, so if they're blanking, ask them if they've eaten anything sour. The human tongue's sour taste buds actually test specifically for acid; sourness is basically acidity.

An investigation of how acids and bases work is beyond the scope of this lesson, but you can let students know that acids and bases are present in many chemical reactions. (*Spoiler alert:* Do not explain at this point that acids and bases counteract each other, or are at opposite ends of the pH scale. Students should discover this on their own during this investigation.)

At this point, demonstrate how pH strips work on a number of household beverages. If time is tight, or if you don't have pH strips on hand, you can skip this demonstration. (Any pH strips you get should come with instructions, but if not, it's pretty simple. You'll dip the pH strip into a solution, and the color or colors on the strip will change in a few seconds. The colors will match up with colors on a chart, which will tell you the pH. A pH of 7 is neutral. A solution with a pH lower than 7 is acidic; higher than 7 is basic. The farther from 7, the stronger the acid or base.) The pH of many sodas, for instance, is closer than most people realize to that of a standard solution of hydrochloric acid or sulfuric acid, the ones that some students may have heard of that burn through things. You want to make the point that many things are acids, and that acids come in different strengths.

Acids are very common in the kitchen (for example, lemon juice, vinegar). The same is true of bases, but (safe) household bases are less common.

Explain to students that acids and bases can be present in water, sometimes making it unsafe to drink, and that it's not entirely possible to reliably detect them via sight or smell (or taste) alone. Students are going to test the effects of acids and bases on life forms between now and the next session—but first, they have to figure out a way to test for the presence of acids and bases without using a pH strip.

This is your cue to bring out the cabbage juice indicator and copies of the "Cabbage Rainbow pHun" handout. Cabbage juice indicator works a lot like a pH strip, turning solutions a different color based on their pH level.

For the next ten to fifteen minutes, students are going to come up with as many colors as they can. Let students mix whatever they like in clear plastic cups (tap water or carbonated water plus salt, vinegar, or baking soda). They should measure whatever they use using measuring spoons, then record the recipe on the "Cabbage Rainbow pHun" handout. (Remind them to rinse the measuring spoons between uses, to avoid cross-contamination.) Then, using a new cup, they'll combine a table-spoon of their solution with a teaspoon of cabbage juice indicator, observe what color the solution turns, and record it on the handout (colored pencils are useful here).

You want a lot of colors, so once that first mixture has been tested, let students mix up several more. (They can wash and reuse the first cup—the one that held the solution before they added the cabbage juice indicator—to conserve cups.) Remind them to measure and record what goes into each solution on the handout.

As anyone who's ever accompanied a preteen to a self-serve soda fountain knows, the temptation is to mix in *everything*. And it's fine if they want to combine the vinegar, baking soda, salt, and water into one supersolution. After that, though, encourage them to experiment with one or two ingredients at a time. If students don't test individual substances, it'll be harder for them to understand their relative acidity and basicity. They'll also be less likely to come up with a relatively full pH spectrum. Students may find that baking soda and vinegar mixtures have a pH close to neutral (because together these ingredients balance each other out) and incorrectly assume that each individual substance is only mildly basic or acidic.

Once your students have a lot of colors, their next task (which should take another ten to fifteen minutes) is to arrange the whole class's colors in order based on transitions between the shades (and if they have succeeded in producing a broad palette of colors in their earlier explorations, the arrangement should be pretty self-evident—colors transition clearly from one to another). Once students have worked out the order, challenge them to start with a solution with a color at one end of the scale (say, blue) and transform it to the color of a solution at the other end, hitting all the shades in between.

If, after a few minutes of this investigation, you feel like your students could use a little hint, ask them all what color pure water tests as. (It's purple, or close.) Then ask what happens if they add a little something of their choice to the water. (It'll shift toward pink or blue.) You've basically given them one point on the pH scale, and also given them a new piece of information to wrestle with. Water is the weakest, safest possible substance, but there are apparently at least two different ways to make it less neutral. Hmm . . .

At the end of this segment, if students have figured it out, they'll have a scale that goes something like the following: (yellow → green →) blue → purple → pink (→ red → orangey), from basic to neutral to acidic. Ask students if anyone's mixed anything from the pink end of the scale with any-thing from the blue end. The answer is probably yes, and the indicator should have tested closer to purple, which is what water tests as. In essence, the substances they mixed (acids and bases—you can reintroduce those terms here) cancel each other out, similar to adding positive and negative integers.

ACID, GAS, AND WATER We've seen students get pretty excited about testing the pH of substances. They've primarily tested liquids, but also some solids (salt, baking soda) dissolved in water. Time permitting, with this additional demo, you can show them that they can even dissolve something they cannot see into water and change its pH: gas!

Have a solution of 1 tablespoon distilled water and 1 teaspoon cabbage juice indicator ready, along with a straw. Insert one end of the straw into the solution, and the other into your mouth. You're not going to drink it. (You could, though, if you wanted to—it's basically really watery cabbage soup.) Instead, you're going to blow bubbles into it while your students watch. After a while, there should be a slight change in color toward the acidic end of the scale (the vinegar end), probably something like a shift from a purple to a slightly pinker purple. What might happen if you blew continuously into a basic solution (something on the baking soda end of the scale)? (Note that if you have students try this in class, you will want to warn them to take a break if they start to get lightheaded from exhaling continuously.) Ask students questions like, If you leave your now-pink cup of liquid out uncovered overnight, what color will it be in the morning? Why? Do you think it will make a difference if you cover it?

When carbon dioxide dissolves in water, it forms an acid. This is where acid rain comes from, actually. It's the reason why carbonated beverages like cola are acidic. More critically, it is the reason why our oceans are becoming more acidic as the amount of carbon dioxide in our atmosphere increases. You can use a pH strip to test cola before and after you shake the bottle and remove some of the gas from the water.

Many gases can dissolve in water. Animals and plants that live underwater breathe the same gases (oxygen and carbon dioxide, respectively) as animals and plants that live above water. This isn't to say that you, as a human, can stick your head underwater and breathe the oxygen there. You would drown, because human lungs cannot extract sufficient oxygen from water (compounded by the fact that water irritates the lungs and interferes with their function). Many creatures that live underwater have specialized organs—gills—that efficiently gather and process the oxygen necessary for life.

BAKING SODA AND VINEGAR EXPLOSION! All of the materials in this session are commonly found in kitchens. Although they're not Dangerous with a capital *D,* they can cause chemical reactions (or irritation, if you get some in your eyes). So, it's a good time to go over some basic chemical safety.

To be safe, have gloves and goggles for your students, and instruct them not to eat or drink anything. Make sure the room is well ventilated.

If you are so inclined (and we **do not** recommend this for anyone but experienced laboratory teachers), you can provide students with a wider range of chemicals to test, including

(continued)

household cleaners like ammonia (but **definitely not bleach,** or any cleaner that contains bleach, which happens to be dangerously reactive in several ways)—which are absolutely Dangerous with a capital *D*. In this case, make sure to follow the full National Science Teachers Association (NSTA) safety guidelines (in "Handy Lesson Links" in the appendix). (For ammonia specifically, we recommend diluting it with water, or using a cleaner like original Windex, to minimize irritation from the fumes. We'll also take this opportunity to remind you again: **do not use bleach or any cleaning agent containing bleach.** When bleach is mixed with ammonia, it produces a poisonous gas.)

Note that two of the substances in the standard set, baking soda and vinegar, are infamously part of the ubiquitous science experiment volcano. They will react with each other, producing a frothing, foaming liquid. (The reaction produces carbon dioxide gas, which is responsible for all the bubbles.) You could forbid the combination of the two to prevent a mess, but preferably you would allow it under controlled circumstances—in essence, students should add one to the other slowly. This'll allow students to see that some solutions test like pure water, which is really, really helpful. If you do decide to allow it, you may want to demonstrate the reaction first to get all the oohs and aahs out of your students, before advising them to be more careful and scientific in their explorations.

Testing Water's Effects (15 minutes)

It's time to bring out your rubber chicken bones and naked egg. Let the students know that an acid led to the damage of both the bones and the eggshell. For dramatic effect, place a fresh egg into some vinegar, and note how it starts to bubble pretty immediately.

Ask your students what effects they think the water contaminated with acids or bases will have on plants. They'll be testing this over the coming days or weeks, depending on how you've scheduled the sessions.

Make sure each student or student group has plant cuttings—basically, a little bit of stem with one or more leaves—from an easy-to-grow plant like a begonia, coleus, or philodendron. They should mix a solution in a clear plastic cup (just as they did in the Cabbage Rainbow pHun segment), note what's in it as precisely as possible, indicate the color of the indicator when tested, and predict what will happen to the plant.

They should then place the cutting so the bottom of the stem segment is underwater, along with part of the lowest leaf. Hang on to these, as students will record root growth from the stem for the duration of this lesson sequence. (In all likelihood, quite a few plants will die soon enough for a point to be made about the negative effects of acidity or basicity on living things, and most of your class won't need to measure root growth.)

Make sure that students collectively duplicate as many experiments as possible. Have them think of solutions they'd like to grow their plants in, and write these up on the board. If necessary, be sure to suggest that students test pure water, in addition to solutions that contain water and only one other dissolved substance. (For a refresher on why it's important to isolate the substances, see the discussion of variables in the Science-O-Pedia.) Once a number of experiments have been suggested, ask students to sign up for the experiment they'd like to do, and to work together to make sure that all the experiments that have been suggested are done.

The Thirstiest Person in the World: Are You Going to Drink That? (15 minutes)

Students at this point ideally will have a slightly expanded idea of what can contaminate water. Have them extend their original narrative a bit, bringing their thirsty character to a situation where he or she finds water that may or may not be safe to drink. Note that they, as authors, probably don't have a very complete picture yet of what makes water drinkable or not, and this is okay. Some of the author's uncertainty can and should translate to uncertainty on the protagonist's part.

Discussion (15 minutes)

Students can share a bit of their writing. Steer the discussion toward whether or not the water sources in their narratives are safe to drink. Ask students what they think some signs of good or bad water are. (They should extend beyond the obvious things likely to have been brought up earlier in the day. We probably should not drink from cesspools. But what about water that's just there in a hole in the ground?) Debate!

Again, your students only have a partial picture of what clean water is and isn't, so it's not likely that any definitive answers will surface. Focus instead on maintaining a flow of questions so that students stay curious. Along the way, keep the focus on how the students know something, or why they think the way they do. If brackish water is unsafe to drink, why? Or if water in a stream is good to drink, what about the stream makes it good? Let them know that as they learn more about cleaning water, they'll learn more about where to find clean water.

When wrapping up, remind students that they'll see some of what happens to an organism that ingests bad water next time, and that in the next session they'll also start the task of cleaning water.

Session 2: Filtration

In this session, students will continue investigating ways to detect things in water, and they'll start learning how to purify it.

Preparation

Before this session, you'll need to prepare a few things. You should already have your cabbage juice indicator from last session. Now, mix up your salt tester; you'll use these in the next session as well. Then make two solutions of dirty water by stirring potting soil or dirt into water in a couple of clean containers. You'll be using these for an alum demonstration, and it's a good idea to experiment with the alum beforehand so you'll know how much to use. Too much or too little alum won't flocculate (that is, clump) the dirt! Watch the MIT-produced video on Khan Academy in "Handy Lesson Links" in the appendix to see how flocculation works.

Introduction and Demos (20 minutes)

Show students the plants from last class. If it's been a week, some of the cuttings in more hospitable solutions may have some root growth. And even if it's only been a day or two, some of the plants in some of the solutions are likely to be at death's door. Probably only the cuttings in water, and maybe those in carbonated water, are doing well. But why? (Here's a hint—have students think back to the "Acid, Gas, and Water" demonstration suggested earlier, if you did that.)

Some of the least well-off plants are probably those in salt solution. Your class's project now: testing water for the presence of salt. You can't use a pH tester for that; you'll use the salt tester you prepared ahead of time instead. Show students the salt tester, and demonstrate that it does not go off in pure water.[2] (It is super important that you get distilled water. Deionized water is okay. Tap water is no good here, nor is purified water or natural spring water.)

If you like and time permits, you can give students a few minutes to use the salt tester on other solutions they mix up using water and additives like vinegar and baking soda, asking them to record any observations they have. Later on, they'll use the salt tester in conjunction with the cabbage juice indicator.

Before moving on to the next section, let students know that you have something cool to show them. Show your students your two containers of dirty water, add alum to one, and stir both. Let them know that you'll show them what happens in a bit! Before getting to that, though, students will explore what really happens when people drink bad water.

Why You Shouldn't Drink That (20 minutes)

Distribute CDC handouts about waterborne contaminants and diseases. Go over the handouts together, discussing anything the students are puzzled or curious about. If your students have access to the Internet, they can go online to find answers to their questions, or to learn more about various contaminants (see Handy Lesson Links in the appendix for useful sites).

The Thirstiest Person in the World: A Bitter End (15 minutes)

Time for a writing session. Have students write about a grisly fate for the Thirstiest Person in the World. Students should draw on what they've just researched about water pollution. Note that having the character die immediately is maybe a little too easy here. The character is likely to go through some rough times, which may end in death. Perhaps the most important thing is why the character suffers—dehydration from not drinking water? Disease from drinking dirty water? Nervous system damage from having to survive on heavy metal–polluted water for months?

If your students have grown attached to their protagonist, let them know the character will have a chance at redemption further on.

Alum Video and Demo (20 minutes)

At this point, again show students your dirty water from earlier. The container with alum mixed in should have the dirt mostly settled out! Wait for oohs and aahs, and then show them the video on flocculation.

Ask them how the video affected their understanding of the results of the live alum demonstration, and use this as a launch point for discussing what makes good science communication.

Purification Experiments: Filtration (30 minutes)

Ask students if they've ever made pasta or squeezed orange juice. How did they remove the pasta from the water, or the pulp from the juice? Most likely, students have used some sort of strainer. Let them know that they're going to try something similar—they're going to create filters for water.

---

2. Pure water is deionized or distilled water—the critical part here is that it must be water that has had the ions (that is, the salts) removed.

Show students the filter materials: soil; sand; cotton balls; pebbles or rocks; and charcoal chunks (activated carbon, preferably). Let them know that they're going to test each of these to see how effective they are at removing pollutants (the same ones added to water in the previous session). Demonstrate using a one- or two-liter soda bottle that's been cut in half to create a simple filter. Put a bit of cheesecloth in the neck and weigh it down with one or more filter materials (see the figure).

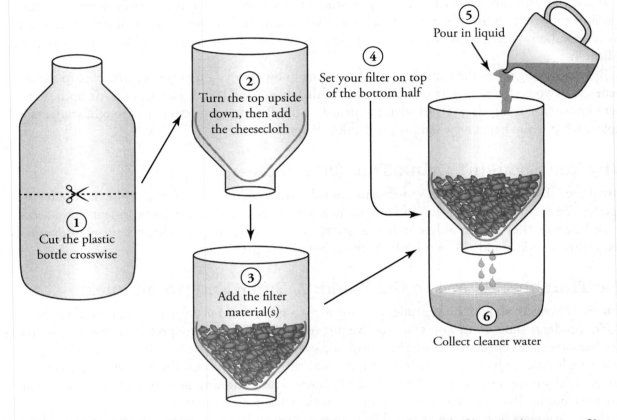

Next, explain the procedure. Students will make their own soda bottle filter (with just one filter material). Then they'll create a polluted water solution just like they did in the previous session, using a pollutant of their choice (baking soda, vinegar, or salt). They'll test the solution beforehand for contaminants (using the salt tester and cabbage juice indicator), filter it (which will take a bit), and test it again afterward. The goal is to test each type of filter with each pollutant to see how effective the different filter materials are. Ideally, after the first session, students will recall the importance of testing variables independently wherever possible, and will organize their experiments accordingly. You can, of course, help them by assigning tests to students, aiming to get at least one test of each filter material–pollutant combination. Students should have time to do a couple of tests, probably; allow them some leeway in the solutions they test, but keep the filters made of just one material. *Note:* The filters should be washed with tap water (or, even better, filtered or distilled water) after each test.

Discussion (15 minutes)

Go through the experiment results with students, and have them share what they think an ideal filter would be. If the discussion goes quickly, students can write and/or draw this design. Let them know that in the next session they'll be doing THE ULTIMATE TEST! Time permitting, students can also share some of their Thirstiest Person in the World narratives so far.

Session 3: Final Challenge

In this final session, students will use what they've discovered to purify water. They'll each finish their story as well, hopefully ending on a happier note.

Preparation

Although this session doesn't use many new materials, it's possible you and your students will have run low on or out of some things from the previous session. Make sure to stock up!

You'll also need to prepare a few new things. First up: Mystery Mud. (A lot.) Basically, mix a bunch of soil or dirt with water. Test it yourself with a pH strip or cabbage juice indicator. If it's neutral (if the pH is 7, or if the cabbage juice indicator remains the original color), make it basic by adding baking soda.

Finally, you'll need to mix up a simple salt solution of salt and water. It should, ideally, smell significantly salty.

The Challenge (10 minutes)

Distribute copies of the "Purification Challenge" handout (you might want to give students extra copies so that they can do multiple tests), and show students what they'll be testing their filters against: salt water, orange juice, and Mystery Mud. Their goal is to get the liquid as clean as possible, by any and all criteria they know. (Earlier in the lesson series, they've done both pH testing and salt testing. Also, they've heard a bit in passing about **turbidity**—the cloudiness of a liquid—from the flocculation video. All of these things are referenced on the "Purification Challenge" handout, and if any other criteria for water purity come up, those can be tested for and referenced as well.)

Purification (30 minutes)

Lead the students in a discussion of what they learned during the previous session. Give them about ten minutes to consider a strategy and build a filter. They should document exactly what their process is and how they built any equipment used. Once they're done, they can test their filter using the "Purification Challenge" handout. The more tests (on different solutions) they can run before this segment is up, the better! This might not be possible because it'll take time for the solutions to drip through each filter, and some solutions and filters are particularly slow.

Better Purification (20 minutes)

After a handful of tests, have your students briefly discuss what worked well. What kinds of filters worked well with different solutions? What kinds of filters were effective at purifying acids or bases, or removing gunk from the water?

Students should take this shared knowledge and build an improved filter, again taking care to document what they've done. Of course, once they've built their improved filter, they should test it!

Final Test and Review Discussion (20 minutes)

Your students have probably built significantly better filters this time around, some of which should have removed a lot of the stuff suspended in the water, and some of which should have neutralized acids or bases somewhat. Again, ask what worked and what didn't, as there's probably one thing that no filtration method got rid of—the salt.

When leading out, emphasize that the purification methods explored so far aren't perfect. They're very helpful, but they don't catch everything. As just mentioned, one thing difficult to filter out is salt—a very important concern in dry climates close to the ocean (Australia, for example). Another is microorganisms. They may remember from the flocculation video that filtration (especially combined with flocculation) can reduce them. But is there any way to get rid of them entirely? Or salt entirely?

If students have any ideas, they can share them. In any case, let them know that you'll be exploring some possible answers later. For now, they're going to do some more writing to convey what they've learned.

The Thirstiest Person in the World: A *Better* End! (15 minutes)

But wait! Have students write an alternate ending to their story so that the Thirstiest Person in the World meets a better fate! This may involve finding a more reliable source of water, or figuring out a way to clean water. To bring the narrative to a resolution, students may also wish to write about how their character escaped his or her thirsty predicament.

If it helps, you can have your students think of these as DVD-style alternate endings, or as options in a Choose Your Own Adventure story.

A Refreshing End (20 minutes or more)

If students would like to share their writing, they can. (Given the scope of their work, it might be best to share the narratives later, maybe even in a more public forum.)

Now come back to salt and microorganisms. For the latter, ask students how they kill germs in general. How might they apply that procedure to water? Some students may bring up chemical disinfectants; you can then let them know that chemical disinfectant tablets exist. (Such water treatment tablets are readily available at camping supply stores. Many such tablets are iodine based, so iodine is an option here as well.) Students might also mention boiling. Let them know that boiling water for a minute (or for three minutes at high altitudes) is the most reliable method, recommended by the Environmental Protection Agency. Another option is to use a few drops of bleach. (See "Handy Lesson Links" in the appendix for instructions, though we really, *really* hesitate suggesting that you tell your students to drink bleach, no matter how small the amount.) If you like, you can demonstrate these purification methods, but because they're visually as interesting as watching water boil, you might want to skip it.

As for salt—ask your students where salt water can be found. (Answer: the ocean.) What about freshwater? Students will probably talk about inland water sources, rivers and lakes and such. But where does that water come from? We hope that students will recognize that a lot of it comes from rain. And where does the rain come from? Surface water and groundwater. Is rain ever salty? Hmm . . . Students may remember a lot of this information from learning about the water cycle, which they probably encountered in elementary school. Let them know that when water evaporates, it leaves the salt behind, and that we can use this to our advantage.

If you're so inclined, you can show students videos of distillation in action (see "Handy Lesson Links" in the appendix for some online videos of steam distillation and solar stills). The inquiry will probably be more engaging, though, if you have students brainstorm their own distillation methods.

After introducing these new aspects of purification, revisit one of the key questions from the first session: How do we know water is clean? We know that distilled water is salt-free in large part because something similar to distillation happens in nature (and we tested it using the salt tester). So perhaps there are similarities between things students have done in this lesson series and water purification in nature! A key discussion question is, Where might nature filter water, and what does that tell us about clean water sources? (Wetlands are a good example; read more in this lesson's "For You to Know" section.)

To contextualize everything and lead out, ask students how what they've learned during this lesson series might help them survive in the wild (or a rural area) or after a disaster. Acknowledge what they've learned, and encourage them to keep investigating! It is, after all, through continued STEM exploration that we're able to find better outcomes for big, global challenges.

MORE WRITING AND STEM OPTIONS If you have time, you can do a lot more with both the writing and the hands-on STEM activities.

For the writing, you can have students practice their informative writing skills by asking them to create public service announcement (PSA) posters that warn people about the consequences of drinking bad water. There are also more potential PSA topics—where to find clean water; why water might become unsafe after a disaster (water infrastructure can be compromised, resulting in many places where contamination may occur); and so on. For more inspiration, you can look up clean water resources online. Pick some that are interesting to you, and task your students with creating similar ones! (You don't have to show them the original resources as models.)

For the STEM part, you can have students come up with a complete water purification system. Filtration will be a centerpiece, of course. Students can experiment with alum to find the optimal amount for flocculation, too. And, for a really intense engineering task, have your students build a desalination system (desalination is the process of removing salts from water—rendering seawater drinkable). (For even more of a challenge here, don't show your students any solar still or steam distillation demos or videos.) Note that students could also explore desalination with the STEM@Home sheet "Be Still My Dirty Water."

There are more purification steps that your students can explore. One of the most accessible is aeration, which helps remove gas (carbon dioxide, for instance, and more harmful ones like ammonia) from water. By enabling a chemical process called precipitation, it also makes some dangerous substances (like heavy metals) easier to filter out.

To demonstrate aeration, it'll help if you've done the exhaling into water demonstration in the "Acid, Gas, and Water" activity. If not, you can do it now. Once that's taken care of, ask students what experiences they've had with carbonated liquids. Shaking a soda bottle will almost certainly come up. Carbon dioxide leaves water (more quickly) when agitated. You can demonstrate this particular aspect of aeration by testing the pH of carbonated water, shaking up a small amount in a plastic bottle, and testing the pH again after the gas fizzes out. Students can experiment with aeration using used plastic soda bottles or food storage containers with tight seals.

FOR YOU TO KNOW (AND YOUR STUDENTS TO DISCOVER)[3]

Water covers about 70 percent of Earth's surface. Water is the only naturally occurring substance on Earth that exists as a solid, a liquid, and a gas. Even though a water molecule has only three atoms, they are put together in a way that results in some really interesting chemical properties. For instance, water can absorb a lot of heat without changing temperature, which helps keep our planet pleasant for humans (not to mention every other form of life we know about). Water is also one of relatively few substances that is less dense as a solid than it is as a liquid (which has lots of benefits for us and other living things—including the fact that it prevents our streams, lakes, and even oceans from freezing solid and killing all creatures unfortunate enough to be in the ice).

Water isn't only helpful: as far as we know, it's essential. It makes up 50 to 70 percent of a human's body weight. Without it, the chemical reactions that drive life could not occur. One way it helps such reactions along is by being a solvent—a substance that can dissolve other substances (solutes). Water can dissolve more substances than any other chemical, which is why it's called the universal solvent.

On the one hand, it's really helpful that a lot of stuff dissolves in water, because vital chemical reactions in the human body, and in all cells, take place between molecules that are dissolved in water. On the other hand, water's ability to dissolve many substances has a downside—water can contain substances harmful to people and can help those foreign substances enter the human body.

Water can also dissolve substances that, once in solution, turn that solution acidic. Despite the popular perception, very few acids will burn through metal, or scar the faces and psyches of supervillains-to-be. Though most people don't think of them as such, acids are necessary to life. (DNA is, after all, an acid. Other acids form essential parts of cells, like membranes. And acids have important macrobiological functions as well; some living things produce acid as a defense mechanism, and many animals use acid to aid in digestion.) Some organisms, humans included, have mechanisms to control acidity levels, but these have their limits. As with salt, ingesting too much acid via water can be harmful. (The chemical opposite of an acid is a base, and bases have their functions as well. One of them is regulating acidity levels in organisms. As with acids, ingesting too much of a basic substance can be harmful.)

Of course, there are other things besides salt, acids, and bases that can make water harmful to humans—heavy metals, household and industrial chemicals, bacteria and viruses . . .

---

3. Information is derived from the following sources: "Functions and Values of Wetlands," *http://water.epa.gov/ type/wetlands/outreach/upload/fun_val_pr.pdf*; "Functions and Values of Wetlands," from *http://www.ecy.wa.gov/ programs/sea/wetlands/functions.html*.

(continued)

In industrialized countries, we take it for granted that the water that comes out of our taps is safe. Those of us who receive water from a municipal water source probably don't think about water safety at all when we are home, as there are strict standards for what amounts of various chemical contaminants are allowed in this water. Many municipal supplies in the United States are treated with a chlorine-containing compound to kill most microorganisms in the water. Many homes, however, particularly in more rural areas, use a well as their water source. The CDC recommends that people on well water test their well at least annually for both disease-causing microorganisms and chemical contaminants.[4] Underground water supplies, called aquifers, can be contaminated by aboveground activities (such as routine farming practices or industrial accidents), or by things that happen underground (for example, leaking underground storage tanks [for gasoline, oil, or any other chemical] or septic tanks, or mining activities, among many other possibilities).

Water safety in the United States can become a big issue after a natural disaster, such as a major earthquake or hurricane (think Katrina or Sandy), when supplies are disrupted due to lack of power (preventing water treatment) or because of a broken water main. It is also an issue for hikers on backpacking trips in the wilderness. And, of course, it is a daily concern for the more than one billion people living around the world without access to improved water supplies.

It turns out Earth has invented a pretty good natural water filtration system in wetlands. Wetlands collect water runoff from the land's surface that occurs during rain and storms. Storm runoff moves slowly through wetlands, which provides time for the sediments present in the runoff (loose soil, dirt, and rocks) to settle in the ground before the water reaches streams and rivers. In addition, the roots of plants in the wetlands absorb nutrients and chemical contaminants present in storm runoff. This process can greatly reduce the toxicity of water flowing into rivers and streams. Finally, the soil in wetlands can absorb other contaminants, again removing them from the water that eventually flows into rivers and oceans.

It took humans a long time to learn the value of wetlands—many were paved over or filled in and built over as we developed cities and towns. Now that we understand their importance, many wetlands are being restored, and in some areas we are building synthetic wetlands to help improve water quality.

---

4. "Well Testing," *http://www.cdc.gov/healthywater/drinking/private/wells/testing.html*.

CABBAGE RAINBOW PHUN

Combine ingredients to make as many different colored solutions as you can. Record your findings here.

Solution 1

What's in the solution?

What color is it?

Now combine 1 tablespoon of the solution and 1 teaspoon cabbage juice indicator. What color is the new solution?

Solution 2

What's in the solution?

What color is it?

Now combine 1 tablespoon of the solution and 1 teaspoon cabbage juice indicator. What color is the new solution?

Solution 3

What's in the solution?

What color is it?

Now combine 1 tablespoon of the solution and 1 teaspoon cabbage juice indicator. What color is the new solution?

Solution 4

What's in the solution?

What color is it?

Now combine 1 tablespoon of the solution and 1 teaspoon cabbage juice indicator. What color is the new solution?

PURIFICATION CHALLENGE

What are you trying to purify? _____

What color is it? Describe, or, if you have colored pencils, use them to indicate the color of the solution here.

Before Purification   After Purification

What color do you get when testing with cabbage juice indicator?

Does the salt tester detect anything? Circle one.   Yes   No   Yes   No

How turbid is the solution?   1 2 3 4 5   1 2 3 4 5

Any general observations?

What evidence do you have for change in the water?

Is your purified water safer to drink? How do you know?

Any general observations?

What evidence do you have for change in the water?

Is your purified water safer to drink? How do you know?

STEM@HOME: PHABULOUS KITCHEN SCIENCE

pH plays an important role in the kitchen. Bakers and chefs make regular use of acids and bases—and without this kitchen chemistry, the foods we love would be very different.

Thinking back to the experiments in class, what "chemicals" did you experiment with in the workshop that are also commonly used in kitchens? Baking soda (whose chemical name is sodium bicarbonate) is a very common ingredient in baked goods. It is a base. What happens when you mix baking soda with an acid (such as vinegar or lemon juice)?

A Tale of Two Recipes

By following two almost (but not quite) identical pancake recipes, you can explore the role of acid-base reactions in cooking.

Recipe 1	Recipe 2
¼ cup milk	¼ cup milk
½ teaspoon vinegar or lemon juice	½ teaspoon vinegar or lemon juice
¼ cup flour	¼ cup flour
½ teaspoon baking soda	1 tablespoon vegetable oil for cooking (optional)
1 tablespoon vegetable oil for cooking (optional)	
Mix together the milk and vinegar. In a separate bowl, stir together the flour and the baking soda until well mixed. Add the liquid ingredients to the dry ingredients and stir until just combined.	Mix together the milk and vinegar. Add the liquid ingredients to the flour and stir until just combined.

With a parent's permission and supervision, set a frying pan on the stove over medium-high heat. If you're not using a nonstick pan, add a tablespoon of oil to the frying pan.

On the left-hand side of the pan, add approximately ¼ cup of **recipe 1** to the pan. Then add about ¼ cup (be sure to use a different cup measure so you don't contaminate the formula!) of **recipe 2** to the right-hand side of the pan.

Flip the pancakes when they begin to bubble, about 2 to 3 minutes. Cook through, then turn off the stove and remove the pan from the heat, keeping track of which pancake was made with recipe 1 and which was made with recipe 2.

(continued)

STEM@HOME: PHABULOUS KITCHEN SCIENCE (continued)

What did you notice? What ingredient is missing from recipe 2? What is the difference between the pancakes made from the two recipes?

Why do you think this difference occurred? (*Hint:* What happened when you mixed baking soda and vinegar together in the workshop?)

What's Going On?

When you mix together an acid and a base, a chemical reaction occurs. Lots of recipes for baked goods take advantage of this. In particular, recipes that include baking soda (or baking powder) as an ingredient also include an acid. Sometimes this acid is obvious—such as the vinegar or lemon juice in the pancake recipes you tried. Sometimes it is less obvious—like buttermilk.

When the liquid and dry ingredients are mixed together, this brings the acid and base into contact with one another, and the reaction begins. Bubbles start to form. If you cut into the pancakes you made, can you see bubbles "trapped" in the cooked pancake of recipe 1? There will probably be some bubbles in the pancake from recipe 2—the result of air that was introduced into the mixed ingredients when you stirred them together—but fewer.

Interested in Exploring More?

What recipes can you find that take advantage of this reaction between baking soda and acid? What do you think would happen if you added more baking soda? More acid? More of both??? Make a prediction, be systematic, and ask your parents for permission to try it.

Pro tip: Clean up after yourself, or you may not be allowed to experiment in the kitchen for a while.

pHun pH pHacts

▸ There is a category of acids called superacids, which are so strong that they can't be measured by the pH scale. The strongest superacid is fluoroantimonic acid, which is more than a million times stronger than pure sulfuric acid.

▸ There are also superbases. These are named not because they are superstrong, but because they are made from two or more bases and have properties different from those of other known bases.

▸ pH is a logarithmic scale. This means that a solution with a pH of 4 is ten times more acidic than a solution with a pH of 5.

STEM@HOME: BE STILL MY DIRTY WATER

As the world's population continues to grow—and its climate continues to change—there is significant concern about there being enough freshwater to meet the needs of people and agriculture. One strategy that is often talked about is to purify seawater, essentially turning it into freshwater by removing the salt. This is called desalination. Desalination takes advantage of the fact that when water evaporates, it leaves behind the solutes that had dissolved in the water (such as salt). You can build a home desalination plant to test this.

MATERIALS

▸ A solution of salt water (Seawater contains 35 grams of salt per liter of water. To make your own seawater, measure 2 tablespoons of salt into 4 cups of water. A cup is approximately ¼ liter.)

▸ A safe way to heat your salt water (for example, in the microwave in a microwave-safe bowl, or on the stovetop)

▸ Your engineeringuity* (to figure out a way to collect the evaporating water's vapor)

Note: Although you will probably need to heat your salt water on the stove to the boiling point, your engineering should happen off of the stove. And **beware, the solution will be HOT.** Don't do this experiment without a grown-up.

Your challenge is to come up with a way to separate the salt from the water you dissolved it in—to desalinate the water, using a still (see sidebar). (*Hint:* What have you noticed when you have cooked before? Have you noticed what happens to the inside of the lid of a pan when it is over a pot of boiling water? Can this knowledge help you engineer a solution?)

How can you tell if your still is successful? Can you come up with some tests? (*Another hint:* What did your salt water taste like? What does the water you collected in your still taste like?)

(*continued*)

> **WHAT'S A STILL?** A **still** is a device or apparatus that is used to separate the solutes (things dissolved in a liquid) in a solution from the solvent (the liquid that is doing the dissolving). Stills typically involve heat (and changes of state from liquid to gas to . . .). You may have seen the word root "still" in the words "distillation" (the act of purifying a liquid in a still) and "distilled water" (water that has been purified in a still, through the process of distillation).

---

*Engineeringuity (ĕn´jə-nîr´ĭng-oo´ĭ-tē) *n.* A clever or inventive approach to engineering.

STEM@HOME: BE STILL MY DIRTY WATER (continued)

Fun Water Facts

▸ Bottled water companies add salts back to water after purifying it for two reasons. First, pure water actually doesn't taste good to us because we are used to water with low levels of salts dissolved in them. Second, just as it isn't healthy for us to drink seawater, it is also not healthy for us to drink pure water—for the opposite reason. If we drink pure water, we flush important salts (called electrolytes) from our body. We need electrolytes to keep our muscles (including our heart) working properly.

▸ Large-scale desalination plants require a lot of energy (to heat the water). That makes the water they generate very expensive, limiting the number of these plants in use.

▸ Water is heavy and expensive to transport, particularly to space. On the International Space Station there is a water recovery system that uses a process like desalination (with a twist to deal with zero gravity) to purify 93 percent of the water on the space station—this includes astronaut urine and sweat.

It's no secret that superheroes' superpowers are all about the science.

Superman can fly because of the greater gravitational pull of his home planet of Krypton and his ability to absorb and metabolize our sun's energy. Peter Parker spider-swings and spidey-tingles because he was bitten by a radioactive spider. Green Lantern can beam his green light and do stuff because . . . I'm not really sure. I never liked him, and never read his comics.

But you get the idea.

If you are going to be a superhero, you better know your science. I can't tell you exactly what supersecrets are revealed in this top secret "Science of Superpowers" document, because then it wouldn't be top secret, would it? But trust me. Get busy with the strawberries, cotton swabs, paper airplanes, and eggs, and you will become a science superhero.

Oh, and while you are superhero-ing—don't forget to write a poem or story or comic about your heroic self. People are going to want to know about just exactly how super you are.

Jon Scieszka

Jon Scieszka is the author of *The True Story of the 3 Little Pigs!*; *The Stinky Cheese Man and Other Fairly Stupid Tales*; *Knucklehead*; and a bunch of other books, most recently the kid science genius Frank Einstein series.

THE SCIENCE OF SUPERPOWERS

BASED ON THE ORIGINAL WORKSHOP BY
MARIAMA J. LOCKINGTON
AND PETER CALHOUN HALL

4 SESSIONS, 2 HOURS EACH
STEM DISCIPLINES: *Physical sciences, life sciences, engineering*
WRITING ACTIVITIES: *Technical writing, narrative writing, poetry*

LONGER THAN A LONG WEEKEND, MORE thorough than a thoroughbred, and more fun than a funhouse, it's . . . "The Science of Superpowers"! True to its subject, this is a superlesson, covering a whole lot of stuff in its four action-packed sessions. But don't feel like you need to be a hero—do as many or as few as you like.

We all know some heroes have special powers. But how, exactly, do their powers work? What lets Iron Man fly? How did the Black Widow get her superhuman strength? In this workshop, students explore the science and engineering behind superpowers and heroic adventures using DNA extraction, paper airplane construction, cotton swab tower building, and egg drop design. In addition to lab note-taking, each activity is paired with a different genre of poetry inspired by the session's theme and hands-on activity.

This is a very flexible lesson. Of course, it was designed to be taught as a series, and although the science content is different in each session, there is a flow to the overarching themes. That said, it also works well as an abbreviated series—doing only sessions 1 and 2, or teaching only sessions 3 and 4.

MATERIALS

SESSION 1

☐ Water

☐ Dawn dish soap

☐ Salt

☐ Capped tubes (2 per student, holding at least 12 milliliters)

☐ Isopropyl (rubbing) alcohol

☐ Rubber bands (2 per student)

☐ Hero costume (completely optional, but cool)

☐ Computer with Internet access, to show video (optional)

☐ Digital projector, to show video (optional)

(continued)

- ☐ Items that may or may not have DNA, like tortilla chips, a kiwi, and a flower

- ☐ Lab coats (completely optional, but cool)

- ☐ Safety goggles

- ☐ Copies of the "Secrets of Strawberries" handout (included with other handouts at the end of this lesson)

- ☐ Coffee filters (1 per student)

- ☐ Clear plastic cups (1 per student)

- ☐ Strawberries (1 per student, plus a few extras in case of strawberry catastrophes)

- ☐ Ziplock bags (1 per student)

- ☐ Plastic coffee stirrers (1 per student)

- ☐ Small (1.5 milliliter) Eppendorff microcentrifuge tubes (1 per student)

- ☐ Copies of the "Supercookbook" handout

- ☐ An example of a "Where I'm From" poem (See "Handy Lesson Links" in the appendix.)

SESSION 2

- ☐ Images of various flying things (such as planes, birds, gliders, and fictional flight devices)

- ☐ Science journals (optional)

- ☐ A ball

(continued)

Session 1: I Am From . . . (Origin Poems and DNA)[1]

All heroes have an origin story. Where did she come from? How did he get his superpower? Like Superman, does she have a secret weakness? The ultimate origin story for every living thing is written in its genetic code, or DNA.

But DNA isn't the end of the story. How living things develop depends not only on their genetic code but also on their environment. In the same way, heroes are defined as much by their choices as their innate powers—Spider-Man had to *choose* to shoulder great responsibility; he didn't have to be a hero just because he had great power.

In this session, students explore the **heritable** qualities (meaning characteristics that can be passed on from parents to offspring) of living things. Students look at the interplay between that inheritance and who a person becomes, sometimes discussed as nature versus nurture.

Preparation

Before the first session, you'll need to prepare the chemicals the class will use to isolate strawberry DNA. Each student will need his or her own tube of Lysis buffer, which is easy to make. This formula makes enough for thirty students. Combine the following:

- ◇ 360 milliliters (1½ cups) water

- ◇ 40 milliliters (2 tablespoons plus 2 teaspoons) Dawn dish soap

- ◇ 8 grams (1¼ teaspoons) table salt

Transfer twelve milliliters of mixture to each tube and secure it with a cap. (*Measurement tip:* twelve milliliters is about 2.5 teaspoons.)

You'll also need to prepare a ten-milliliter tube of isopropyl (rubbing) alcohol for each student. Wrap these tubes with a rubber band to identify them (rubber band, rubbing alcohol—easy to remember!). If you'll be doing the experiment on a hot day, you'll probably have better results if you can keep the alcohol tubes cool until you need them.

---

1. This session is adapted from "Strawberry DNA Extraction," *http://seplessons.org/node/217.*

Introduction (10 minutes)

Begin class with an official welcome to the science of superpowers. Brief the students on your mission: You will create and explore together. You will extract real DNA, learn some physics, and engineer solutions to superchallenges. In the process, you will envision heroic adventures for your hero and use poetry to communicate the science of superpowers.

If you are awesome, you will give this welcome wearing a hero costume yourself.

The first session focuses on origins and what makes us (and heroes) who we are. Your students will reflect on and explore the dimensions of their identity, from the parts they control to the parts they don't. Ask the class:

◇ What are some of the traits or characteristics of a hero?

◇ Can you think of examples of traits that a hero is born with?

◇ What about characteristics that are shaped by a hero's environment—where she lives, what he learns from his parents, some sort of conflict or dilemma she experiences?

Make a T-chart on chart paper or the board documenting students' ideas of hero traits, noting which are heritable and which are environmental.

The distinction between the two types of traits parallels the nature versus nurture debate that is prevalent in biology and in particular in the study of animal, including human, behavior. Some heroes are shaped by their environment, others by their genetics (or a change to those genetics), and still others by a tool or agent that conveys power (such as Green Lantern's ring). Ask students for some examples of heroes and their traits, both inborn and environmental. Following is a sample list in case the discussion gets off to a slow start, though students will probably know more:

◇ Spider-Man undergoes a genetic change when bitten by a spider (but is also shaped by his uncle's values: "With great power there must also come great responsibility").

☐ Prefolded paper airplane

☐ Paper airplane templates (See "Handy Lesson Links" in the appendix.)

☐ Paper of varying weights and types for making airplanes

☐ Tape measures

☐ Rulers for plane design stations

☐ Copies of the "Paper Airplane Tech Specs" handout

☐ Stopwatches (or smartphones or other devices with stopwatch functionality)

☐ Masking tape

SESSION 3

☐ 8.5-by-11-inch paper to fold, accordion-style, into drying racks (2 to 3 per student)

☐ Cotton swabs (40 to 60 per student plus extra for demonstration, possibly including some extra-long swabs for variety)

☐ Clear rubber cement (at least 1 bottle for every 2 students)

☐ Newspapers, scissors, and tape (optional)

☐ Sample haikus

(continued)

- Copies of the "How to Be a Superengineer!!!!" handout

- Copies of the "Secret Lair Blueprint" handout

SESSION 4

- A balcony, window, or ladder (10 feet tall or more) that the egg vehicles can safely be dropped out or off of

- Waterproof tarp, tablecloth, or large garbage bags to cover the floor area where drop testing will occur

- Masking tape

- Copies of the "Saving the Egg" handout

- Assorted packing materials (cardboard boxes, cups, disposable takeout containers, Styrofoam, Bubble Wrap, newspaper, balloons, air-filled packaging, shredded paper, toilet paper or paper towel tubes, and so on)

- Eggs (1 per student)

◇ X-Men are born mutants.

◇ The Hulk experiences a change to his genetic makeup caused by exposure to radiation (and exacerbated by anger control issues). Is this a heritable change or an environmental change?

◇ Superman's powers derive from his origin on another planet and the differences in physiology (how the body works) due to differences in gravity between Krypton and Earth. It is likely that his powers are heritable, as his cousin, Supergirl, has similar abilities. That said, Superman's, or Clark Kent's, adoptive parents had a strong value system they shared with their son.

What About You? (10 minutes)

Authors create a backstory to explain the history of a character before the story begins. A hero's backstory—often called an origin story—explains how and why the hero came into being, the origin of her superpowers, what experiences and influences shaped him into who he is in the comic series, and so on. Essentially the hero's backstory explains the role of nature and nurture in making her who she is.

Unsurprisingly, as most heroes are people, these stories mirror our own. This session helps students investigate their own backstory. Ask them, "What makes you who you are?"

It's fine if there are lots of different interpretations of the question. Record student responses on the board, and start moving the discussion toward genetics. What makes you you, a cat a cat, and Spider-Man Spider-Man? (You'll return to the nurture bit eventually.) Write their responses on the board.

When students introduce more complex ideas, encourage them not to just state a label (for example, "It's because of genes"), instead asking them to explain, in their own words, their understanding of what that label means to ensure that everyone has the same understanding of the word or concept.

What Is DNA? Discussion and Activity (10 minutes)

At this point, explicitly ask students if they have ever heard of DNA. We like to introduce the concept with a music video from They Might Be Giants.[2] Next, show students a variety of objects, and ask them if DNA can be found in them: a kiwi, tortilla chips,[3] and a flower (these can be substituted out for anything else you might have on hand).

---

2. The video can be found at *http://www.youtube.com/watch?v=ZK6YP1Smbxk&list=PL44C7ADBD6A22FF0B&index=1.*

3. Even some top graduate students in biology have gotten tripped up by the question, Is there DNA in your food?

GENETICS Although this topic of genetics is covered in much more detail in this session's "For You to Know" section, there are a few key ideas that may come up in this discussion:

- Offspring (babies) are similar to their parents. Humans give birth to humans, elephants to elephants, and mice to mice. The same idea holds true with plants, bacteria, and so on.

- The instructions to make a creature are encoded in a chemical compound called **d**eoxyribo**n**ucleic **a**cid (DNA). DNA is chemically the same in all organisms—thus either with your naked eye or with a microscope, DNA from a strawberry looks the same as DNA from a human.

- DNA in a cell makes up a structure called a **chromosome.** Different organisms have different numbers of chromosomes.

- An offspring receives one set of chromosomes from its (biological) mother and another set from its (biological) father.[4]

- The complete set of genetic information inherited from your parents is called your **genome.**

- One analogy to explain how DNA works is to think of the whole genome as a cookbook and the DNA as the language (or code) that the cookbook is written in. Most cookbooks have similar recipes (for example, breakfast recipes, cookie recipes, and vegetable recipes), but the actual recipes in the cookbook are different because they use different amounts of the same ingredient or different ingredients entirely. The variations in genetic cookbooks are what make different organisms who or what they are. The cookbook for monkeys and the cookbook for humans are fairly similar, but there are a lot of differences between the cookbooks for humans and plants.

- Much like a cookbook, the genome is broken into smaller units of information— the recipes (or **genes**). Some recipes provide the instructions for a complete dish (a **trait**)—for example, to make pancakes you only need one recipe. For other dishes (that is, human characteristics) you may need two recipes (spaghetti with tomato sauce requires a recipe for spaghetti and a recipe for tomato sauce), and a cake may require many recipes (one recipe for the batter, one for the filling, and one for the frosting).

- With the exception of mature red blood cells—which don't play a role in the activity today—every cell in your body has the complete set of instructions (cookbook)—though each cell may only use a subset of the instructions (recipes) to help it specialize. (In other words, eye cells are not using the same recipes as skin cells.)

---

4. Because it is biology, there are always exceptions. Most notably, some creatures reproduce asexually, so there is only one parent. In this case, the parent passes on its complete set of chromosomes (rather than just one set) to its offspring.

Reinforce the idea to students that some traits are inherited (for example, eye color), some relate to learned behaviors (for example, being polite), and others are a combination of what is often called nature (inherited) and nurture (learned or in some way supported by your environment)—like height, which is dependent on both the height of your parents and your access to nutrition.

DNA Extraction Experiment (35 minutes)

Tell the students it's time to put on their lab coats and see actual DNA. If you don't have lab coats, don't worry. All the materials used in this session are common household materials.[5] Nothing here is inherently dangerous. Real science requires real protocols, however, so you'll want to remind your students of the following:

◇ Strawberry juice will stain—so don't wipe fingers on your clothes, and try to avoid splashing, spilling, engaging in flying strawberry battles, and so on.

◇ Don't eat or drink anything while doing the strawberry experiment. This will prevent you from mistakenly drinking the Lysis buffer, or some other mishap. This is also a very critical laboratory safety practice to get used to.

◇ Wear safety goggles. Even though everything being used in this experiment can be found in either your kitchen or your medicine cabinet, getting into the habit of wearing eye protection is good science.

◇ Wash your hands thoroughly when finished—another good laboratory practice.

Break students into groups of two or three (although ideally, even in these small groups, each student will extract DNA from his or her own strawberry). Distribute the supplies: copies of the "Secrets of Strawberries" handout, coffee filters, clear plastic cups, rubber bands, strawberries, ziplock bags, test tubes of Lysis buffer and isopropyl alcohol, stirrers, and Eppendorff tubes.

If adult helpers are available, have each helper oversee a few groups as they work through the extraction (step-by-step instructions are on the "Secrets of Strawberries" handout). If helpers are not available, go over the instructions with the class as a whole group before handing out materials. Then set them loose to conduct the procedure as described on the handout, circulating to help as necessary.

Note that students will be able to see a *mass* of DNA (and it looks like a big clump of snot), not individual strands. They will *not* be able to see the double helix shape. (Scientists cannot see the double helix either, even using a microscope. With a very special and powerful type of electron microscope that magnifies more than twenty thousand times, scientists can see a single strand of DNA, but they still cannot see the helix shape. That takes an indirect visualization technique called X-ray diffraction.)

Origin Stories (20 minutes)

Gather students back together. Explain to students that DNA is the ultimate origin story, because the DNA code in every organism on Earth tells a complete history of the organism. When isolated and decoded, the DNA can reveal who the organism's parents are and who it is related to, both its recent ancestors and those from the very distant past. Understanding the DNA story has helped us

---

5. If lab coats aren't available and your students want to wear *some* kind of uniform, invite them to make hero capes out of towels or jackets tied around their shoulders. Scientists are heroes, too!

to figure out how life evolved on our planet, to better understand where diseases originate, and to develop new treatments that save lives.

Now you want to shift to creating *new* heroes that will encounter a series of adventures and scenarios. Let students know that you want to understand how their new hero became super—the hero's origin story, which students will write in poetry form.

Because DNA is a cookbook for an organism, students will use the "Supercookbook" handout to develop their hero. An important part of this work is thinking about the powers the hero will have. Where did these powers come from? How does she use them? How does his environment shape how he uses his powers? Does he have a moral code for how the powers are used? Where did this code come from? What types of pressures influence the hero, for good or bad?

Brainstorm Breakout (10 minutes)

Have students use the "Supercookbook" handout to begin developing a description of their hero.

Personifying Your Hero (15 minutes)

Once students have filled out the "Supercookbook" handout, it's time to use their powers for poetry.

After making some time for questions and sharing, task students with writing a "Where I'm From" poem in the voice of their hero that explains who the hero is, as well as the origin of his or her powers and abilities. In doing so, they're writing a **persona poem,** or a poem that is written from the perspective of another character—in other words, you step into the shoes of someone who is not you!

Read an example of a "Where I'm From" superpower poem with the group. George Ella Lyon's poem "Where I'm From" is a fantastic introduction to the form (see "Handy Lesson Links" in the appendix). We highly encourage instructors, when introducing a superpower spin on this type of poem, to share one they have written. Creating your own hero will be helpful throughout the workshop.

OWL GIRL Here's a "Where I'm From" poem that one of our students wrote:

I am from a family of owls.
They adopted me.
I now fly around on my owl wings
With my side cat, Snice.
By day I sleep in a comfy mountain,
But by night I climb into
My tree house and zip-line
To my secret headquarters.
I fight against Lo and JB,
Who try to hypnotize their fans.
I dart through the sky eating marshmallows
That shoot out of my hands.
I also love to bake.

—*Athena Murray, age eleven, New York*

Have students find a quiet space to write their own "Where I'm From" poem in response to the following prompt:

> Imagine that your hero has to leave his or her home, and venture out into the world to fight evil. How will your hero explain to strangers where he or she is from? What powers will your hero carry with him or her? What was the role of genetics in shaping your hero? What about his or her environment? How did your hero get those powers? Was there some event that led him or her to develop the powers? Be sure to use some of the traits outlined on the "Super-cookbook" handout to tell your hero's story.

"Where I'm From" poems are often open ended and quite personal, even in comic book persona form. In poet George Ella Lyon's original "Where I'm From," which inspired the form, lines like "I am from Artemus and Billie's Branch, / fried corn and strong coffee" evoke strong images of southern heritage and rough mornings, but they don't often suggest future directions. We recommend challenging your students with an additional twist. Have them think back to the concepts of nature and nurture, and consider how these relate to personal choice. Students should think about possible choices for their hero, and how these might be informed by any moral responsibilities that come with the hero's powers. Toward the end of their poem, students can envision their hero's future actions as they move from "I am from" to "I am going."

THE SUPERPOWER OF IMAGERY Poets—and writers in general—can create powerful mental pictures in their readers' minds by using imagery. One of the most basic and most effective ways to do this is by using the five senses: touch, taste, sight, smell, and sound. How does a hero experience these things? Brainstorm a few lines beginning with "I feel," "I taste," "I see," "I smell," and "I hear."

Wrap-Up (10 minutes)

As students finish writing their poems, ask them to help clean up the materials left over from the DNA extraction activity. Note that the capped tubes can be saved and reused. (If you plan to repeat this workshop in the near future, simply refill the tubes with the Lysis buffer and rubbing alcohol, and you're ready to go!)

Once cleanup is completed, gather students together and build excitement for the next session by summarizing this session and foreshadowing the next. Now that they are beginning to understand how humans and heroes develop their traits, they'll begin to go a little deeper—or should we say higher? In the next session, students will continue their study of heroes by exploring why—and especially *how*—they fly. Many heroes use flight to help them protect a city, rescue an innocent civilian, or battle a supervillain. How do they do it? Are they able to fly naturally (without assistance), or do they get help from an engineered system (a plane or rocket suit)? What are the structures in these devices that help them fly, and what can we learn about flight by studying these structures?

FOR YOU TO KNOW (AND YOUR STUDENTS TO DISCOVER)

Locked away in every cell of every living thing is a molecule with the tongue twister of a name, deoxyribonucleic acid (DNA). DNA is the ultimate origin story—written in a secret code. For within the code of DNA are not only the instructions to build a living thing (whether a bacterium, plant, dog, human, or something else), but also a genetic history of the organism—whom the individual is related to, who the species' closest relatives and ancestors are, and how the species has changed and evolved. DNA is a remarkable molecule.

A Spiral Staircase

The DNA of all organisms is made of the same chemical stuff. It is impossible to tell the difference between the DNA of a strawberry, an elephant, or a human by just looking at it (either magnified or unmagnified). Because all DNA is made from the same ingredients, it all looks the same.

At the molecular level, the structure of DNA is like a spiral staircase—it is a twisting ladder that is made of a sugar phosphate backbone (the railings) as well as nitrogen-containing "bases" (the stairs). But this structure is so small that it is impossible to see using a microscope. To discover the structure of DNA, scientists used a technique called X-ray diffraction. This technique provides information about the positions of atoms in a molecule. Figuring out the structure of DNA was one of the great aha moments in modern science. Particularly exciting was the fact that identifying the structure led immediately to hypotheses about how some very important cellular processes might work—and to experiments that could test these ideas. This information led to a biological revolution through which researchers have unlocked many secrets of cells, helping us to better understand and treat diseases, among many other benefits.

Recipes for Life

As discussed in the lesson, a helpful analogy for explaining DNA is to think of DNA as a cookbook. All organisms have their own unique cookbook—and that book is full of recipes (genes) to make the complete organism. There are, of course, similarities between cookbooks. The human cookbook and the monkey cookbook are fairly similar (both need recipes for eyes, hearts, intestines, and so on), whereas there are huge differences between the human and plant cookbooks. This is of course an imperfect analogy because the genes in DNA encode the *building blocks* of parts, not entire parts. It takes many recipes (genes) to make an eye.

(continued)

Another important idea to understand is that every cell of a human being contains the complete cookbook for making a human. Said differently, a skin cell does not only have the recipes (genes) for making skin. It also contains all the information to make eyes, kidneys, blood, and so on, but it's only making use of the skin cell information (just like you might only look at the spaghetti recipe when cooking dinner, even though it's contained within the larger collection of recipes inside the cookbook). Specialized cell types only use the DNA instructions they need (if you want to make a cake, you don't also use the spaghetti recipe in your cookbook) at any given time.

Why Can I Extract DNA with Dish Soap, Salt, and Rubbing Alcohol?

It's pretty cool and unbelievable at the same time that simple household ingredients can enable you to hold DNA in your hand.

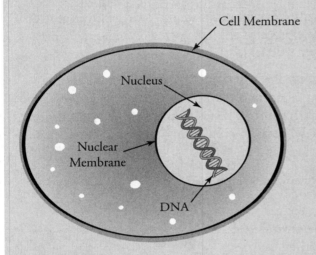

The ingredients used to extract the DNA take advantage of some simple biological chemistry. DNA is found in the cells of living things (and in multicellular organisms, the DNA is kept in a special compartment within the cell called the nucleus). Cells and the nuclei are each surrounded by membranes made of fats. Detergents (like those in dish soap) break up fats (this is why they are helpful for cleaning greasy pans). Scientists take advantage of this. When they add soap to a mixture containing cells, it breaks down the cell and nuclear membranes, releasing the DNA into the solution. The detergent and salt also help separate other cellular components (proteins from the DNA), but just adding detergent and salt would not be enough for you to see the DNA. To do this, we add rubbing alcohol (isopropanol). This takes advantage of another cool bit of chemistry: different materials can be dissolved in different liquids. Both DNA and salt, for instance, can be dissolved in water. However, DNA is insoluble (cannot be dissolved) in rubbing alcohol. So . . . if you add alcohol to a solution with DNA, the DNA becomes insoluble and precipitates (comes out of the solution). You see the DNA precipitate as a cloudy (snotty-looking) mass in your tube.

Session 2: Up, Up, and Away! (Secret Power Poems and Flight)[6]

Humans have been fascinated by flight and have longed to fly for hundreds of years, with recorded attempts at human flight appearing as early as the ninth century. No surprise, then, that we love to give our heroes the power of flight. In this session students will explore flight and engineer a flying vehicle for their hero. During all of this, students will grapple with the idea of structure-function

6. This session is adapted from "Take Off with Paper Airplanes," *http://www.teachengineering.org/view_lesson .php?url=collection/cub_/lessons/cub_airplanes/cub_airplanes_lesson06.xml.*

relationships and the important roles they play in both natural and engineered systems. Along the way, students will continue their hero's narrative in verse, writing about the way their hero anticipates and overcomes obstacles—just as engineers make their job easier by looking ahead and preparing for expected challenges.

Preparation

Before class, set up two or three airplane testing stations. At each station place a tape line on the floor (this is the start [or launch] line). Ideally, there will be a clear path leading from the launch strip so there are no obstructions that might get in the way of a test flight. Each station should also have a tape measure for students to measure the flight distance, and a stopwatch to measure flight length. You many need to set up stations in the hallway, if the classroom isn't conducive.

Introduction (15 minutes)

Display some images of flying things (natural and engineered, real and fantastic). You could include birds; butterflies or other flying insects; planes; gliders; Icarus; Da Vinci flying machines; heroes who fly on their own; and the devices that support the flight of others (rocket suits, helicopters, or planes, for example).

Prompt the students to think about what helps each of these items (animals, heroes, or vehicles) fly. If your students are using science journals, they can take notes of their ideas there.

After a few minutes, ask students to think specifically about the shapes of the items. How does the shape help an item fly? Does it have any other qualities—size, weight—that also help it fly?

At this point, it's useful to define what a **structure** is—for example, bridges and houses are structures. And each serves a **function**—bridges help you cross over something (a highway, a river, a canyon), and houses provide shelter. Structures can also be components of an item: doors are a structure on a house, and their function is as an entry way and exit from the building; and the head of a nail functions as a surface for a hammer to connect with (to either push in or pull out the nail). What about in natural systems, such as a human? Ask students to name some structures on a human, and to describe their function (you could record responses in a T-chart). Structures could include legs (for mobility), thumbs (for grasping), eyes (for seeing), teeth (for chewing), and many, many others.

Today's function: flight! The ability to get off the ground has been pursued by heroes and humans since ancient times. Most of the time, they have failed. Icarus flew too close to the sun and came crashing down. The eleventh-century British monk Eilmer didn't do any better when he fashioned wings for his arms and feet and jumped off a tower. And in Judy Blume's *Tales of a Fourth Grade Nothing*, when Fudge tries to fly off the monkey bars, he ends up with two fewer teeth.

But some heroes overcome gravity and genetics to become airborne. Sometimes superpowers let them, and sometimes their supergear does. Superman can fly unassisted, Spider-Man can swing from building to building using his web, and the modern Batman has all manner of nifty black vehicles to get him off the ground to where he needs to go. These flight devices (themselves structures) often comprise several component structures, which students will investigate here. (And later, they'll see how writing structures can be combined into superstructures as well.)

Continuing from the preceding discussion of structure and function, ask students what structures in birds, heroes, or vehicles make flight possible. Are there parts of any of the objects that help them fly? What about particular shapes that are common in many different flying things? Are these structures? How do the structures contribute to the function (flight)? Students might have difficulty answering this last question. That a wing may be important for flight is something many students will know intuitively, but the science behind this idea is much more complicated. Fortunately, your class is about to do some exploration that will help students develop their ideas about how things fly.

Also ask students what things might hinder flight. Students may have a variety of responses to this question—from the lack of wings (or more generally structures to support flight) to gravity (which pulls things back to Earth).

Engineering Flight (55 minutes)

Throw a ball into the air and let it fall to the floor. Ask students if they are surprised that it fell; why or why not? Then ask why an airplane, which is much heavier than a ball, doesn't fall out of the sky. Take a paper airplane and then drop it. Ask students why this didn't fly, and what you'd need to do to make it fly. Students will suggest throwing rather than dropping the airplane. Test their suggestion by throwing the plane. Ask them why throwing it makes a difference. Collect student ideas on chart paper or on a blackboard.

Now it's time to give the students their mission:

> You have been challenged to engineer a vehicle for your hero to fly in. You have just discovered that the world's greatest supervillain has a hideout in Antarctica, and you need a fast way to get there. Because of the cold, it has to be enclosed—jetpacks, capes, and flying carpets won't cut it. As engineers, you have decided to use paper airplanes as your model system.

Believe it or not, aerospace engineers also use paper prototypes, which let you plan, prototype, test, and refine designs quickly. Each student will design and test two different plane models in the session today.

Provide students with paper airplane templates and rulers. Use of the templates is optional; however, if students choose to use a template, encourage them to refine the template design for their second plane rather than picking an altogether new template to test. We want them to be involved in some of the design decisions and to experiment with how changing a plane design changes how it behaves in flight.

Students should use the "Paper Airplane Tech Specs" handout as they design and test their planes. Encourage students to test their planes with at least two—and hopefully three to four—trials so that they can calculate the average flight length, duration, and speed.

Once students have designed and folded their first plane, they can move to a testing station. They'll need to work in pairs: one person will launch a plane while the other records the duration of the flight in seconds. After the plane has landed, the partners should measure the flight distance, or the distance from launch line to landing site.

This is also a good time to talk with students about isolating variables (see "Variables" in the Science-O-Pedia). The more consistent they are with their flight launches during trials, the more reliable and informative their data will be. Time permitting, you can have students brainstorm possible variables that might affect their flight tests and encourage them to limit and control them as much as possible.

After they have tested their first plane, have students reflect, using the "Paper Airplane Tech Specs" handout, on the strengths and weaknesses of that plane. Challenge them to refine their design to result in a plane that can fly either longer or farther (or both!). Have students use the handout to repeat all design and testing steps with their second plane design.

Have students compare and contrast the two planes on the handout. Ask students how they might further improve their plane. Are there structures that hindered their flight performances? What would they change? Add? Remove? Why?

Understanding Flight (15 minutes)

Have the class think back to the demonstration from earlier, when you dropped a plane and it fell without flying. Why didn't it take off? Gravity, they might answer. But gravity still acts on planes (and heroes) when they are in the sky. There must be some other force that can counteract gravity. What other ideas do students have about why throwing the plane helped it fly and overcome gravity? Now that they have experimented some more, have their ideas changed or developed further?

We hope a student will say that the plane flew because you gave it a push. This is an important point. This pushing force is called **thrust.** Ask them why thrust makes a difference. What is happening when the paper airplane is pushed (thrust) forward? Why does a forward push on a plane keep it from falling down? Thinking beyond planes, what gives a bird thrust? Or a hero beginning an unassisted flight? Though all of these fliers' thrust comes from different mechanisms, they have something in common. It has a lot to do with what is going on around the flying thing, as well as with the design of the flying thing itself.

Ask students what they feel on their face when they ride a bike, a scooter, or even a roller coaster. Does the feeling change if they are going faster or slower? Alternately, you could ask students if they have ever flown a kite. What type of weather is best for flying kites? The answer: windy! How can you get a kite "started" or in the air if it is not a very windy day? Students may offer the suggestion of starting by running with it. There's a lot to consider here!

Now is a good time to circle back to thrust. Thrust pushes flying machines through the air (in a plane, the thrust is created by the engines; in a paper plane, by the launcher's push; in a kite it may be created initially by running, but it can also be caused by the wind). The thrust causes air to move over the wings (a structure designed for a specific function), just as when you ride a bike or a scooter, you feel the air moving past your face. This is where the science gets really interesting. When there is a rock in a river, the water flow changes to go around the rock. In the same way, air must flow around any object, whether it's your face as you ride your bike, or the wing of a bird, plane, or kite. As Isaac Newton noted, for every action there is an equal and opposite reaction. The wing pushes and pulls the air around it in a very particular way, and the air pushes and pulls back up on the wing. This upward force is called **lift,** and good wing structures are shaped in a way that maximizes it. The lift generated by air flowing over the plane's wings creates enough force to overcome the downward pull of gravity and carry a huge aircraft loaded with passengers into the air. If the thrust stops or decreases, the speed of the aircraft decreases, so the flow of air over the wings slows, decreasing the lift—and gravity can then pull the plane back down.

There are some cool things you can do to have your students experiment with lift. The first involves a strip of paper. Have students tear a length of scratch paper at least an inch wide. Ask them to hold the strip by a narrow end and ask for observations about what happens when you hold it from that side. (It droops.) Now, ask students to hold the strip to their lips and blow over it. What happens? (The paper lifts up.) Ask students to experiment a bit further—What happens if you blow under the paper? (Not much.) There is a second experiment they can possibly try, with their parents' permission. Ask students to stick their hand out the car window (when the car is in motion) and experiment with changing both the shape of their hand (flat versus cupped, fingers open versus held closely together, and so on) and the angle of their hand in relation to the wind. Their hand can pretty closely approximate the shape of a wing. You can read more about lift and these experiments in the lesson "Technically Speaking." Lots of cool discovering to be done!

If I Could Fly . . . (25 minutes)

As your students have seen, flight isn't all that easy—and neither is being a hero, superpowered or not. Before engaging in all sorts of daring adventures, heroes have to hone and harness their abilities. Think Peter Parker in the 2000s Spider-Man movies, Bruce Wayne in *Batman: Year One* (the graphic novel), the many X-Men who literally go to school to learn to control their powers, or even Violet and Dash Parr in Pixar's *The Incredibles*. And once their talents are under control, things can still go wrong, like when Tony Stark's armor runs out of power or Superman encounters some Kryptonite.

Heroes must persevere, and planning ahead helps them do so, just as anticipating challenges helps engineers create structures that function according to their plans. If a civil engineer is overseeing a bridge being built in an earthquake zone, he can plan ahead and use materials and designs that are flexible but strong. Or if she's in charge of a skyscraper along the stormy tropical coast, she can think of building designs with high wind resistance.

Whatever a hero's goals, it helps to predict obstacles in an effort to overcome them. Here, ask your students to consider what their hero wants to do, and what might be in the way. Then, give them time to write a poem whose stanzas each describe an obstacle and how it's overcome. Your students can write about how their hero becomes a hero in the first place (and has to build equipment, control powers, or both), or how their hero uses his or her preparedness and ingenuity to survive a power- or equipment-related disaster. Students could even include how their hero had to revise his or her plan either mid-course or before attempting to overcome an obstacle a second time—persisting and succeeding!

Flying Out the Door (10 minutes)

Before students fly off, you want to wrap up today's session and build excitement for the next one. Ask students to share what they have learned about how structures serve specific functions in living and engineered systems (they can use flight as an example) and how they might like to continue to refine their plane design at home. (Are there any structures they would like to adapt or change at this point, to see how those changes affect flight?) Encourage them to continue their flight engineering—this is a particularly accessible activity to take home and keep exploring and discovering. Connect back to heroes, saying, "Heroes who fly without mechanical assistance often have capes. Using what you know about structure and function—and how flight works—what do you think the cape might be doing? Do you think it helps or hinders flight? Why?" If there is extra time, invite them to share some of their poetry.

Next session, students will continue their focus on engineering by designing a safe place for their hero to fly to: his or her secret lair.

Session 3: Quick, to Safety! (Secret Lair Building and Haikus)

Shelter is one of the basic needs of most animals. Shelter provides protection from extreme weather (heat, cold, precipitation) and predators. Shelter provides a safe place to sleep, to care for young, and to rest and recover from injuries. Human shelters are the most elaborate in the animal world. They are engineered to meet the needs of those who live in them with specialized rooms for different functions, though other creatures like bees and ants also build specialized structures (or rooms) within their shelters. Heroes have some of the most amazing shelters around—secret lairs that conceal their secret identity, protect them from supervillains, and allow them to rest and recuperate (and sometimes study or invent) between adventures.

Preparation

Before class, make some drying racks for the cotton swabs by folding paper accordion-style. You'll also want to build a simple structure with cotton swabs predipped in rubber cement to give students an idea of how this building material works.

For this session, the students will also do a little prep (and be sure to see note on rubber cement at the end of these preparation instructions). As soon as students walk in, have them start prepping their cotton swabs. Preparing cotton swabs is quick—simply dip each swab end in rubber cement and set it on the accordion-folded drying rack to dry. Students will want to wipe the dunked swabs on the edge of the glue jar when pulling them out. If there is too much glue on the end of a swab, it will take a long time to dry (drying time is typically ten minutes). Once the swabs are "tacky"—dry but sticky—they can be used for building. *Tip for instructors:* If time allows, we recommend that you try this activity in advance of the workshop to get a sense of the right amount of dipping and tackiness.

Cotton swab prep can be done at stations with small groups of students working with adult helpers. In the absence of helpers, teach the early arrivers how to dip the cotton swabs in the rubber cement and place them on the racks to dry. Ask students to share how to prepare cotton swabs with any students who join their table later. Each student will need about forty to sixty prepared cotton swabs.

A note on rubber cement: It can get a little fumy, so you'll want to **be sure you're working in a well-ventilated room.** If your classroom is on the small side, crack some windows. Keep an eye on the students to make sure they're not hovering over the jars of rubber cement too much, and instruct them to screw the caps back on once they're done.

Introduction (15 minutes)

In the first session, students used the "Supercookbook" handout to design a new hero. They then used their understanding of structure-function relationships to engineer a flying vehicle to help their hero get where he or she needs to go. Today, students will continue engineering to fill an important need of every hero: a secret lair. When that's done they'll engineer a haiku that mirrors the secret lair's structure.

The session starts out with a discussion of retreats. Humans, like many other animals, need a place to feel safe and protected. Ask your students where they go to feel safe. Many will say they go to their home; ask them where specifically in their home. Others will say school or church, or a friend's house, or the neighborhood park or library. Whatever the response, make sure students are as specific as possible, and then ask what about that place appeals to them. Some will say they like the solitude; others will say they enjoy the company. Some will like that they can relax; others will look forward to challenge and excitement. Heroes have all the same reasons and more.

Move on to the next bit of the discussion, asking, "Where do you think a hero goes to feel safe and hide out?"

Discuss some well-known hero lairs. Where are they, what do they look like, what are the essential elements? What unique features do they have that help the hero be successful? Examples might include Superman's Fortress of Solitude, Batman's Batcave, the X-Men's Xavier's mansion, and the Teenage Mutant Ninja Turtles' sewer hideout.

Brainstorm the elements that make up a "secret lair," writing the results on the board. Students ideally will mention the following:

◇ Location: Secrecy and camouflage

◇ Solitude: A place to rest, heal, and think

◇ Space: A command center for learning, practice, planning, inventing, and storing the hero suit

◇ Entrance/exit: Easy accessibility

Unfortunately, most superfolks are not also superbuilders. They need someone else to design and create their secret lair: an engineer. And engineers have superpowers, too: they can design solutions to important problems, making the world better. There are engineers who design airplanes so that they can safely take hundreds of passengers from one point to another, engineers who study the flow of traffic and design streets (and time traffic lights) to reduce traffic jams, and engineers who design and build video games that you enjoy playing.

Heroes need engineers to help them solve a variety of problems. They need engineers to design gadgets that help them evade supervillains. They need engineers to design high-tech fabrics that protect them from their enemies' onslaughts (and their own derring-do), and they need engineers to build their secret lair—a safe place where they can work, plan, practice, and recover from their stressful adventures.

Give students their task:

> Today you will design a secret lair for the hero you created in the first session. Your hero needs you—to be an engineer.

Distribute the "How to Be a Superengineer!!!!" handout and spend a few minutes going over it. Engineering is like a superpower, and it's what will help them—and their hero client—succeed in their assignment.

Engineering a Lair (75 minutes)

Distribute the "Secret Lair Blueprint" handout, and set the students loose to start designing. After a few minutes, announce a challenge. You can use one of these or come up with your own:

> We've just learned that there is a worldwide shortage of lair building materials. Given this crisis, your hero client has challenged you to build the biggest lair possible, using the fewest materials.

or

> Today's newspaper includes an announcement by the Decimator, the world's most powerful supervillain. He has sworn to find and destroy all hero lairs (and the heroes who inhabit them). He has developed a powerful new radar tool that can detect most lairs. Currently, there is one form of camouflage or shielding that can evade detection, but it only works when the surface area of the lair is under a certain size. Design a lair that can escape detection by shielding it with no more than a half sheet of newspaper (about eleven by ten inches, depending on the format of newspapers in your region). Note that you can be creative about how you apply the newspaper (think scissors and tape)—but the total paper area cannot be more than one sheet.

or

> There has been a huge uptick in villain activity in Metro City, and all heroes are relocating there to protect the populace. Given several heroes' need to construct a new secret lair (and zoning restrictions that require new buildings to be at least twenty-five stories tall), you need to design a stable skyscraper lair at least twenty-five centimeters tall.

All of these are model constraints, or limitations, that engineers face. There are often cost constraints on projects (a limit on how much money can be spent, or on how much of a certain material is available for use) or size constraints (How do we build a new freeway or bridge that doesn't require us to demolish entire neighborhoods?), among others.

Once students have each sketched their design, disperse students into groups at tables to start building with the prepared cotton swabs. Show them the sample structure you made as an example. After they're done, debrief with a discussion. You can ask:

◇ Did any of you have a structural failure that you would like to share? How did you solve the problem?

◇ What are some ways that you were able to add stability to your structure? Did connecting the swabs in certain patterns lead to a more stable structure than others? If so, how?

◇ What was the most challenging part of building your lair? The most rewarding? The most exciting?

◇ The next time a hero asks you to build a secret lair, what will you do differently? Are there any particular questions you might ask your client this time around? Are there different approaches to the problem that you think might be more effective? How might you test and evaluate these options to determine which is best?

Lair-Upon-Lair Haiku (20 minutes)

After students have done a bit of engineering, bring them back to writing, and highlight some similarities between writing and engineering. There's a purpose to things people write, like there's a purpose to things people engineer. And in both there are constraints to work around. Engineers may have size constraints (as with earlier in this session) or cost constraints (which, as already suggested, aren't necessarily monetary—the amount of available resources, such as cotton swabs, is another kind of cost). Writers have constraints as well. A writer may only have a limited amount of time for a radio or TV commercial, or may have to hold back on complicated vocabulary so an audience can understand. Sometimes, these constraints are more codified or formalized—five hundred words on a statement of purpose for a college application, or an ABABCDCDEFEFGG rhyme scheme for a Shakespearean sonnet.

Here, students will further explore the client-engineer relationship, as well as structure and form, in their writing. Ask if they know what a haiku is; they probably do, but if they've forgotten, remind them of their five-seven-five syllable structure. Show some traditional and nontraditional examples of haikus (maybe show an example of your own haiku you've written about a hero, or see a student's example in the "Acorn Avenger" sidebar). If need be, go over what a syllable is and have students practice counting how many syllables are in their own name to get warmed up for writing.

THE ACORN AVENGER Here are some hero haikus one of our students wrote:

Surrounded with green,
a silver horn and curled tail
is where you'll find me.

* * *

Abundant with gear,
woven from a straw basket,
hidden in the woods.

* * *

A perfect hideout,
a pyramid of supplies,
the place where I spy.

—*Jalen Lisbon, age twelve, New York*

To give the students a little more structure, ask them to write a client-engineer haiku. The first two lines will be a client request from a hero. For example, "Help build my lair, please. / I need to heal after fights." or "I need to hide out / Where the Fox Man can't get me!"

And the last line will be by an engineer, in response to the request. For the previous examples, finishing lines might be "Look, infirmary!" or "Have these iron walls!"

Encourage your students to write as many first and second lines as possible, taking on the persona of their hero client. Ten or more is not unreasonable to ask for.

Once that's done, have them hand their partial haiku to a partner, who, as the engineer, will write final lines with resolutions to the problems. The completed haiku should be returned to the first author, the client.

Finally, the client will take a look at the completed haiku and decide which of the engineer's solutions they like best. If time and awesomeness permit, students can revise their cotton swab model. For major bonus points, they can use the haiku as walls.

WANT TO KEEP WRITING?
OPTIONAL ADDITIONAL WRITING PROMPT

For more writing, give your students the following prompt:

Imagine that your hero has to get a quick note to the rest of his or her friends about being safe and hidden. Using the haiku structure, write a "secret lair haiku" from the perspective of your hero that also acts as a secret message to his or her friends and family. How can you reveal your location and surroundings without giving away too much? How will they know you are safe? Go!

Safe, for Now . . . (10 minutes)

After students have assembled their haiku, bring them back into a large group discussion. Have students share some of their writing, and marvel appropriately at the solutions they came up with and the clever concrete haiku arrangements.

Ask them to talk about how they made their choices about which resolutions they chose to include or not include in their lair poems. It's likely that several chose to leave out certain resolutions because things didn't fit—an ice hero might melt going through a hidden volcano entrance, or jet engines would ruin the stealth capability of a submarine. Note that sometimes structures don't work well on their own, and that sometimes they work well on their own, but don't make sense with other structures. Can your students think of structural designs on paper airplanes that work well by themselves but not with each other?

To finish, let your students know that the final session in the lesson will continue the engineering focus: students will design a safe vehicle to help their hero save the day.

FOR YOU TO KNOW (AND YOUR STUDENTS TO DISCOVER)

The focus of this workshop session is on students designing a secret lair for the hero they created during the first session. Engineers in general and your lair design engineers specifically have to base their design solutions on the expressed needs of their clients. In this lesson, the expressed needs are the fictional needs of their hero. In addition, the lair design engineers also have to work within the constraints of the lesson's design challenges. This is a big idea in engineering—responding to client needs and working within constraints. Although students won't complete a full engineering design cycle in this session, they will focus this very important piece—how to make sure their design is relevant to the problem that needs to be solved. Be sure to read the "How to Be a Superengineer!!!!" handout to brush up on your engineering principles.

The Shape of Stability

Note: What follows is a brief description of the stability of different shapes, and some examples that you can use with students if they bring up these ideas. Beware of giving spoilers. It's best if the ideas are discovered by your students in their building and their discussions, and then reinforced by you, the instructor.

Children building with blocks often build towers and—even at a very young age—are thrilled by the wobbliness of a tall tower and the challenge of balancing just one more block on top (then one more, and one more) until the whole thing comes crashing down. It's a primitive exercise in the field called structural engineering, in which different shapes serve different purposes.

Over time, those same children building block towers are likely to discover that they can build taller if they give the tower a wide base and the tower narrows as it goes up. The Empire State Building is a particularly elegant real-life example of this principle. Students with

(continued)

experience riding on trains, buses, or subways (or skateboards and surfboards) may have some relevant personal experience with this notion . . . they will probably know that, when standing, they are more stable if they have a wide base (if they have their legs spread apart, as opposed to standing with their legs together).

Triangles are the most stable shape for building because of the way they distribute forces. The ancient Egyptians built the tallest buildings in the world (at the time) using the triangle as their base shape. The result was the Great Pyramids—still standing after four thousand years. (Try this out: create a triangle out of rubber cement and cotton swabs, then try and deform it. You'll only be able to do so by bending the cotton swabs. But if you were to assemble, say, a square, it would be very easy to deform at the joints without bending the cotton swabs at all.)

Even when modern structures are not shaped like a triangle, you can probably find many triangles in their "skeleton"—the framing that keeps them stable. Bridges offer a great example of this—look at old railway bridges and trusses and notice the number of triangles in the frame. Even buildings will be cross-braced for added stability against wind or earthquakes.

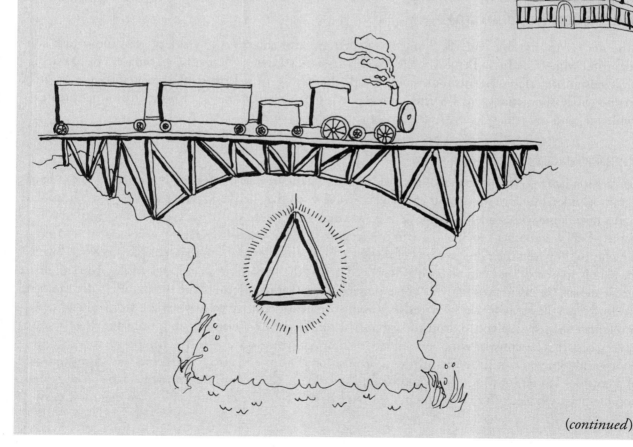

(*continued*)

One architect, whose primary concern was hurricane damage, built a house in the shape of a dome. This was unconventional, certainly, but the shape allowed tall waves and strong winds to flow smoothly around the house, and in storms in which conventional houses were destroyed, the dome house survived essentially unscathed. Dome homes are a fantastic example of how engineers apply scientific principles to solve problems.

Session 4: Saving the Day (Prose Poems and the Great Egg Drop)

Whether it's an invisible plane, a flying silver surfboard, or a custom van, safety is an important consideration when creating a hero's vehicle. In this session, students will explore principles of physics while designing safety systems for a supervehicle that will get the hero to the scene without a scratch. To end the lesson, students will write a prose poem in which their hero confronts his or her greatest challenge, and tells the tale of whether he or she succeeds or not.

Preparation

This session has a pretty big materials list. All students will not use all materials—but you do want to have a good selection available so students can have access to what they need and have planned for. It's helpful to send a note home with students (or speak directly with parents) after the first session, asking them to collect recyclables and other supplies to use in this session. When it's time to build, we encourage you to ask students to show you their design plan before they grab their materials from the available supplies. Once the plan is approved, they can take what they need, rather than hoarding a bit of everything. You can make sure materials are distributed fairly by not approving plans that require all of the Bubble Wrap, for example.

Students will be using these materials to build vehicles to safely convey an egg from a height, so you'll also need someplace to drop the vehicles from. There are a number of options for this. If you have access to a balcony or window (ten feet or more off the ground—but no higher than a second-floor window), you can drop them from that position. Drops can also happen indoors, from the top of a ten-foot ladder (only adults should be on the ladder). Tape down a disposable tarp—a large disposable plastic tablecloth or several large garbage bags—to make cleanup of broken egg mess easy.

Introduction (10 minutes)

All heroes, and those with superpowers in particular, are known for their dedication and commitment—their willingness to put themselves in harm's way. But you don't need to have superpowers to help someone in distress. Even little actions (offering to have lunch with another student who is sitting alone, volunteering to do a chore or task at home before a parent asks) can do a lot. Ask students to go around and tell a short story about a time when they chose to be a hero (by helping someone or doing a good deed). Ask, "What happened? How did it make you feel? How did the other person respond?"

Today, they'll have a chance to be a hero again. Their task: to engineer a vehicle that will get their hero to the scene quickly and safely; safely most of all.

Ask students to think about their experiences with various modes of transport (cars, planes, bicycles, and so on). What types of safety devices are either in place as a part of these vehicles or worn while riding them? Let students brainstorm a list of as many safety structures as they can think of, listing their responses on the board. (If you like, you can give the students a couple of minutes to jot down their ideas first; you'll get more fleshed-out ideas, and the pause is helpful to English language learners.)

SAVING THE DAY . . . ON MARS! NASA engineers are the heroes behind rover expeditions to Mars. Engineers designed a complex sequence of events to correctly orient the rover, slow its descent, and absorb the energy of impact, so the rover would land intact on the surface of Mars with all of its delicate scientific equipment in working order. There are several good videos produced by NASA that describe the landing sequence and how the rover's "safety" features work together for a successful landing. See "Handy Lesson Links" in the appendix.

Next, ask students what the function of these safety structures is. At this point, convert the list on the board to a T-chart. The headings "Safety Structure" and "Function" may be helpful. If the students need some clarification, remind them that the function is what the structure does and how it contributes to safety.

Designing an Escape (70 minutes)

It's time for each student to start building his or her vehicle. At this point you can let the students know who will be playing their hero today: an egg. Yes, they'll need to design and create a vehicle that will safely get the fragile cargo from point A to point B, with point A being very high, and point B being the ground.

Encourage students to think about how they will integrate safety features. Revisit the list of safety structures and group them into themes based on their functions. For example:

◇ <u>Reducing momentum:</u> Brakes (slowing the vehicle and reducing the chance of impact or momentum at impact)

◇ <u>Restraining passengers:</u> Seat belts (preventing passengers from being thrown from the vehicle and from hitting objects in the vehicle, and positioning them correctly to be protected by airbags)

◇ <u>Absorbing and distributing impact:</u> Crumple zones, airbags

◇ <u>Protecting passengers:</u> Strong passenger compartment, roll cage, and so on

Discuss prototyping, or building a model to test a design, and ask students what they know about how the safety of vehicles is tested. Have they heard of crash test dummies? Why do they think these are used? What do car manufacturers do to test the safety of a vehicle? (For a video of a crash test, see "Handy Lesson Links" in the appendix.) Explain that students each will use a crash test dummy in their vehicle—a raw egg. The goal is for their egg to survive the crash unbroken (and ideally uncracked).

Remind students that engineers plan before they begin building. They draw a design plan, and perhaps even conduct some small-scale tests along the way before building the complete prototype. Distribute the "Saving the Egg" handout and give the students about fifteen minutes to complete their design plan. Tell students that they should bring their plan to an engineering supervisor (you) for approval prior to gathering materials.

Once students have completed their design plan and have approval to gather materials, provide approximately twenty minutes for building their prototype vehicle.

After the structures are built—and the eggs are secure inside—it's time to put them to the test and drop them from the drop station. Allot ten minutes or more. Note that an adult should do the dropping, and that drops of different vehicles should be as consistent as possible (that is, a simple release from the same height—do not throw or otherwise accelerate the vehicle). Students should stand around the perimeter of the drop area at a distance where they will be unlikely to get splashed by broken egg mess. Assign a student or volunteer to "collect" each vehicle after its test and put it to the side so other students' vehicles are not landing on top of those already dropped.

After everyone's dropped his or her egg, give the class about ten minutes to record what worked and what didn't work on their "Saving the Egg" handout. Once that's done, assemble the group for a discussion. Ask students to share how their passenger fared. Then move to a more reflective discussion about what they learned from their prototype and what they would do differently next time. Were there particular types of safety features that seemed to provide the most protection? Things that didn't work at all? Is there a way to combine different features from different students' designs to create an optimal passenger safety experience? Put up a piece of chart paper or use the board to collect students' ideas and collaboratively draw a revised supervehicle that, based on students' experiences in this session, should be supersafe.

Writing a Prose Poem (25 minutes)

A prose poem lives between standard verse and standard prose. You can think of it as a paragraph of prose that uses poetic style, language, rhythm, and flow. Or you can think of it as a poem that's arranged in sentences and paragraphs instead of verses and stanzas. The end result should look like a standard paragraph, but sound like a poem. (For more on prose poems, see "Handy Lesson Links" in the appendix.)

After testing the egg drop devices, whether they've succeeded or failed, students should have a heightened sense of the stakes associated with choices. They'll mainly at this point consider the choices of the engineer (the design of the vehicle), but you should also ask them to consider the choices and challenges facing the hero.

After a little bit of discussion on this, task your students with writing a prose poem about their hero's most colossal challenge. This prose poem should . . .

◇ Describe the challenge the hero is facing. Is it the Decimator, another villain, an impending natural disaster, or something else entirely?

◇ Explain why the challenge is too big for our hero right now. Our hero at this point shouldn't be able to successfully confront the challenge head-on, or get everyone to safety (or both).

◇ Describe the outcome. Students may write this based on the outcome of their egg drop, but it's okay if they write about a success here even if their egg drop failed (or vice versa). In any case, students can still draw on aspects of their egg drop as inspiration (for example, even if the landing legs on the egg drop fell off entirely and the egg was obliterated, in the poem the hero might be able to escape the wreckage with only a broken arm).

◇ Include vivid descriptions and figurative language throughout.

Teach-Backs and Close (15 minutes)

Time permitting, have students share shorter or longer bits from their prose poem. Discuss, with the class, how the heroes' choices affected the ends of the stories. More indirectly, how did engineering design choices affect the egg drop experiment, and how were those reflected in the prose poems? What other choices were there, and how might things have changed as a result of making different choices?

To end the lesson, have students reflect on all the choices their hero has made. How do those choices relate to the hero's natural abilities and nurtured tendencies? How do those choices affect the client-engineer relationship, and the quality of everything the students built? How do those choices affect the hero's world?

Bring the idea of choice back to the students' world. How can your choices influence who you are and where you are going?

Remind students that although we can't change our nature and nurture up to this point, we still do have choices, and our own choices are powerful determinants of who we become. Persisting through challenges and overcoming adversity are hallmarks of successful heroes, scientists, and engineers—but continuing to move forward and not giving up are choices that these real and imagined heroes make, on various scales, every day.

FOR YOU TO KNOW (AND YOUR STUDENTS TO DISCOVER)[7]

Automakers spend huge amounts of money engineering systems within cars to keep the occupants comfortable and to protect them in the event of a crash. Similarly, NASA engineers carefully design systems that enable the Mars rovers to fall safely to the planet's surface without damaging the sensitive (and very expensive) components that will be crucial for a successful mission.

In designing a landing pod for their egg, your students will be engaging in a very similar task, and using the principles of physics will help them be successful.

What's Going On in a Crash

There are several important physics concepts at work in a collision:

▶ Although it is almost too obvious to state, objects tend to stay where you put them unless a force acts on them to change their state of motion (this is really Newton's first law). If you put a cup on the table, it will stay on the table until someone picks it up or pushes it over. The act of picking up or pushing over is a force acting on the cup. The converse—namely, that objects in motion stay in motion until a force acts on them to change that motion—is also true. It is, admittedly, harder to see, because there is always a force—friction—acting on forces in motion. The tendency of objects to resist a change in motion is called **inertia.**

▶ **Momentum** is essentially a measure of the amount of motion an object has. It is dependent on both the **mass** (a measure of how much stuff the object is made of—or on Earth, its weight) and its **velocity** (speed and direction).

▶ An **impulse**—a force acting over a period of time—changes the momentum of an object. If a car driving down the road runs into a brick wall, it comes to an abrupt stop. There is a large force that acts on the car over a short period of time. If the same car traveling at the same initial speed (and with the same mass) runs off the road into a sand pit, it comes to a stop much more slowly—there is a smaller force acting on the car over a longer period of time. The change in momentum in these two situations is the same—the car comes to a stop, but the effect on the vehicle and its occupants is dramatically different.

What does this all mean when we put it together? If you are sitting in your chair in your dining room, it is obvious that you are not in motion, unless someone pushes the chair (or you stand up and walk away). If you are sitting in a car moving at fifty-five miles per hour, although you perceive that you are sitting still, your body is moving at the same velocity (speed and direction) as the car you are traveling in. In this example, the system (the entire car and you) has momentum that is equivalent to the momentum of the car plus the momentum of the passenger.

---

7. Information is derived from the following sources: "How Crumple Zones Work," *http://www.autoevolution.com/news/how-crumple-zones-work-7112.html*; "Physics in the Crumple Zone Demonstrate How Less Stiff Materials, Like Plastic, Can Help Prevent Injury and Save Lives," from *http://www.plastics-car.com/Todays-Automobiles/Automotive-Safety/Physics-in-the-Crumple-Zone-2.html*.

(continued)

Most of the time, when all is going smoothly on a drive, the momentum of the passenger and the momentum of the car act as a single system. When you brake your car to come to a stop, the slowing wheels apply a force to the car, and the car applies a force to you via friction or the pull of seat belts—and your momentum and that of the car decrease roughly simultaneously. If something forces the car to stop abruptly, however, like hitting the brick wall just mentioned at fifty-five miles per hour, the force has acted on the car, but you'll still keep moving. You still have momentum because of inertia (if you're not wearing a seat belt, the low force of friction in the car hasn't had enough time to stop you—that is, there has not yet been a sufficient impulse acting on you to stop your motion). Your body (and your internal organs) continues to travel at speed until a force changes your motion (brings you to a stop). You will slide forward in your seat until something stops you (and your organs will continue to slide forward until something, such as your rib cage, stops them—not good). Hopefully you are wearing your seat belt and have other safety systems in your car, as all of these safety systems are designed to either (1) absorb or distribute the force of the impact or (2) increase the time over which the force is acting, thereby decreasing the impulse.

That's the Way the Car Crumples

Newton's second law states that the size of a force depends on how quickly an object changes speed. If a car stops quickly, there must be a very large force acting on the car. If it can be slowed down at all before impact, the size of the force necessary to stop it decreases. That is, the longer the car takes to come to a stop, the bigger the decrease in the force needed to stop it. The brakes in a car help slow it (ideally enough so that an impact never takes place). Car manufacturers have also built what are called crumple zones, which harness the power of Newton's second law, into the body of the car surrounding the passenger compartment. If you hit a brick wall in a car with a crumple zone, the front end comes to a stop at the wall, and the body of the car continues to move forward, collapsing or crumpling the body of the car between the front and the passenger compartment. This takes time and absorbs energy—meaning that the force experienced by the passengers is reduced.

Once upon a time, car manufacturers made car bodies very rigid. This meant that there was little crumpling, and the passengers felt the full force of impact (the car may have been less damaged than in accidents with modern cars, but passengers did not fare so well and were terribly injured). Modern cars couple crumple zones with rigid passenger compartments (to limit intrusion of, say, the engine into the passenger area), and together these two improvements (with those described in the following paragraphs) have greatly improved passenger safety.

Don't Burst My Airbag

Just like how crumple zones decrease the force of the impact by slowing the car, airbags decrease the force of impact experienced by the passenger by slowing the passenger. An airbag inflates as a passenger is sliding forward in his or her seat as a result of the impact. The passenger then hits the airbag, rather than a rigid structure like the dashboard, and the airbag

(continued)

deforms (much like how a pillow changes shape when you hit it). This deformation absorbs some of the energy of impact and slows the passenger so he or she does not come to an abrupt stop (big force, short time).

In addition, because airbags cover a large area, they distribute the force of impact. You probably have experience with this carrying a heavy backpack. If your backpack strap is twisted, it quickly becomes painful as the weight of the backpack (the downward force from gravity) is only distributed over a small area on your shoulder. If you untwist the strap, the weight is distributed over a greater area, and although the backpack is still heavy, it is less painful to your shoulder. Before airbags, drivers would hit the steering wheel, and the force of the impact was distributed over a very small area on the driver's body. By distributing the impact, the passenger is less likely to experience a severe injury.

Use Restraint

Seat belts serve several functions. Seat belts connect you to the car, so in a crash, you are no longer a separate body moving independently of the car. This allows you to benefit from safety features like crumple zones that slow the car (and you) and decrease the force of the impact you feel. Seat belts are designed to stretch a little, and so, like the other safety features just described, seat belts slow a passenger and thereby reduce the force of impact. Seat belts also prevent a passenger from hitting objects inside the car, like the dashboard, steering column, or windshield, and prevent the passenger from being thrown out of the car altogether. Finally, like airbags, when worn properly, seat belts distribute the force of impact over the passenger's body.

SECRETS OF STRAWBERRIES

Follow these steps to discover the DNA hidden in strawberries.

Directions and Observations

1. Put a coffee filter over the top of a plastic cup and secure it with a rubber band.

2. Put a single strawberry in a ziplock bag and seal it. Remove as much air as you can.

3. Smash up the strawberry with your hand and fingers for 1 minute. Then pass it to a partner and let him or her smash it for another minute. Be careful not to break your bag. The best way to mash it is to massage the mixture at the bottom of the bag. Describe the smashed strawberry specimen:

I smell . . .

I feel . . .

I hear . . .

4. Add 12 milliliters of Lysis buffer (in the clear tube **without** a rubber band, made of dish soap, salt, and water) to the bag and zip it closed. Mash again for a minute, then pass it to a partner and let him or her mash it for an additional minute. Describe the sample now:

I see . . .

(continued)

I smell . . .

I feel . . .

I hear . . .

5. Tilt the bag so that the mush collects in one bottom corner of the bag, and open the bag. Carefully pour the mush into the coffee filter. Let the liquid drip through into the cup for about 5 minutes. You can gently stir with the small coffee stirrers. **NOTE:** Be careful not to poke a hole in your coffee filter with the stir stick!

While you wait, figure out whether the following statements are true or false, and discuss with your partner(s).

If the total DNA in one person were laid in a straight line, it would stretch to the sun and back over thirty times (it's ninety-three million miles from here to the sun). True or false? Discuss.

If you had really strong reading glasses, you'd be able to see the double helix or spiral ladder shape of DNA. True or false? Discuss.

6. After most of the reddish liquid has dripped into the cup, carefully remove the filter paper with the strawberry mush and throw it in the trash. Tilt the cup a little and gently pour the 10 milliliters of isopropanol (also known as rubbing alcohol, in the tube **with** a rubber band) into the cup, letting it slowly pour down the side of the cup. **DO NOT MIX!** Describe the sample now:

I see . . .

I smell . . .

(continued)

I feel . . .

I hear . . .

7. Observe and wait another 5 to 7 minutes. You'll see the DNA start to collect as a goopy glob, and you can "spool it out" on the tip of the plastic stick. Then describe the sample:

I see . . .

I smell . . .

I feel . . .

I hear . . .

While you wait, discuss the following statement with your partner(s) and figure out whether it is true or false:

DNA is chemically the same, whether it comes from a fish, a flower, a bacterium, a human, or a hero. If you were to isolate DNA from any of these life forms (like you're doing for your strawberry today), it would all look the same in your test tube. True or false? Discuss.

8. Transfer the spooled DNA into an Eppendorff tube with some isopropanol (eyeball the amount until the tube is about one-third full). You can take the DNA home with you, but keep it tightly closed to avoid evaporation of the alcohol. The DNA is stable in this form for many years.

SUPERCOOKBOOK

	YOUR TRAIT	YOUR HERO'S TRAIT	IS THE TRAIT INHERITED (IN THE DNA)?
Eye color			
Hair color			
Height			
Wears glasses?			
Favorite color			
Talent (for example, singing, playing an instrument, sports, math, magic tricks)			
Favorite "street" clothes			
Hero suit	**Not applicable**		
Ways similar to parents			
Ways different from parents			

What is your hero's superpower?

Do your hero's parents also have this superpower?

Do your hero's grandparents also have this superpower? Do other family members have this superpower? If yes, who?

How did your hero discover his or her superpower?

Was your hero born with this power? Or did something happen later in life that changed the hero and conveyed the power?

What is the planet of origin of your hero? If this planet isn't Earth, what are some of the characteristics of other "people" from this planet?

What is your hero's greatest desire?

What is your hero's greatest fear?

PAPER AIRPLANE TECH SPECS

Record your paper airplane specs here.

Plane 1 Specifications

Complete this section after folding your first plane.

Plane length (tip to tail): _____ centimeters

Plane width (wing to wing): _____ centimeters

Schematic diagram:

I made the following design decisions to help the plane fly:

PAPER AIRPLANE TECH SPECS (continued)

Plane 1 Flight Data (Trial 1)

- Flight distance: _____ centimeters

- Duration (time) of flight: _____ seconds

- Speed (Speed = Distance ÷ Time): _____ centimeters per second

Plane 1 Flight Data (Trial 2)

- Flight distance: _____ centimeters

- Duration of flight: _____ seconds

- Speed: _____ centimeters per second

Plane 1 Flight Data (Trial 3)

- Flight distance: _____ centimeters

- Duration of flight: _____ seconds

- Speed: _____ centimeters per second

Plane 1 Flight Data (Trial 4)

- Flight distance: _____ centimeters

- Duration of flight: _____ seconds

- Speed: _____ centimeters per second

Plane 1 Average Flight Data of Trials

- Average flight distance: _____ centimeters

- Average duration of flight: _____ seconds

- Average speed: _____ centimeters per second

PAPER AIRPLANE TECH SPECS (continued)

Engineering Reflections

1. I liked that . . ._____

_____

2. I was surprised that . . ._____

_____

3. One change I would like to make to my plane is . . ._____

_____

4. I think this change will . . ._____

_____

_____

Plane 2 Specifications

Complete this section after folding your second plane.

Plane length (tip to tail): _____ centimeters

Plane width (wing to wing): _____ centimeters

Schematic diagram:

I made the following design revisions to help the plane fly:

PAPER AIRPLANE TECH SPECS (continued)

Plane 2 Flight Data (Trial 1)

- Flight distance: _____ centimeters
- Duration (time) of flight: _____ seconds
- Speed (Speed = Distance ÷ Time): _____ centimeters per second

Plane 2 Flight Data (Trial 2)

- Flight distance: _____ centimeters
- Duration of flight: _____ seconds
- Speed: _____ centimeters per second

Plane 2 Flight Data (Trial 3)

- Flight distance: _____ centimeters
- Duration of flight: _____ seconds
- Speed: _____ centimeters per second

Plane 2 Flight Data (Trial 4)

- Flight distance: _____ centimeters
- Duration of flight: _____ seconds
- Speed: _____ centimeters per second

Plane 2 Average Flight Data of Trials

- Average flight distance: _____ centimeters
- Average duration of flight: _____ seconds
- Average speed: _____ centimeters per second

PAPER AIRPLANE TECH SPECS (continued)

Engineering Reflections

1. I noticed that my second plane flew . . . _____

_____

_____

2. I was surprised that the change I made . . . _____

_____

_____

3. If I could change one more thing, I would . . . _____

_____

_____

4. I think this change will . . . _____

_____

_____

Any other notes or comments you might have:

HOW TO BE A SUPERENGINEER!!!!

Engineering is like a superpower. It's what lets you design the tallest buildings—and the vehicles that can leap over them in a single bound. Fortunately, it's a superpower you don't have to be born with. You can learn how to do it! Here are the steps every good engineer follows:*

_____

* These steps are drawn from the following sources: "Engineering Design Process," *http://www.teachengineering.org/ engrdesignprocess.php*; "Engineering," *http://www.engr.ncsu.edu/theengineeringplace/educators/*.

(continued)

Step 1: Understand

Engineers can't solve a problem for a client if they do not understand the problem that the client needs solved. Engineers take considerable time at the start of a job to understand the project. Imagine that you have been asked to build a bridge. It might be great fun to go off and start designing the bridge, but without some really critical pieces of information, you are unlikely to solve the right problem (though you may design a lovely bridge), and you will be unaware of any design constraints. In this case, important questions to ask the client might include: What is the bridge over? How long does the bridge need to be (span length)? Does anything need to be able to pass under the bridge (for example, tall ships)? Who will use the bridge? For what? What are the weather conditions the bridge will experience? Your plans for a pedestrian bridge over a creek on a hiking trail would be very different from those for a bridge over a river that carries lots of traffic on a busy interstate highway.

Step 2: Brainstorm

With this information, engineers (individuals or teams) will brainstorm ideas for how to solve the problem. The goal of a brainstorm is to come up with lots of ideas—a wide variety of possible solutions. Expert brainstormers will tell you that you shouldn't judge ideas at this point. You want to have a lot of possibilities.

Step 3: Select an Idea

After brainstorming, go back over your problem and constraints again, and with these criteria in mind, review your ideas; compare them to one another (perhaps mixing and matching different components of different ideas) to see which ideas are likely to provide the best solution; and add information (about materials, costs, and so on). Finally, select the design you want to take to the next phase.

Step 4: Plan

Draw a diagram of your design. What materials will you use? What do you know about how those materials work (or when they fail)? In drawing your plan, look to see if you notice anything that could cause problems when you build and test your design. If so, how will you correct it?

Step 5: Create and Test

Now it is time to build a prototype—a first-draft model—of your plan, and test it against your design constraints. Does it meet your (and your client's) goals? Is there anything that can be improved?

Step 6: Improve

Think about what went well, and what could be improved in your design based on what you learned in your tests. Using these new ideas, refine your ideas. This process could include drawing new designs, rebuilding, and retesting. Your goal should be to make the best product you can—something that you can be proud of that solves the stated problem and meets the client's needs.

SECRET LAIR BLUEPRINT

Engineers use science and math to design and build solutions to solve important problems. And a hero without a lair is definitely a very big problem. Fortunately, you have the engineering skills to save the day.

The first step to building a good lair is to understand what your hero client needs.

Client name: _____

Lair location (circle one in each row):   Urban (in a city)   Rural (in the country)

Aboveground   Underground

If the lair is in a city, what type of building is it likely to be in or under?

_____

_____

If the lair is in the country, will the lair be a stand-alone structure or part of another building or landform?

_____

_____

Types of activities the lair will be used for (circle any that apply):

Hiding   Storing vehicles

Inventing tools and gadgets   Changing from everyday identity into hero

Tracking nemeses

Other: _____

How many rooms will the lair need?_____

What will keep the secret lair secret (how will it be camouflaged)?

_____

_____

Engineers draw plans for a given solution (in this case a secret lair), then they build a prototype or model to get a better idea of whether their plan meets the needs of their client. They then revise their model based on both their own ideas and feedback from others to make it better.

Draw a schematic (diagram) of the lair you plan to build. If you need more drawing space, use the back of this sheet.

SAVING THE EGG

Egg Protection Device Design Plan

Materials used:

Design plan:

SAVING THE EGG (continued)

I chose the materials for my protection device because . . .

_____

_____

My device is designed to protect the egg by . . .

_____

_____

Drop Data

Height of egg drop: _____ feet

Name of drop engineer (person who drops egg): _____

Status of egg after drop (circle one):

Intact   Small cracks   Large cracks   Oozing egg   Completely smashed

Describe the appearance of your device and egg after the drop (in words or in pictures):

Engineering Reflections

1. I was surprised that . . . _____

_____

_____

2. One change I would like to make to my device is . . . _____

_____

_____

3. I think that this change will . . . _____

_____

_____

STEM@HOME: SESSION 1 (TRACING TRAITS)

All humans (including heroes) are unique, but they share many **traits** with their parents and siblings. Traits are observable characteristics that are passed down from parents to a child. What traits do you share with your relatives?

Trait Inventory

Interview your relatives to track who inherited which traits. If you want to interview even more relatives—great!—track their traits on a separate piece of paper.*

	Me		Relative Name		Relative Name	
Can roll tongue?	Yes	No	Yes	No	Yes	No
Has dimples?	Yes	No	Yes	No	Yes	No
Is right-handed?	Yes	No	Yes	No	Yes	No
Has freckles?	Yes	No	Yes	No	Yes	No
Has naturally curly hair?	Yes	No	Yes	No	Yes	No
Has allergies?	Yes	No	Yes	No	Yes	No
Can see the colors red and green (is not color blind)?	Yes	No	Yes	No	Yes	No

Traits are passed down from parent to child in **DNA** (deoxyribonucleic acid). DNA is like a cookbook—every cell of a human includes all the recipes needed to make a human. Small differences in the DNA of individuals (for example, between you and a classmate) make us unique and account for our individual traits (hair color, eye color, whether or not we can roll our tongue, and so on).

Fun DNA Facts**

▸ DNA is chemically the same, whether it comes from a fish, a flower, a bacterium, a human, or a hero. If you were to isolate DNA from any of these life forms (like you did for your strawberry today), it would all look the same in your test tube—just like if you look at two books from very far away, you cannot tell that there are any differences in the books. You would have to get close enough to read the books to see the differences between them. Similarly, you would have to get a close-up of the DNA to be able to "read" the differences between fish and flower DNA.

---

*Adapted from *http://teach.genetics.utah.edu/content/begin/traits/traitsinventory.pdf*

**Facts are adapted from "Genes in Common," *http://genetics.thetech.org/online-exhibits/genes-common*; "Amazing DNA Facts," *http://sciencecentres.org.uk/projects/handsondna/4.8%20-%20Amazing%20facts%20and%20quiz%20 questions.pdf*; EmilyC, "Genetic Similarities of Mice and Men," *http://blog.23andme.com/23andme-and-you /genetics-101/genetic-similarities-of-mice-and-men/*.

- Humans and chimpanzees share 98 percent of their DNA (and humans share 7 percent of their DNA with bacteria!).

- Each human cell contains about 3.5 billion base pairs of DNA.

- If you were to unwind the DNA in just one of your cells, it would be approximately six feet long.

- If you unraveled all of your DNA from all of your cells and laid out the DNA end to end, the strand would stretch from Earth to the sun hundreds of times (the sun is approximately ninety-eight million miles away from Earth).

- You could fit twenty-five thousand strands of DNA side by side in the width of a single adult hair.

STEM@HOME: SESSION 2

Paper airplanes may seem simple, but there can be some pretty advanced engineering involved.

Challenge Yourself

There are lots of different ways that you can launch a paper airplane. How does changing the way you launch a plane change its behavior?

Some variables to try:

▸ Light throw versus hard throw.

▸ Nose pointed up on release versus nose parallel to the ground.

▸ Holding the plane closer to the nose versus holding it closer to the tail.

▸ Pointing the plane toward the wind (fan or air conditioner) versus pointing it away from the wind (fan or air conditioner). Note that this mimics planes having a head- or tailwind.

Think of some more variables to test!

Fun Flight Facts*

▸ Aerospace engineers, aircraft manufacturers, and scientists all use paper aircraft to test aircraft behavior—just like you did.

▸ Ken Blackburn holds the Guinness world record for longest (duration) paper aircraft flight—27.6 seconds!

▸ Tony Fletch holds the world record for longest distance flown by a paper aircraft—193 feet (longer than the distance of the Wright brothers' first flight)!

▸ The largest paper airplane ever built had a wingspan of 40 feet. It flew 114 feet before crashing and smashing its nose.

Learn More

▸ Ken Blackburn explains how paper airplanes fly (*www.paperplane.org/paero.htm*) and has patterns for making additional planes (*www.paperplane.org/patterns.htm*).

▸ There are lots of other great plane patterns available at *www.augq07.dsl.pipex.com/paamain /links.html*.

---

* Facts are adapted from "Paper Aircraft Association 'Amazing Facts,'" *http://www.augq07.dsl.pipex.com/paamain /facts.html*.

STEM@HOME: SESSION 3

Today you solved an important problem for your hero by designing and building his or her secret lair. Can you keep thinking like an engineer?

Talk to your family members. What are some important problems that you can help them solve? Are there things that frustrate them? Is there something they wish were different?

For example:

► Do you ever not know if the dishes in the dishwasher are dirty or clean?

► Do you or your parents have a hard time keeping track of important notices from school?

► Do you wish you had a way to know if your younger sibling went into your room while you were at school?

► At dinner, have you and your family members ever all wanted different things to eat?

► Have you ever been really, really hot on a summer's day and wanted to invent a way to cool off?

► Have you ever misplaced an important item, like the keys to your house, and needed a way to keep track of it?

Brainstorm a list of possible problems you could engineer a solution to, then get down to work and design a solution. Test your design, and after getting feedback from your family, refine or revise it.

STEM@HOME: SESSION 4

Humans have invented lots of devices that save the day—and save lives. A few examples:

▶ Seat belts save nearly eighteen thousand lives each year.[*]

▶ Vaccines save more than three million lives worldwide each year.[**]

▶ Installation of modern sewer systems eliminated deadly cholera epidemics from the world's major cities beginning in the late 1800s.[†]

▶ The discovery of penicillin, the first antibiotic, has saved more than eighty-two million lives.[‡]

▶ Invention of the incubator for premature babies has increased survival rates from only 15 percent to 85 percent.[§]

You don't have to save a life to save the day, however. Ask your parents, grandparents, an aunt, an uncle, or an adult friend about something they did that made them feel super. This could be an accomplishment they were proud of or something they did to help someone else.

Are there ways that you can imagine saving the day? What are some choices you can make in your life that will help you save the day sometime in the future?

---

* "Seat Belts: Your Single Most Effective Safety Step," *http://www.nsc.org/safety_road/DriverSafety/Pages/SeatBelts.aspx.*

** "F.A.Q," *http://www.sanofipasteur.com/en/faq.aspx.*

† "Cholera Prevention," *http://wonder.cdc.gov/wonder/prevguid/p0000002/p0000002.asp.*

‡ "Lives Saved," *http://www.scienceheroes.com/.*

§ Stina Caxe, "The Baby Sideshow: A History of the Incubator," *http://stinacaxe.hubpages.com/hub/caxe21incubator.*

INFINITE RECESS

BASED ON THE ORIGINAL WORKSHOP
BY EMILY CLADER AND DANIEL RECK

2 SESSIONS, 2 HOURS EACH
STEM DISCIPLINE: *Mathematics*
WRITING ACTIVITIES: *Technical writing, narrative writing, poetry*

WE'RE LETTING YOU IN ON A BIT OF A SECRET here: math and writing are pretty much the same thing. This might come as a surprise, but think about it. Like writing, math helps us understand the world by allowing us to describe the rules it follows and explore what would change if we broke those rules. In this lesson, students learn how imposing structure on writing can inspire them even while constraining them. By developing an awareness of mathematical structure in life, they will be able to imagine the world in a different and exciting new way. Together, you'll create infinite poems using fractals, imagine life on a doughnut, and speculate about a universe where time goes crazy. Along the way, everyone will learn some cool math facts and some helpful writing strategies.

Session 1: Fractal Poetry

In this session, students learn that shapes don't have to be silent, and poetry doesn't have to be linear, as they write shapes in verse, and verse in shapes.

MATERIALS

SESSION 1

☐ Copies of the "Fractal Poetry: A Step-by-Step Guide" handout (included with the other handout at the end of this lesson)

SESSION 2

☐ Modeling clay or the like

☐ Foil

☐ Copies of the "Leaving Space and Time" handout

☐ String, pipe cleaners, or long strips of paper

The Lesson Takes Shape (20 minutes)

Start by asking students to share their favorite shape and why they like it. A triangle? A rhombus? Will someone go wild and choose a dodecagon? Once everyone's had a chance to voice his or her polygon preferences, dive into some meatier topics:

◇ What is math? What does it do, or what is it about? Why do you do math?

◇ Does math have anything in common with writing? What about creative writing?

After allowing the students to share their ideas on these questions, offer a definition of math, such as the following:

> **Math** is a *language* in which we can give precise definitions of concepts that would otherwise be hard to pin down.

Multidimensional Math (10 minutes)

Your students probably have some idea of what dimensions are. They know that a sheet of paper is two-dimensional, or that the planet Earth is three-dimensional.[1] But what about a collection of dots (or points, mathematically speaking)—does that have a dimension? In the language of math, it's possible to give a definition of dimension. Then, equipped with that definition, we suddenly have the power to make sense of new ideas—we can figure out what dimension that collection of dots has. And we can know what four-dimensional means, or one hundred–dimensional, or even one half–dimensional or infinity-dimensional. (Check out this lesson's "For You to Know" section for some helpful explanations related to this concept, as well as a few other mathematical ideas that come up in the activities.)

When viewed as a language, mathematics becomes a tool both for describing the world and for expanding the scope of our imagination. In this way, it is similar to creative writing. A mathematician, like a writer, uses the familiar as a springboard to conceive of new worlds, and gives those worlds substance by putting them into language.

Zooming In (30 minutes)

In this session, students will learn about a mathematical object known as a **fractal.** Before you explain exactly what a fractal is, it's helpful to show a few pictures to spark imagination and curiosity. (There are a ton of great images to choose from online; just search for "fractal" and select a handful of eye-catching examples, ideally looking for ones that clearly illustrate the definition.) You can also show students a video. Search online for "fractal zoom," which will yield some stunning videos of fractals in motion.

Allow the students a moment to try to articulate what these images have in common, or, more simply: What's so cool about these pictures and videos? After a short discussion, define the term:

> A **fractal** is a shape that contains a copy of itself *inside of itself.* If you zoom in on one part of the shape and keep zooming in, you'll eventually see something that looks just like what you started with.

---

1. If you have time and access, showing a clip from "Homer[3]" in the "Treehouse of Horror" episode of season 7 of *The Simpsons* is a very entertaining way to get the point across.

We've found it's helpful to return to the images while explaining this concept to students, pointing out the smaller copies of the fractal inside the larger shape. There are even examples of fractals in nature, like Romanesco broccoli, where each floret is made up of smaller florets that each look like a whole piece of broccoli. Some simple fractals, like the Sierpinski triangle or the Koch snowflake, are easy to draw on your own. (We highly recommend that you have students try to draw one or the other; there are instructions in the "For You to Know" section of this lesson, so you can teach the students how to draw them if time and interest permit.)

We've come up with a simple method for turning *any* shape into a fractal. It will take students fifteen minutes the first time, give or take. Here's the method:

1. Draw a simple shape.

2. Pick any two points on the perimeter of the shape. Label one of the two points with an *X* and the other point with an *O*.

3. Draw a smaller copy of the shape (about half the size of the original one), with its own *X* and *O* in the same places as on the original shape. But here's the key: draw it so the *X* on the smaller shape is *on top of* the *O* on the original shape. This will probably require you to rotate the smaller shape, but that's good.

4. Draw an even smaller copy of the shape (about half the size of the previous one), with its *O* on top of the *X* on the previous shape.

5. Repeat until the shapes get too small to draw.

It's a bit tricky to explain the procedure in words, but an example should make the idea clear:

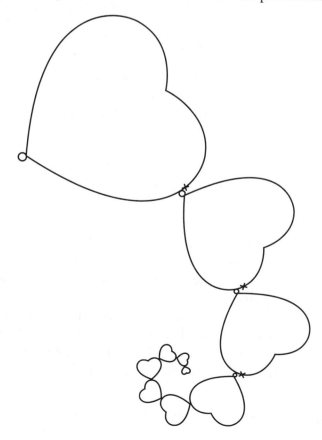

Model the procedure for your students first. Then ask them to try it for themselves with a very simple shape to get the hang of the method. If your students have no problems with triangles, circles, or hearts, see what they can do with smiley faces, airplanes, or trees! Be sure to leave time for sharing.

Putting the Writing in Writing (25 minutes)

So, what do fractals have to do with creative writing? To make the connection, we need to think about the idea of **recursion.**

Recursion, roughly, is when something feeds back into itself. Fractals are recursive, because when you zoom in you wind up back where you started. There is recursion in some works of art, like M. C. Escher's *Drawing Hands,* in which one hand is drawing a picture of another hand, which is drawing a picture of the first hand, and so on. Students may have seen images where someone is holding up a picture of him- or herself holding up a picture of him- or herself (and so on). They may also have experienced this phenomenon themselves by standing in front of a mirror with another mirror in their hands. That's recursion, too. Music can be recursive, like "The Song That Never Ends,"[2] which loops back into the beginning whenever it reaches the end. All recursion is in some way infinite, because when something feeds back into itself, it can always keep looping back and back forever.

In this session, students are each going to write a poem that has the same form as "The Song That Never Ends" (but that is, we hope, less annoying); the end of the poem will loop back into the beginning. Here's an example of a recursive poem that a student wrote in a previous version of this lesson:

Always Dreaming

A person is always dreaming
about a cool dude that
is himself because he
wants to be cool
so he keeps on dreaming
of
A person is always dreaming
about a cool dude that
is himself because he
wants to be cool
so he keeps on dreaming
of

—*Harrison Li, age eleven, Michigan*

Distribute the "Fractal Poetry: A Step-by-Step Guide" handout and challenge students to write their own recursive poem. Tell them not to worry about the length; even if it's only five or six lines long, when it loops back on itself, it will become infinite! The only important thing is that the ending gives a way to go back to the beginning.

There are a couple of ways students can do this. Much like "The Song That Never Ends," their poem can end with an incomplete phrase like "because . . . (This is the song that never ends)" or "I say . . . (My name is Yon Yonson)." A similar option is ending the poem with a question ("What is your favorite color?") and starting it with the answer ("The color blue").

---

2. The Song That Never Ends. *Wikipedia, http://en.wikipedia.org/wiki/The_Song_That_Never_Ends.*

For even more wordplay, have students write an acrostic—a poem where the first letters of each line spell out a word—and have that word start or end the poem. Here's an example:

CAT

Can't stand it anymore
All I want to do is get away from
That . . .

Encourage students to experiment here. Can they come up with new structures for recursive poems? Have them try different things and find something that they like. Again, it doesn't have to be all that long.

Get That Writing in (a) Shape (20 minutes)

With the rest of the handout, you can show your students how to turn their recursive poem into a fractal. First (step 2 on the handout), they pick a shape related to the theme or idea of their poem. This is going to be the basis for a fractal. They'll need to draw it a lot of times, so they shouldn't be afraid to keep it very simple. (Of course, don't discourage ambition.) Students can use the back of the handout or a piece of scratch paper to practice drawing their shape until they've figured out something they like and can draw easily.

For step 3, students should find a way to arrange their poem inside the shape. It can go through the inside or around the edge, in lines or in crazy loops. Here's how a poem might look if it were arranged inside a speech bubble, as imagined by 826michigan student Angela Zhang, age eleven, in her poem "Once Upon a Time":

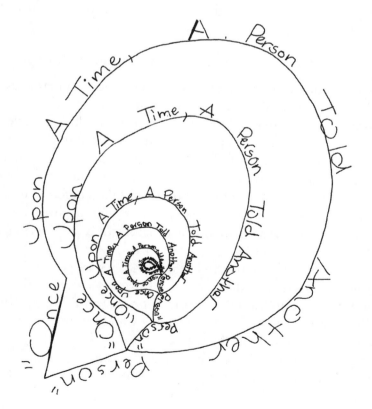

Finally (step 4 on the handout), students make their shape and poetry into a fractal! To do this, they'll use the procedure you practiced together earlier. First, they will mark the spot where the poem begins with an *O* and the spot where the poem ends with an *X*. Then, as before, they will make smaller and smaller copies of the shape, with the *O* of each new copy sitting on top of the *X* of the previous copy. In each shape, they will write their poem, so the end of the poem on one shape flows directly into the beginning of the poem on the next shape.

From Beginning to End and Back Again (15 minutes)

At the very end of the session, ask everyone to share and marvel at the results.

Session 2: Leaving Space and Time

In this session, students will use ideas from mathematics to imagine and write about worlds in which space and time behave strangely. The first half of the session will be devoted to space, leaving the second half to think about time.

Introduction: Playing with Shapes (30 minutes)

For playing with space, the most important mathematical tool is the subject of **geometry.** Once again, start the class by asking students to share their opinions. Ask them:

◇ What is geometry?

◇ If you think geometry has something to do with shapes . . . what's a shape?

These are hard questions with no single right answer, but one combined definition might be as follows:

A **shape** is a collection of points in space, and **geometry** is the study of properties of shapes.

For example, some common properties of shapes that a geometer (a mathematician who studies geometry) might study are length, area, angle, and dimension.

Mathematicians sometimes talk about shapes as abstract things, like "a circle of radius 2" and describe their properties without having any particular circle in front of them. But you can also think about the geometry of the world around you: What is the geometry of our world like?

To get students started, you might note that Earth is a sphere (roughly, but with mountains and valleys). Ask students to think about some of the specifics of this geometry, such as the size of that sphere (very big), and the dimension of the space we move around in (three, but stuck to a two-dimensional ground). They might even notice the fact that Earth is a finite thing, whereas outer space might very well go on and on forever.

There are many stories about characters who live in worlds whose geometry is very different from that of our own. Putting a character in a different sort of space is a way to present him or her with challenges (and sometimes, opportunities) that would not occur on Earth. In Antoine de Saint-Exupéry's *The Little Prince,* for example, we learn of a boy who lives on a very small planet, who worries that a few trees will overtake the entire surface of his world.

Size is actually a minor difference in geometry; there are much bigger ones. To get students thinking about different geometries, give them some modeling clay, and have them make a planet in a fun shape. Let them know that some of the craziest math is in the field of topology—a cousin of geometry. In topology, a circle and a square are the same thing because, roughly speaking, you can stretch and bend one into the shape of the other. However, a doughnut (mathematically called a torus) is not the same as a ball; you would have to squish the hole in the middle of the doughnut, and that's not allowed. Topologically you can bend and stretch one shape into another, but you're not allowed to close holes or cut out new ones. (Remember from the first session that definitions and rules are important!) Ask your students if they can stretch their shape into a ball—if so, topologically it's the same as the planet Earth. Challenge your students to create a shape that's topologically different from a ball, and then as many topologically different shapes as they can!

Edwin Abbott Abbott's *Flatland* offers another classic example of interesting geometry; this late-nineteenth-century novella describes a two-dimensional world where the inhabitants are all objects like lines and triangles and squares. (See "Handy Lesson Links" in the appendix for a link to the text.) Among the many difficulties faced by these two-dimensional inhabitants is the challenge of recognizing each other from afar, because any two-dimensional object looks just like a line segment when viewed head-on.

After they wrestle with that for a bit, bring up Vi Hart's *Wind and Mr. Ug*.[3] Ask your students what's going on! (The quick answer is that Wind *is* Mr. Ug! Wind is on a Möbius strip, a special shape that has only one side.) It's fine if they don't understand; let their curiosity and wonder linger. If they do understand that they're seeing a Möbius strip, you can let them know that there's another crazy shape with only one side, the Klein bottle. It can only exist in four dimensions, and its inside is also its outside! (For more on the Klein bottle, see "Handy Lesson Links.")

We've discussed a number of examples of weird geometry in fiction, but there's another great source of interesting geometries: video games. The Mario games have some awesome geometry; *Super Mario Bros.* and many of its sequels are great two-dimensional fun, and *Super Mario Galaxy* and *Super Mario 3D World* have amazing three-dimensional mechanics. (*Super Paper Mario* actually requires switching between 2-D and 3-D views of the world; if you can show a video of this—see "Handy Lesson Links"—it's a really great example of how geometry and perspective are connected.) The game *Portal* shows you what might happen if jumping through one point in space suddenly put you at a different point somewhere entirely different. Ask students if they can think of other examples of video games (or examples from fiction that were missed earlier) in which geometry works differently from the way it does in our world.

Speaking of video games, here's a fun fact students may not have known: Pac-Man actually lives on a cylinder rather than a square. To see why, remember that when Pac-Man moves off the left side of the screen, he reappears on the right side, and vice versa. This suggests that his world operates as though its left side and its right side were glued together. A square with its left and right sides glued together, though, is nothing but a cylinder. The same kind of reasoning explains the shape of *Asteroids*, an arcade game that takes place on a doughnut. In that game, moving off the left side of the screen makes you reappear on the right side, but *also*, moving off the top of the screen makes

---

3. "Mobius story: Wind and Mr. Ug," *https://www.khanacademy.org/math/recreational-math/vi-hart /mobius-strips/v/m-bius-story-wind-and-mr-ug*.

you reappear at the bottom. So the world of *Asteroids* is a square with its left and right sides glued together and its top and bottom glued together. Try that for yourself (with a very flexible piece of paper or a piece of tinfoil) and you'll see that you get a doughnut-shaped world.

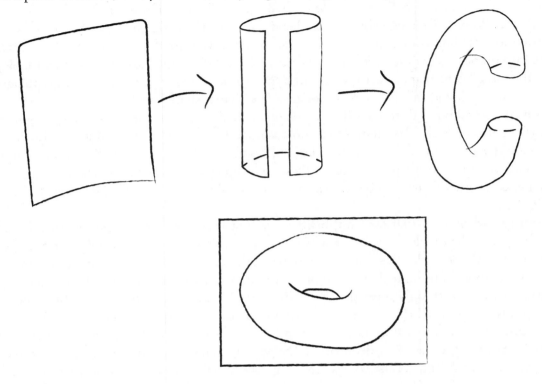

Shaping the World (20 minutes)

With this perspective in mind, it's time to start writing. Today, students are going to generate an idea for a story that takes place in a world with different geometry from that of our own. Geometry, in their stories, should be more than just a setting; it should be a source of conflict, presenting obstacles or opportunities to the characters that they wouldn't encounter in our world. (If it helps them think about geometry, let students manipulate modeling clay and foil.)

To come up with ideas, it can be helpful to think more about the aspects of our own world that we take for granted.

◇ How does the shape of the planet Earth affect how we live? (See "Handy Lesson Links" for some ideas!)

◇ What about its size?

As a group, you can try to answer these questions, and also to imagine how you might live if Earth's shape or size (or dimension, or some other property) were different. You may also want to keep in mind that the same world can look drastically different depending on your point of view:

◇ How might a shape look different from the perspective of someone living on that shape, as opposed to someone looking on from the outside? In Abbott's *Flatland,* for example, the inhabitants see each other as line segments, but an outsider looking on from above sees full shapes. If you showed students *Super Paper Mario* in action, it helps a lot here!

Even the planet Earth demonstrates this idea of perspective; it took a long time for humans to realize they were living on a sphere, because a sphere this big looks just like a flat surface to a person walking around on it.

Equipped with these ideas to get them started, students should fill out the first part of the "Leaving Space and Time" handout to help them start thinking of a premise for a story that takes place in a world unlike ours.

Transitioning to Time (15 minutes)

Now's when things get *really* interesting. So far, we have been thinking about the space we live in as a three-dimensional space. It has length, width, and height. But what about time? Albert Einstein taught us that time is really just another dimension, the fourth dimension, of the space in which we live. Time works a little differently from other dimensions, though. We cannot move freely in time like we can along other dimensions, but instead our consciousness experiences time as always moving in the same direction at the same pace. Even more weirdly, time is *relative:* if you and I are moving at different speeds, time will pass differently for me than it does for you. Although you'd need much more time to explain how this works in detail, for interested students—and instructors!—the Wikipedia page on the theory of relativity is very good (see "Handy Lesson Links").

Just like they did with three-dimensional space, students can imagine time working differently than in the linear fashion we're used to. Our favorite examples come from a book of short stories by physicist Alan Lightman called *Einstein's Dreams*. In one story, called "14 May, 1905," there is a center at which time stands still. As one approaches this center, time slows down. Characters wishing to stretch out a particular emotional moment move toward the center. However, spending time near the center means that one ages much more slowly than others farther away. This story, and perhaps several others from *Einstein's Dreams,* are worth reading if you have the time. Ask the class, "Can you think of other examples of stories that play with time?"

If students struggle to come up with examples, a whole host of stories they probably know involve time travel. Here are a few examples we like:

◇ *Back to the Future*

◇ Time Turners in the Harry Potter series

◇ *The Time Machine,* by H.G. Wells

◇ *A Wrinkle in Time,* by Madeleine L'Engle

◇ *Groundhog Day*

Another example a lot of students will know is the ability of the character Titan Kronos to manipulate time in Rick Riordan's *Percy Jackson and the Olympians* series. Kronos can slow down time to help him defeat his enemies. Being on the receiving end of this is very confusing. If you were slowed down by Kronos's powers, would you feel like you were moving in slow motion or like things around you were moving unnaturally quickly? Have your students ever been in situations where they felt like time was slowing down or speeding up, for themselves or for the world around them? For example, have any students felt like they suddenly slowed down when they passed a train or bus travelling in the same direction going almost the same speed as they were? What other examples can they think of?

Time permitting, if your students are really into video games, you can bring up examples of games with different time rules. Older examples include *Chrono Trigger* and Zelda games like *Ocarina of Time* and *Majora's Mask*; recent indie games include *Braid* and *Super Time Force.* (Interestingly, among other time mechanics, *Braid* has location-based time-slowing mechanics similar to those of "14 May, 1905.") Ask your students if they're familiar with any video games in which time plays a role. What do these time powers allow you to do? What problems do they cause, and what are their limitations?

Time to Brainstorm (20 minutes)

Now we are ready to experiment with changing the rules of the fourth dimension of our world. The second part of the "Leaving Space and Time" handout guides students to think about time in new ways, inspiring a premise for a story.

If it helps students brainstorm, have them use a piece of string, a pipe cleaner, or a long strip of paper to create a simple time line. Then have them twist the string or paper around, maybe tangling things up in a knot or two. How would the time line be affected if different events collided?

Time and Space to Write and Reflect (35 minutes)

Now, ask students to pick one or both of the two ideas generated earlier on their handout, about a different kind of space or time, and flesh out as much of a story as possible, using the third part of the handout. Try to save enough time—five or ten minutes—to allow a few of your students to share some of their work aloud.

To end, after students have shared, conclude the lesson by revisiting the question with which the lesson began, What is math? Ask students whether their answer to this question changed over the course of the two sessions.

We think math is awesome. Students often think of math as a collection of facts and methods for solving math problems. Formulas are extremely important for you to be able to understand and use, but there's so much more to math! The formulas and methods students learn in class have not always been known by human beings. They are the fruits of countless hours of labor by people trying to figure out how the world works, in many cases thousands of years ago. These people imagined the world in tons of different ways until they stumbled on the right rules to describe it (and many other worlds besides). And mathematicians are still learning more all the time!

By studying math, we can learn to think logically about the world, to use reason and imagination to understand something in a completely original way. How cool is that?

FOR YOU TO KNOW (AND YOUR STUDENTS TO DISCOVER)

Here is some more information on a few of the mathematical ideas that arise in the lesson, in case you'd like to know more before discussing them with students.

Dimension

Dimension, roughly, refers to the number of degrees of freedom one has when moving about a geometric object. For example, a flat plane is two-dimensional because motion on it can occur in two basic directions: horizontally or vertically. The space we live in, in contrast, is three-dimensional because motion can occur forward and backward, left and right, or up and down. A four-dimensional universe would be one in which movement was possible in *four* different directions, which, of course, is nearly impossible to visualize.

(continued)

It is slightly more difficult to understand the dimension of a geometric object that isn't as basic as the two- or three-dimensional spaces we're familiar with, but the trick is to imagine the perspective of a tiny person living on the object. When viewed up close in this way, almost any shape you can think of looks very simple. The surface of a sphere, for instance, is a two-dimensional object. To see why this is the case, pretend you are a tiny person living on the sphere; that shouldn't be hard, because we live on a very big sphere ourselves: Earth. From your point of view on the sphere, it looks just like a flat plane, and this is why we consider the sphere to be two-dimensional. For another example, a squiggly line is one-dimensional, because it looks just like a regular old straight line from the perspective of a really small person standing on it.

Using these ideas, one can make sense of what a four-dimensional or five-dimensional or hundred-dimensional object might look like, but what would it mean to say the dimension of a shape is something weird like $\frac{3}{2}$? Fractals have fractional dimension. To see why, we'll need to think of dimension a bit differently.

Dimension dictates how the size of a shape changes when its side length doubles. Consider, on the one hand, the two-dimensional square. If the square has side length 1, its area is 1, whereas if it has side length 2, its area is 4. That is, doubling the side length yields a square that is four times the size of the original one. Cubes, on the other hand, are three-dimensional, and doubling the side length of a cube gives a new cube that's eight times larger. If you could visualize the four-dimensional analogue of a cube (which is called a **tesseract**), you'd see that when its side length is doubled, the resulting object is sixteen times the size of what you started with. To summarize in somewhat more mathematical terms: if doubling the side length of an object yields an object **2^d** times as large, then that object has dimension *d*.

To see why fractals have fractional dimensions, let's play with a relatively simple one: the Sierpinski triangle (see the first figure in this section). First, draw a triangle of side length 1 and subdivide it into a Sierpinski triangle by the procedure described in the "Fractals" section that follows. Then, do the same, but starting with a triangle with side length 2:

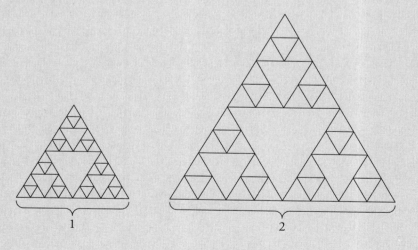

(*continued*)

The larger Sierpinski triangle contains three copies of the smaller one. In other words, doubling the side length gives an object three times the size of the original.

This is bizarre, because we would expect the size to increase by a power of 2; remember, if the size increases by a factor of 2^d, then the dimension is d. But 3 *is* a power of 2, it's just a really weird one: you can check on a calculator that $2^{1.58} \approx 3$. The conclusion, then, is that the dimension of the Sierpinski triangle is approximately 1.58.

Fractals

Two examples of fractals that are easy to draw are the Sierpinski triangle and the Koch snowflake. They both have good Wikipedia pages (see "Handy Lesson Links"), so you can go there to get a better idea of what they look like.

To draw a Sierpinski triangle, start with a triangle of any size. Subdivide it into a stack of three triangles like so:

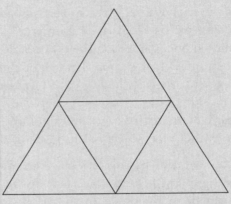

Then, take each of the three triangles in the stack and subdivide them in the same way:

Repeat with each of the nine triangles that result, and so on.

(continued)

The Koch snowflake also starts with a triangle. In the middle of each of its edges, draw a smaller triangle jutting out:

Then draw an even smaller triangle jutting out of each edge of the resulting shape:

Repeat forever. Which brings us to . . .

Recursion

As mentioned in the lesson, recursion occurs when something feeds back into itself. An example would be two identical mirrors positioned exactly across from each other, reflecting each other into infinity. Another example would be the box of cocoa that depicts a model holding the same box of cocoa, and so on, and so on. Fractals are also recursive; when you zoom in, you're led back where you started.

(continued)

Topology

We'll say it: topology is crazy (cool), if a little mind blowing. Topology is similar to geometry, only geometry looks at rigid things (angles, lengths, area, volume, and so on), whereas topology looks at things that can be stretched, twisted, bent, and squeezed—but not torn.

For an example, think of a coffee cup and a doughnut. If you make the cup's handle fatter and its bottom thicker, eventually it would look like a doughnut. And although it would be different in some ways, in others, it would be the same—for instance, it would still have a path, or a "tour," around the hole in the middle.

On a sphere, any tour that returns to its starting point can be retraced with shorter and shorter ones, until it shrinks to a point. But on the cup/doughnut, the tour around the hole is "noncontractible"—if you try to shorten it, you'll get stuck at some point, when it goes around the hole as tightly as possible.

You can also think of a tour as a closed loop; so a tour on a sphere divides it into a section inside the tour, and a section outside the tour (although you're free to decide which is which!). But the tour around the hole or handle of the cup/doughnut doesn't divide the surface into two parts—you can get from one side to the other without crossing it.

These sorts of things are topological properties: they stay the same as long as we don't cut the object, or punch new holes, or fill an existing hole in all the way.[4]

One of the most important results in recent mathematical history in regard to topology was Grigori Perelman's proof of a nearly century-old problem—the Poincaré conjecture, which is about what three-dimensional shapes are the same as other three-dimensional shapes. The proof involved something called a "Ricci flow with surgery."

Fun facts aside, it'll be more helpful for you to know a couple of cool world shapes used in science fiction. One of them, which we just discussed, is the torus (doughnut)—it features prominently in Larry Niven's *Ringworld* and in the *Halo* series of video games. The other is the Dyson sphere—essentially, the inside of a hollow surface surrounding a star—which was featured perhaps most prominently in an episode of *Star Trek: The Next Generation*.

The torus is definitely not the same topological shape as our world, remember, because there are two tours that cannot be shrunk to a point, and because there are tours that don't divide the torus in two. However, the inside of a sphere is the exact same thing, topologically, as the outside—mathematicians have found ways to turn spheres inside out.

---

4. Thanks to Cristopher Moore, a professor at Santa Fe Institute in Santa Fe, New Mexico, for the preceding explanation of topology.

(*continued*)

Time Travel and Paradoxes

Some people hypothesize that time travel is impossible because we haven't seen any evidence of it. Now, absence of evidence is not evidence of absence, but time travel does have its problems. A lot of these come down to paradoxes—apparent contradictions. Many of these paradoxes follow a particular pattern:

1. Time travel into the past.

2. Change things in the past.

3. Prevent yourself from being born.

4. Prevent step 1 from happening (because if you're not born, you can't time travel into the past).

Rather grimly, one of the canonical examples of a time travel paradox is the grandfather paradox, where step 2 in the preceding pattern involves killing your grandfather. You absolutely don't need to share this with your students. A friendlier example comes from *Back to the Future*, in which Marty McFly accidentally prevents his mother from falling in love with his father, and he needs to fix the situation to ensure he'll be born.

Scientists and the like have hypothesized many ways to resolve these paradoxes, including parallel universes.

Time Travel and Relativity

Think about yourself standing, and think about what it's like for someone to zoom past you on a bike. That person seems fast. But if you're biking alongside the other person, she suddenly doesn't seem so fast, right?

So speed is relative, and it is for everything in the universe except one thing: light (generally speaking—this also includes other kinds of electromagnetic radiation). So, no matter how fast you go, light always goes at the ultimate speed, about 186,000 miles *per second*.

The consequences of speed's relativity are really, really cool. When you work out the math, you find that the faster you go, the slower time goes for you relative to anyone else who isn't moving very fast. The thing is, you have to be going very, very fast for time to slow down a lot. So far, experiments we've done have only been able to have fast clocks run fractions of a second slower than stationary clocks.

What does this mean for time travel? Some think that we can get time to slow down so much that it goes backward—the problem is, it means we have to figure out how to go faster than light.

FRACTAL POETRY: A STEP-BY-STEP GUIDE

1. Write a poem whose last line loops back into its first line, so that it can be repeated over and over again.

   ▷ Your poem does not need to be long; five to ten lines is fine.

   ▷ Each repetition can be the same, or repetitions can all be slightly different.

2. Pick a simple shape related to the theme or idea of your poem. Draw it on the back of this sheet.

3. Think of a way to arrange your poem within that shape, and make a draft on the back of this sheet.

   ▷ Your poem should start and end on the edge of the shape. Mark the place where the poem starts with an *X* and the place where it ends with an *O*.

   ▷ You can draw the shape and place the words inside of it, or have the words themselves form the shape.

4. Create a fractal.

   ▷ Use scratch paper first.

   ▷ To make a fractal, take a smaller copy of your shape, and connect the *X* on the smaller shape to the *O* on the larger shape. Then repeat.

   ▷ Once you have an arrangement you like, create your final fractal poem!

LEAVING SPACE AND TIME

Thinking about space and time in new ways can inspire great stories. Use another sheet of paper for your answers as needed.

Part 1: Bending the Rules of Geometry

1. Pick a shape or a way of gluing a shape that interests you. Describe or draw it here.

2. How would life be different if this shape were your world?

- What would be good about it?

- What would be bad about it?

- Who would be most affected by it?

Part 2: Time for Time

3. Pick a twist in time that interests you. Describe it here.

4. How would life be different if time worked this way in your world?

- What would be good about it?

- What would be bad about it?

- What types of people would be most affected by it?

Part 3: Story Time

Pick whichever of the two preceding ideas interests you most. Or combine both ideas!

5. Develop your characters.

- Pick one or two people in your world, and describe them in more detail (personalities, jobs, names, where they live, hobbies, and so on).

6. Outline the plot of your story.

- How do the changes you made to space and/or time in your world introduce conflict into your characters' lives?

- How do the characters react to the conflict?

- How can you resolve that conflict?

STEM@HOME: BENDING THE NUMBER LINE

Can you imagine a world where the rules of math as you learned them don't apply? What if 2 plus 2 did not equal 4?

Can you believe that there is an entire branch of math, called **modular arithmetic,** that describes a completely different way (from the way you learn in school) of adding and subtracting—and that when you do modular arithmetic, you often get completely different answers? (What a great way to confuse your brother or sister.) In some instances of modular arithmetic, 2 plus 2 does not equal 4! We could have 2 + 2 = 1, or even 2 + 2 = 0!

Let's Get Started!

Before we continue, consider the number line. If you were to figure out 2 + 2 on the number line, you would start with the number 2 and move two spaces to the right—this would take you to 4, so 2 + 2 = 4. What would happen, though, if the number line weren't a line? We'll explore exactly this scenario.

To do modular arithmetic, you must first pick a number (the fancy term for this number is the **modulus**). The example that follows shows you how 2 plus 2 might not equal 4. We'll pick the number 3 as the modulus.

1. Draw a circle.

2. Draw three evenly spaced notches on the circle (the modulus you pick determines the number of notches you draw on the circle). Label the notches 0, 1, and 2, Like so:

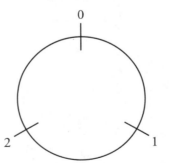

3. Counting and adding in modular arithmetic are the same thing as moving around the circle. Counting upward starting at 0, we'd have 0, 1, 2, 0, 1, 2, and so on.

4. Start at 2.

5. Now add 2 by moving from 2 to 0 to 1.

6. We added 2 to 2 and got 1 instead of 4!

(continued)

Copyright © 2015 by 826 National

STEM@HOME: BENDING THE NUMBER LINE (continued)

There actually is no 4 in this number system! A mathematician might say that 1 = 4 (mod 3). Can you figure out why?

You can also do modular subtraction. What do you think 1 − 2 might be in our example?

What other numbers would you like to try?

To think about how this works, imagine the number line. If we make it into a loop, and have the 3 meet the 0, we get the circle we just created!

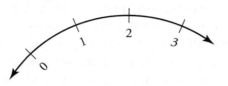

As you might guess, the way that you add and subtract clock times is like modular arithmetic, using the numbers 60 (for minutes and seconds) and 12 (for hours) instead of 3. There are several other examples of ways to replace the rules of math to go to strange, exotic places. For instance:

▶ Some types of arithmetic have addition but no multiplication, or multiplication but no division.

▶ In the regular arithmetic you know, A plus B always equals B plus A; this (the commutative property) is not true in other kinds of arithmetic.

▶ There are kinds of geometry with no straight lines!

STEM@HOME: MATH, LOGICALLY

You may remember learning that division by the number 0 is undefined—that's because there is no answer that fits the rules of arithmetic. (A quick refresher: Division is the inverse, or opposite, of multiplication. $10 \div 2 = 5$ because $5 \times 2 = 10$. You can't multiply any number by 0 to make 10, so the answer to the corresponding division problem is undefined.) This principle also explains why the square root of 4 is +2, even though $(-2)^2$ is also 4; mathematicians need standard rules and definitions.

Mathematicians are often very interested in finding where the rules break, or in coming up with new sets of rules that also work. (Modular arithmetic, from the "Bending the Number Line" STEM@Home sheet, is one.) Often, seeing where the rules break leads to new rules. The square root of 9 is 3, but –9 doesn't have a square root in the real numbers most of us use. And so the real numbers were extended to include the imaginary and complex numbers, where –9 does have a square root: 3i.

To see where rules break, mathematicians start with basic rules, use logic to find more and more new rules, and see if any of those rules **contradict** each other. We won't get into mathematical logic and finding contradictions here; what we will do is explore contradiction in the rules of imaginary worlds.

What Is Logic?

Logic can be defined informally as a way of reasoning that makes sense. Here, we'll explore logical reasoning and illogical reasoning through a classic example: syllogisms.

A **syllogism** is a way of combining two statements that are true to create a third statement that is also true. For example:

All humans must breathe to live.

You are a human.

Therefore, you must breathe to live.

Makes sense, right? This is definitely logical. But sometimes people don't combine statements correctly. Think about this example:

All humans must breathe to live.

You must breathe to live.

Therefore, you are a human.

This time, the third statement is not true! You might actually be an alien, a puppy, or a redwood tree, as they all have to breathe, too.

(*continued*)

STEM@HOME: MATH, LOGICALLY (continued)

People make lots of logical mistakes, unfortunately. Being logical and correct in your thinking is a huge skill in the STEM fields, but also in writing, and in life in general. Here's one last example.

The president is an outstanding person.

Outstanding people are usually right.

Therefore, the president is always right.

Again, untrue! In logic, it's important to differentiate between things being never true, sometimes true, or always true. This particular example relates to something called an ad hominem argument, whereby someone makes an argument for or against the person claiming something, instead of arguing the logic of the claim itself. Even if the president is an outstanding person, and outstanding people are usually right, we should look at what the president says, logically, and not assume things are okay because the president says so!

Logic and Stories

Consider this scenario: You rub an old-fashioned oil lamp, and a genie comes out. The genie says, "I will grant you three wishes and only three wishes. You can wish for anything you want." There's actually a contradiction here! If you wish for more wishes, you can get more wishes than the genie says you get. Now, if the genie instead says, "I will grant you three wishes and only three wishes. You can wish for anything you want, except things that will get you more wishes," there would be no contradiction. A lot of fiction, especially that involving magic or time travel, has rules. Why are rules important in these stories?

Let's have some fun with this. Your goal is to imagine a world like our own, but with one of the fundamental rules—like gravity—changed. What other rules would have to change so that the world would make sense? (In the case of a change to gravity, what new rules would there need to be so that we wouldn't all fly off into space?)

Alternately, you can think of a wildly imaginary world—certainly not limited to a world where magic or time travel exists. Create a bunch of rules for this world, and see if you can find any contradictions! (Your friends and family can help you here.) If there are contradictions, how would you add new rules or change old rules to get rid of them?

I've written books about zombies, but I'm not really a horror guy. I like questions too much. You tell me zombies want to eat people, I say, "Why?" You tell me zombies are the dead risen from the grave, I say, "How?" You tell me zombies can only be killed by a blow to the head (or a chop to the head if you happen to have a katana handy), and I say . . . well, that time I say, "Makes sense!" Because it does, kinda sorta. But lots more about zombies doesn't. Why do only people become zombies? Why aren't there zombie cats and dogs and skunks and squirrels? Why do zombies want to eat brains if they don't need food to stay "alive"? And what happens to all those brains after the zombies eat them? (I actually answered that question in one of my novels. It wasn't a pretty picture.) Some horror fans would probably say that asking questions spoils the fun. I couldn't disagree more. Asking questions *is* the fun. Which is why I love science. Sure, it doesn't always mean studying stuff as cool as zombies. But getting satisfying answers to "Why?" and "How?" always feels cool to me.

Steve Hockensmith

Steve Hockensmith is the best-selling author of Pride and Prejudice and Zombies: Dawn of the Dreadfuls *and other novels. His new mystery series for middle-grade readers, cowritten with educator and professional mad scientist "Science Bob" Pflugfelder, was recently launched with the books* Nick and Tesla's High-Voltage Danger Lab *and* Nick and Tesla's Robot Army Rampage.

REWRITING THE ZOMBIE APOCALYPSE

BASED ON THE ORIGINAL WORKSHOP BY
JULIUS DIAZ PANORIÑGAN

4 SESSIONS, 2 HOURS EACH
STEM DISCIPLINES: *Life sciences, engineering, technology, statistics and probability*
WRITING ACTIVITIES: *Technical writing, narrative writing, creative writing*

IN THIS LESSON SERIES, STUDENTS EXPLORE multiple STEM disciplines, and discover the importance of scientific modeling across various fields, all in the context of an upcoming zombie apocalypse. This is a long workshop—four sessions—but easy to do; for the most part, it doesn't require a lot of prep or materials, and you can do as many or as few sessions as you like. The handy-dandy slides walk you through every zombie step. It's also incredibly fun and active, great for students who need to move.

Session 1 focuses on science: after playing a variant of tag (the classic school yard game), students will understand scientific concepts related to the spread of disease. The middle sessions explore engineering (building and testing structures and vehicles for zombie protection and evasion) and math (employing statistics and probability to explore projected outcomes for zombie survivability). The last session focuses on technology as a tool, not a toy; students will use a simple computer simulation to investigate a big problem (zombies, of course). All along the way, students will write not only notes detailing their discoveries but also an ongoing narrative recording their fight against the undead.

MATERIALS

SESSION 1

☐ Slides to guide discussion (See the thumbnails; slides are also available for download at *www.wiley.com /go/826stem.*)

☐ Overhead projector or computer and digital projector to show slides (optional)

☐ Copies of the "Zombie-Fighting Skills" handout (included with other handouts at the end of this lesson)

☐ Dot stickers (1 sheet per student)

SESSION 2

Note: Amounts given are per station; you may need more.

(continued)

- Overhead projector or computer and digital projector to show slides (optional)
- 200 small craft sticks
- 20 large craft sticks
- A large plastic garbage bag
- Cloth (from old T-shirts or cheap bedsheets)
- String
- Bubble Wrap, cut into small squares
- Aluminum foil
- Rubber bands
- Fishing wire
- Paper clips
- Duct tape
- Bricks
- Low-temperature glue gun (be sure to supervise use!)
- Eggs (2 dozen should allow extra in case of accidents)
- Tables or chairs
- A foam cooler
- Heavy things: dumbbells; bricks; full bottles; or bags of rice, flour, or sugar
- Backpacks (If you have several, this will help things move faster.)
- A bathroom scale
- Copies of the "Zombie Apocalypse Building Supplies" handout
- Copies of the "Zombie Apocalypse Survival Supplies" handout

(continued)

Zombies are fun. Zombies can also be educational. No surprise there; after all, their favorite food is braaaaaaains.

This lesson was inspired in part by an academic paper about stopping a zombie outbreak (see "Handy Lesson Links" in the appendix) and a simulation of a zombie outbreak. Zombieism, especially in the modern sense, has a lot of parallels with real disease outbreaks, and we realized we could use it as a model for exploring epidemics. We came up with other zombie-related models, and here we are. (Before reading any further, check out "Models" in the Science-O-Pedia.)

In this first session, we focus on the first zombie model—zombieism as infectious disease. By playing a fun variant on tag and mixing up the rules (in this case, testing different disease-control measures), students learn a lot about how infectious disease spreads in real life, and how to prevent that. To make things easier, we've prepared slides to guide the lesson.

Session 1: The Day the Zombies Came

It Was Just a Normal Day . . . (15 minutes)

It's a clichéd opener, but here we're going to have fun with it. Students should write about all the normal things they (and their family and friends) have done this week, in response to the following prompt:

> What is a normal week like for you? Who are the people you come in contact with? What are the things you usually do? Where are the places you go, and when and how often do you go?

Let's Get to Know Each Other! (15 minutes)

Even if your students do know each other, this is an opportunity for them to get to know each other better. But really, the reason to do it is that it models the spread of disease.

Distribute the "Zombie-Fighting Skills" handout, and tell the class that their goal is to talk with everyone in the room, asking each classmate about his or her best zombie survival skill (foraging, running, grappling, MacGyvering, and so on). Everyone should write down these names (in the order in which they meet people), and each classmate's skill.

Rewriting the Zombie Apocalypse

The Day the Zombies Came

It Was Just a Normal Day...

What is a normal week like for you?
Who are the people you come in contact with?
What are the things you usually do?
Where are the places you go, and when/how often do you go?

Zombie-Fighting Skills

What's your best zombie survival skill?

What Do We Know About Disease?

Can you catch a cold from being cold?

Infection Tag!

- Everyone will start with sheets of stickers.
- Some of us will start with stickers on our arms. These people are sick.
- Walk around the room.
- If you are sick, and you meet someone who isn't, put a sticker on their arm! They are now sick.
- We'll keep going, and we'll see how long it takes to get the whole room sick.
- NO RUNNING!

Infection Tag with Prevention

This is the same as disease tag, except
- You don't always automatically get sick when you meet an infected person.
- When a sick person meets a healthy person, they play rock-paper-scissors.
- If the healthy person loses, stick a sticker on them! They are now sick.

Infection Tag with Quarantine

This is the same as disease tag, except
- If you're sick, try and hide it! You should still put stickers on other people's arms. Be sneaky!
- There is a quarantine zone. If we think someone might be sick, we can bring them there to stop the spread of disease. Be careful—they might infect you!
- If someone brings you to the quarantine zone, stay there. Infect people as normal if you're sick.

Infection Tag with Immunity

This is the same as infection tag, except
- If you have an immunity sticker, you're safe! You can remove all the disease stickers placed on you.

Best Ways for Stopping Disease?

Now that we've experimented with quarantine and immunization, what do you think the best way for stopping disease spread is? Why might people like or not like these methods?

ZOMBIE TAG!!!

- Some of us will start as zombies.
- Walk around the room.
- If a zombie meets a regular person, that person becomes a zombie!
- STILL NO RUNNING!

Zombie Tag with Resistance

This is the same as Zombie Tag, except
- Non-infected humans can "fight" back by playing rock-paper-scissors.
- If the human wins, the zombie is stunned. The zombie must count to 20 before moving again.
- If the zombie wins, the human dies. The human counts to 20, then becomes a zombie.
- If there's a tie, the human is infected! The zombie is stunned (count to 20). The human also counts to 20, then becomes a zombie.

Zombie Tag with Immunity

This is the same as Zombie Tag with Resistance, plus the following "fight" rules if the human is immune.
- If the human wins, the zombie is stunned. The zombie must count to 20 before moving again.
- If the zombie wins, the human dies, but doesn't turn into a zombie.
- If there's a tie, the zombie is stunned, but the human gets away and stays healthy.

Zombie Tag with Quarantine

This is the same as Zombie Tag with Resistance, plus the following rules:
- There is a quarantine zone.
- If someone is a zombie, or you think they're turning into a zombie, two people can team up and bring them to the quarantine zone.
- If you're bringing a zombie to quarantine, or someone turns into a zombie on the way, "fight" with rock-paper-scissors. If the zombie wins, the human counts to 20 before becoming a zombie.

The Day the Zombies Came

When did you first hear rumors about the zombies coming? Did you believe them? Were those rumors accurate (did some of the facts change)?
And when did you first encounter a zombie? How did you survive?

The Post-Zombie Normal

Think about the everyday activities you wrote about at the beginning of today's workshop session. When the zombies come, can you still do those things? How might your life have to change?

Halfway into this activity, or once someone has talked with everyone, shut it down, and introduce the surprise: there has been an infection! Move everyone to one side of the room. You can declare yourself patient zero, or select a student at random. (True randomness is best; if necessary, shut your eyes and point!) Patient zero will move to the other side of the room. Ask patient zero who the first three people he or she met with are. Those people have been infected! They should move across the room. They should look at their list for the person who infected them (patient zero); the next three people after patient zero have been infected as well!

If you can, draw a bubble map on the board, like the one that follows, detailing the spread of disease. In any case, the class will discover that almost everyone, if not everyone, has been infected. *D'oh.*

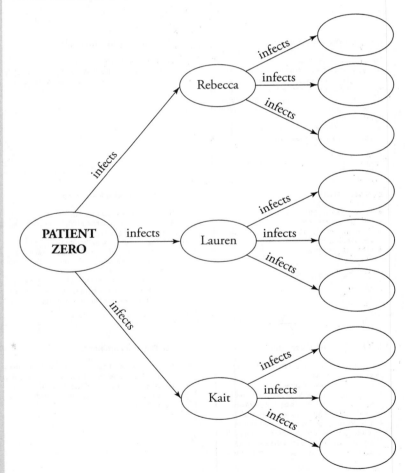

What Do We Know About Disease? (15 minutes)

Ask your students what they know about disease. What is disease, and how do people get a disease? (You can use this opportunity to debunk some common misconceptions.) What does disease have to do with the first activity?

HOW WE DO (AND DON'T) GET SICK Despite all we know about illness, there are still a lot of misconceptions about when, why, and how we get sick. Here are some basic facts:

- There are essentially two broad categories of diseases: infectious and noninfectious diseases. Infectious diseases are the ones you can catch from someone else.

- Many, many infectious diseases are transmitted by what is called the fecal-oral route (poop-related). This generally means that an infected individual went to the bathroom and didn't wash his hands. He touched something (or many things), leaving an invisible trail of infectious particles (bacteria or viruses), which stuck to someone else's fingers when she touched the same surface. When this uninfected person ate her sandwich or picked her nose or wiped her eyes, she transferred the agent into her body. A short time later (usually a couple of days), this second person begins to feel sick.

- Hands are a big culprit in spreading diseases. Whether through contact with feces or a cough or a sneeze, unwashed hands leave millions of microbes lying around for others to pick up.

- Being cold doesn't cause you to get sick; you have to be exposed to an infectious agent, such as a virus (though interestingly, some people have allergic reactions to cold).

- If your immune system is compromised, you can be more susceptible to infection. Your immune system can be weakened if you don't get enough sleep. In addition, certain diseases target and weaken the immune system, and drugs like the chemotherapy agents that are used to treat cancer can also weaken the immune system.

After some good points, switch up the discussion: What do we know about zombies? How do people become zombies? Ideally someone will say that people become zombies after being bitten by a zombie. Sounds a lot like disease spread, right? A lot of modern writers of zombie fiction actually have written about zombieism as a rabies-like disease, spread by a virus or a fungus or something similar.

They're kinda the same, aren't they? And how are they different? Compare and contrast disease and zombieism on the board for a bit, then let students know that they'll explore both through a game—namely, tag.

Infection Tag and Zombie Tag (40 minutes)

This section can vary in length; if it runs short, you can do some optional activities to explore these ideas even further. If it goes long, you can cut a little of the time from the writing prompt.

For all tag variants, have a strict no-running rule. Also, let students know that the goal isn't to win; it's to learn about disease. It is possible to cheat here, but it doesn't help anyone.

Have your students play infection tag for about ten minutes. Start them off with the simplest version: Every student should have a sheet of stickers. Select three to five students to be the initial infected (you can choose randomly, or ask for volunteers—students will happily do this), and have them try to stick stickers on their classmates. Students should walk about randomly, and not as if the infected are attempting to infect others, or as if the uninfected are trying not to get sick—the goal is to simulate random human interaction. (Students will have both of these options later.) When someone has a sticker attached to him or her, he or she becomes infected, and should start sticking stickers on people as well (note that a person can be infected more than once by our sticker disease, as with diseases in real life). See how long it takes for the whole room to be infected.

After the first round, ask students how people might prevent disease spread. Come up with a way to vary the rules of the game to test this. Here are a few examples:

◇ Preventative barrier measures (for example, filtration masks, hand sanitizer): These aren't perfect, but they do work sometimes. Every time students meet, they should play rock-paper-scissors. The uninfected student becomes infected only if he or she loses.

◇ Immunization: Designate a special immunity sticker. If a student has one, he or she can't be infected or infect others! Play this round several times, with varying numbers of students starting with immunity stickers. How does varying the immunization rate affect how far and how fast the disease spreads?

◇ Isolation (for example, staying home, staying in the hospital): There are a few options here. In this scenario, those who are infected can try to stay away from others, or vice versa. Also, the infected can try to hide their infection—sometimes, in real life, people do exactly this, and other times, they don't know they're infected. Students may choose to gather in a "safe" area, and in this scenario may see the disastrous effect of one undetermined contagious individual rapidly infecting a crowded population.

As the game proceeds, you can document the results on the board or chart paper via a T-chart. Have one side list the infection tag scenario (which will vary, normal infection tag, infection tag with immunization, and so on) and the other list the time required to infect the whole room.

After a few rounds of infection tag, help your students reflect for five to ten minutes on what they've learned about the spread of disease, perhaps in small groups and/or in writing, using this prompt:

> Now that we've experimented with quarantine and immunization, what do you think is the best way for stopping disease spread? What are the pros and cons of different methods? Why might people like or not like them?

Next, move on and play zombie tag for fifteen to twenty minutes. Essentially, this is the same as infection tag—except that instead of stickers signifying infection, the infected walk about with arms outstretched, moaning "BRAAAIIINS." Note that the zombie walk, at least in the beginning, should be a slow shamble. Again, as always, track how far and fast the infection spreads!

Here are some starter ideas for more variants:

◇ <u>Fast zombies:</u> Students sprinting around a desk-filled classroom probably isn't the way to go here. Fast walking should be sufficient.

◇ <u>Humans fight back:</u> If a human meets a zombie, they play rock-paper-scissors. If the zombie wins, the human becomes infected. If they tie, the human escapes, for now. If the human wins, the zombie is defeated. (You can choose this to mean that a human can kill a zombie and remove him from the game, or stun a zombie so that she has to count to ten before starting to seek out more brains. Try both options with your students!)

◇ <u>Zombie immunization:</u> Immunized humans no longer have to worry about a fate worse than death—undeath. In this variation, any human who is immunized will not be turned into a zombie. This human will, however, still need to fight the zombie for a chance to escape. When a zombie encounters an immunized human, the basic rules are the same as with the "humans fight back" variation, except that if the zombie wins, the immunized human is killed rather than infected. (Unfortunately, one can't avoid dying after a zombie attack.) As with infection tag, you can experiment with different levels of access to the vaccine.

◇ <u>Zombie cure:</u> This is basically the same as the "humans fight back" version, unless the human wins rock-paper-scissors—in which case, the zombie is cured!

◇ <u>Zombie quarantine:</u> Humans can try to take zombies to a quarantine zone. Two humans can team up to escort a zombie to the quarantine zone. Once the zombie is there, the zombie plays rock-paper-scissors with each human—if the zombie wins, the human is infected. If one human meets one zombie, they play rock-paper-scissors as in the "humans fight back" version.

After all the zombie tag, hammer home this point: There is a big, big world out there. And one of the ways STEM people deal with that is by making models to understand it. Some of the most powerful computers in the world run models on things like weather and climate. Sometimes we build scale models of things like buildings and bridges. And sometimes, yes, even games can be models, like infection tag and zombie tag. Can your students think of examples of models?

The Day the Zombies Came (20 minutes)

Now that your students have zombies on the brain, let them know that they'll be writing a full zombie narrative, piece by piece, throughout the lesson sequence, drawing from their STEM discoveries. Today, they'll begin with the opening. Give them this prompt to get them started:

When did you first hear rumors about the zombies coming? Did you believe them? Were those rumors accurate (did some of the facts change)?

And when did you first encounter a zombie? How did you and others try to avoid being infected?

This can tie into hypotheses about how the outbreak began: perhaps their characters saw in the supermarket an issue of the *National Enquirer* that had an article about zombies in Haiti created by voodoo, for example. Maybe it was via the radio, or a phone call. Maybe it was supposedly a rabies outbreak (as in *World War Z*). Maybe they saw a zombie, and it went for their brains. Whatever it was, let's allow them to get crazy creative here, until . . .

IMAGINATIONS UNBOUND Note that your students may be inclined to write the kind of gory zombie narrative with which they may be familiar. That's not the point of this lesson, and indeed, throughout, you and your students will consider why such narratives are unrealistic (for example, why taking a chainsaw to a zombie horde may be the worst idea). Instead of directly instructing your students to stay away from this kind of writing (which may have the opposite of the intended effect), make sure your directions and questions focus on exploring the human side of things (for example, preparation and aftermath) and on integrating the lessons they've learned into their narrative. Even with this subtle redirection, it may take some time for your students to shift from blood and guts to more thoughtful writing.

The New Abnormal (15 minutes)

After students have written the start of their zombie account, remind them of what they wrote at the beginning of the session. How would the spread of zombies affect their ability to live their lives as they normally do? We're going for some silent, somber reflection and writing here:

> Think back to the everyday activities you wrote about at the beginning of today's session. When the zombies come, can you still do those things? How might your life have to change? How might society have to change?

If time permits at the end, you can have students share their writing and thoughts. Alternatively, you can try some advanced variants on infection tag or zombie tag—for example, students can designate physical barriers (like table forts) to simulate fortified quarantine zones.

At the very end, students' mood may be pretty down. This is intentional. It is important to raise spirits for next time, however, so you should let your students know that humanity strikes back!

Session 2: Humanity Breaks Through (We Hope)

In this session, students return to a type of model that they are likely more familiar with: the physical scale model. Using bits and pieces of household materials to represent things that may be available during the zombie apocalypse (such as a bit of string, representing rope), students will engineer structures and vehicles to aid humans in the fight against zombiekind.

Students will be pretty busy engineering for most of the session. If, by any chance, they find themselves with any idle time, help them figure out how they can expand their notes on their engineered structure and engineering process. And if that's entirely taken care of, students can, of course, work on continuing their zombie narrative.

Preparation

This session requires a little more prep than the others. Students will be building structures (a bridge, zip line, raft, or collapsible ramp) in groups of four, and there are two ways you can do this: (1) you can decide what each group will build, or (2) you can let the students decide. Option 1 requires more prep but ensures things go more smoothly.

If you're going with option 1: Before class, designate building stations, labeling them BRIDGE, ZIP LINE, RAFT, and (optional bonus) COLLAPSIBLE RAMP. You'll need one station for every four students, so if you have, say, thirty-two students, you'll need eight stations, or two of each kind. Try to locate each ZIP LINE station near a door; they'll need the door to set up the line. At each BRIDGE station, you'll need two flat, raised surfaces to bridge (tables and chairs work well). Place them fifteen inches apart, or farther for more of a challenge. Fill the foam cooler with water and place it somewhere it won't get knocked over. Then distribute the building supplies (see the materials list or the "Zombie Apocalypse Building Supplies" handout). Different stations will require different supplies, but the supplies will overlap a bit, so you can do whatever seems easier, either putting the relevant supplies right at the stations or setting up a single central supply area.

If you're going with option 2: Place all the building supplies (see the list of materials at the beginning of this lesson, or the "Zombie Apocalypse Building Supplies" handout) at a central supply area. Fill the foam cooler with water, and place it somewhere it won't get knocked over.

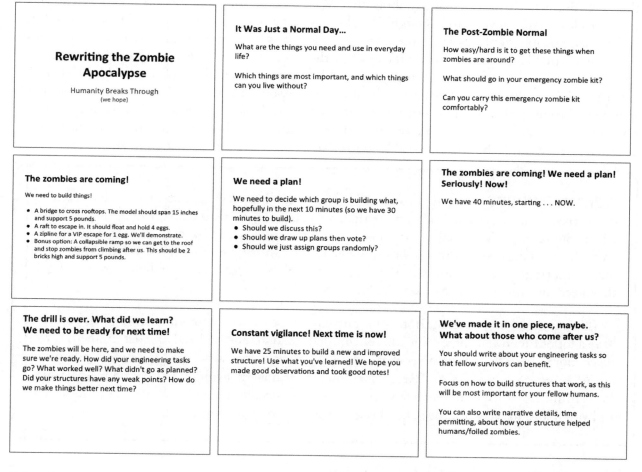

My Stuff (15 minutes)

This is a tweak of the first session's prompt, focusing more directly on things. Ask the students to respond to the following:

> What are the things you need and use in everyday life? Which things are most important, and which things can you live without?

If students generate this list really quickly, have them revisit their fictional narrative from the previous session and extend it, focusing on the supplies they need to gather and use to survive the zombies.

Zombie Stuff (10 minutes)

Now, the class will explore the concrete ways people's lives might have to change. Ask students to respond to the following prompt:

> How easy or hard is it to get these things when zombies are around? What should go in your emergency zombie kit? Can you carry this emergency zombie kit comfortably?

Distribute copies of the "Zombie Apocalypse Survival Supplies" handout to help students consider what they can carry. Try to leave at least a couple of minutes to briefly discuss with your students what they have prioritized and why.

For example, students may think that they can forage for food or water in the wild—and maybe they can. But help them think clearly about this. Where would they find food or water? Would the water be clean? Are a few berries enough? Would they rather move as fast as possible, or have to hunt and gather, possibly in places where there are lots of zombies (like an overrun grocery store, perhaps)?

Students are likely to overestimate the amount they can carry—to drive home a point, you can have some backpacks to fill up with heavy things like weights, bricks, bags of rice, and bottles of water (an eight-ounce bottle of water weighs about half a pound; a one-liter bottle weighs about two). Have a bathroom scale on hand so they'll know what the full backpack weighs. Let them explore how much they can carry, comfortably, for even a few minutes. When they are trying on the pack, ask them if they think they would be able to run—over obstacles—to escape from zombies.

FIGHTING WORDS Anyone who's ever watched a zombie movie or played a zombie video game knows that it typically takes more than a cutting comment to take down a zombie. And when considering what supplies they'll need, your students, naturally, may want to load up on flamethrowers and other forms of heavy artillery. We can see their point, but we don't recommend granting it. Tell the students that weapons won't be on anyone's supply list, explaining, if they need an explanation, that zombies are impervious to them.

The real explanation is that, from a narrative point of view, weapons are lazy. When you have a lot of firepower, there's not a lot of conflict; the outcome is already predetermined. It's *much* more interesting if characters have to rely on their wits instead. As Max Brooks advises in *The Zombie Survival Guide*, "Remember, no matter how desperate the situation seems, time spent thinking clearly is never time wasted." This is basically the unofficial motto of this lesson, and you'll love to see what your clear-headed students come up with.

The Zombies Are Coming (45 minutes)

Take five minutes, and only five minutes, to present the engineering tasks to the students, explaining that they will be tasked with building the following structures to help them escape from the zombies:

◇ BRIDGE—needs to span fifteen inches (you can increase this number for more of a challenge). This will probably take up a lot of craft sticks. It needs to support 5 pounds, but stronger is better (so that more supplies can be carried across).

◇ RAFT—should fit as many eggs (people) as possible, at least four. If it can carry extra weight, that's even better (for supplies)!

◇ ZIP LINE—should get one egg safely to the ground, preferably two, preferably with some weight. The zip line will start at door height, and end at the floor (about seven away, if the door is seven feet high). The egg is your class's VIP, who's essential to fighting off the zombies for good. More on this later.

◇ COLLAPSIBLE RAMP (a bonus option for an advanced engineering team, if your class has groups that are up to it)—should go two bricks high, maybe more. It should support 5 pounds, without the weight sliding down (so it can't be super steep). And it needs to be easily collapsible—via taking out a couple of beams, or something (and not via something unrealistic, like dropping all the weights on it).

Return to the concept of modeling, and explain how various materials in this session (for example, craft sticks, string, and Bubble Wrap) model various things in the real world (lumber, rope, and pillows, respectively). Hand out copies of the "Zombie Apocalypse Building Supplies" sheet to help them see this modeling.

If you've already set up building stations (preparation option 1) for each BRIDGE, RAFT, ZIP LINE, and COLLAPSIBLE RAMP group, assign four students to each station and let them get to work.

If you're letting the students decide themselves what to build (preparation option 2), divide them into groups of four, then explain what's going on—the zombies won't wait for us, so we have to finish on time. Let students know that hopefully they'll be able to decide in the next ten minutes which groups are building what, so that there will be a full thirty minutes afterward to design, build, and test. (And if they can decide more quickly, they'll have more time!) Ideally, the entire class should produce approximately equal numbers of each structure. Two bridges, three rafts, and two zip lines are okay; six zip lines and a bridge are not. Otherwise, don't be too directive here; some chaos will make a point about teamwork and leadership. In addition to deciding which group will build what, students should also come up with the best way to divvy up supplies.

For the remaining thirty minutes, give or take, students will engineer their assigned structure, hoping to be ready when the zombies arrive. They can test and observe while building, and take notes about what works and what doesn't. (*Note:* The zip line group can't test with an egg while building—because an egg, in their miniature world, is a person.)

Although you could ask students about prior knowledge before they start (What kinds of shapes have you seen that form bridges or rafts? What do you know about keeping people or things safe in vehicles?), it is entirely fine, and maybe even preferable, for them to have very little guidance. Engineering does rely on using known principles to devise solutions—but, perhaps more fundamentally, it relies on testing and retesting, building and rebuilding, to refine solutions. The emphasis here, as in other lessons, is on iteration (see "Iteration" in the Science-O-Pedia).

But Does It Work? (10 minutes)

Once time is up, instruct students to stop wherever they are. Let them know that the zombies won't wait for them to finish. It's time to test their structures, taking notes as they do so. What worked or didn't work as expected? What were the weak points in the design that need to be reworked?

Have the RAFT students place their rafts in the water, and the BRIDGE students place the appropriate weight in the center of each bridge. We'll come back to these tests in a few minutes (it's not helpful if a bridge or raft only works for thirty seconds).

While this happens, supervise the ZIP LINE students as they send their vehicles (with eggs) down the zip line, and then return to note the results for the RAFT and BRIDGE students. (*Note:* You may want to place a plastic garbage bag on top of the landing surface for the zip line to make cleanup easier, should the VIP egg not survive.) If time permits, the entire class should watch each test, one by one; it's a great big team-building exercise, and the collective applause after an egg survives the zip line is a great thrill.

The Zombies Are Here (25 minutes)

This is an engineering lightning round. The zombies will be here, so the students' structures and vehicles absolutely need to be ready!

Based on their notes, students need to engineer things better than ever! You can add on challenges, like: An extra person needs to fit on the zip line! We have extra supplies, and it would be great if there were room on the raft! A longer bridge would help us access the supplies in that grocery store!

Students have less time for this segment, but more knowledge. Each group should test by itself toward the end of this window. (After all, if every group gawked at every other group's test, everyone would lose time to prepare for the zombies.) You should be present, of course, to note how groups did the second time around. Some students ideally will discover that they can reuse pieces of their old structure, which is great—and resourceful.

For even more of a challenge: If you feel that the groups are up to it, you can rotate them so they do different tasks and have to rely on the previous group's knowledge and notes. If you have the time and interest, feel free to extend this engineering into an additional session or two!

Paying It Forward in the Zombie Apocalypse (15 minutes)

To help students reflect on their structure and what they learned along the way, have them write instructions on how to build a bridge, zombie escape raft, zip line, or collapsible ramp, to leave for people who come after them. (As with everything else in this lesson, this should be written from the perspective of a character living through the zombie outbreak—so a craft stick is not a craft stick, but instead a two-by-four or a plank ripped from a picnic table.) Students should be drawing from any and all notes they made during their model design and construction, in either phase. (For more perspective on technical writing and instructions, see the lesson "Technically Speaking.")

Session 3: Zombies Evolve

When students are first introduced to probability and statistics, they're usually taught how to calculate things like mean, median, and mode—which summarize the data we have. This is often called descriptive statistics—and although it's important, it's certainly not the only use of statistics.

Another branch, statistical inference, aims for much more than summary. It seeks to pull conclusions and draw meaning from limited data sets. It's how pollsters can draw conclusions from the general population, and be pretty accurate, by only asking a hundred people.

Statistical inference and its associated math are beyond the reach of the average middle schooler, and this session doesn't aim to teach it. What it does do is engage students in a process called resampling. Though it's simplified and simulated here, it still hints at the power of math and statistics in conducting some really cool investigative work—about zombies, of course. Specifically, students here will use resampling of a collection of zombie data to make good guesses about even more zombie data.

Conveniently, while doing this, students will also learn about mutation and natural selection.

Rewriting the Zombie Apocalypse

Are we winning?

We're Outsmarting Them!

Continue your zombie stories, focusing on how thinking ahead, preparing, and engineering helped us fight back.

You can focus on things we've built (i.e. bridge, zipline, boat, or ramp), or things that you imagine you might build.

It Looks Like We're Winning!

With engineering smarts on our side, we're seeing fewer and fewer zombies!

The waves of zombies have taken a toll, though. There are a lot fewer of us. And the places we live, work, and go to school are not in good shape.

Continue your story, writing about how we start to rebuild our lives.

Preparing for the Final Offensive

Some zombies have survived, and instead of going in without a plan, we should study them first. ("Remember . . . time spent thinking clearly is never time wasted." —Max Brooks, zombie expert)

We have reports of three kinds of zombies: red, yellow, and green. Based on these reports, we've built a model on how they attack.

Zombie Dice

The basic rules:
- Each roll of the die represents a fight between a zombie and a human. For basic experiments, we'll do 15 rolls.
- A brain means that the zombie gets a brain.
- A set of footprints means the human gets away.
- A *POW!* means that the zombie has been injured. (Three injuries mean a zombie is dead.)

Let's Investigate Zombies

Using our model and our observation sheet, let's figure out some facts about zombies. (It's safer than actually fighting zombies.)

- How good/fast are they at eating brains?
- How many fights can zombies survive for?
- How many brains can they eat while alive?

Rewriting the Zombie Apocalypse

ZOMBIES EVOLVE

Mutant Zombie Dice

What's this?! The zombies have been mutating! Now we really need to know what we're up against.

Using the mutation sheets and the 20-sided-dice, roll zombie mutations. In your groups, using the mutant dice and observation sheets, learn everything you can about these mutant zombies.

More Mutants?!

The strongest mutants have survived, and are continuing to mutate!

Let's study these new mutants, too, or else we're not gonna make it!

Oh, the Horror . . .

Just when we thought we could rebuild society, the zombies have become stronger than ever.

Write the story about how these mutant zombies and their abilities make a comeback and push humanity back to the brink. Describe the mutations we've seen (and maybe new mutations we haven't).

Preparation

Very simple prep this time—just prepare some stickers for the zombie mutation dice game. You'll need one sheet for every 4 students. On each sheet, on one-third of the stickers, write POW! On another one-third, write BRAINS. And on the final one-third, write FOOTPRINTS.

During class, it's simplest—and the most fun—to have students play the dice games in groups of four. If necessary, rearrange students' desks or tables to facilitate this.

ZOMBIE DICE AND D20S This session is built on a modification of the commercially available dice game Zombie Dice, by Steve Jackson. The game is widely available both online and in retail game stores and bookstores. It also uses D20s. A D20 is a twenty-sided die that is most used in the role-playing game Dungeons and Dragons. Such dice are also really easy to come by, online and at game stores.

The Story So Far—Are We Winning? (25 minutes)

This third session opens with some writing and reflection. First, ask students to imagine how they might use engineering not just to escape but to fight back. Have students spend ten minutes responding to the following prompt:

> Continue your zombie story, focusing on how thinking ahead, preparing, and engineering helped us fight back. You can focus on things we've built (that is, the bridge, zip line, raft, or ramp), or things that you imagine you might build. What will help us win this war?

Make sure to remind students how scarce resources are in the new, zombie-scarred world—so they probably won't be able to build antizombie robot exoskeletons or anything like that. But they might be able to come up with clever antizombie traps—we're sure your students can think of some.

After this, ask them to think about how they might start to rebuild the world after pushing back the initial wave of zombies. Give them fifteen minutes to respond to the following prompt:

> With engineering smarts on our side, we're seeing fewer and fewer zombies!
>
> The waves of zombies have taken a toll, though. There are a lot fewer of us. And the places we live, work, and go to school are not in good shape.
>
> Continue your story, writing about how we start to rebuild our lives.

Meanwhile . . . (25 minutes)

Of course, some zombies have survived. We haven't gotten them all. Ask your students what kinds of zombies might have escaped their traps and other devices. They might answer with strong zombies, fast zombies, and/or smart zombies—which all may potentially cause trouble later.

Let your students know that the folks in charge, whoever they might be, have sent out research patrols to find out more about the surviving undead. There seem to be three different strains: red, yellow, and green. Conveniently, researchers have made six observations of each zombie strain meeting a human, and they've been able to create a mathematical model that fits on a set of dice.

Show students the zombie dice. They come in green (representing the green zombie), red (representing the red zombie), and yellow (representing the yellow zombie). Explain that each side of the dice represents one of the observations researchers have made. For example, for the yellow zombie, there have been two observations of humans being successfully attacked and turned by a zombie, two observations of humans successfully escaping, and two observations of humans fighting back and injuring the zombie. Researchers have also been able to determine that three major injuries to a zombie usually mean it's taken out of commission.

Students are going to use this model to simulate the life of a zombie, and see what kind of havoc it might wreak on the human population.

Explain the rules:

◇ Each die roll represents an encounter between a zombie and a human.

◇ If you roll a BRAIN, it means the zombie gets a brain. (Poor human.)

◇ When you roll a set of FOOTPRINTS, the human gets away. (Lucky human.)

◇ A POW! means the zombie has been injured. (Three injuries mean a zombie has died. Go humanity!)

Distribute the "Zombie Modeling" handout, and take a few minutes to go over it. Everyone will need three copies, one for now and two for the zombie mutation rounds that follow in just a bit. Students should choose a red, green, or yellow zombie die, and use the handout to record the result they get for each roll. (The handout has space for fifteen rolls. It's not unheard of for a green zombie to survive seventy-plus rolls without accumulating three POW!s. You can encourage students to do longevity studies later.)

It's fun to play in groups of four. Have groups do a couple of runs through the different zombies, and discuss the differences. Have them make a game of it, hypothesizing which zombies are best at living long, can eat the most brains before dying, and so on. Note-taking is important!

YES, THIS IS ACTUAL STATISTICAL WORK It's simplified, but yes, this is definitely statistics. A lot of the time, researchers have limited data—a sample—about a phenomenon. They might want to understand something about an entire group of people or things (for example, What happens when zombies and humans interact?), but they can't possibly test every possible scenario (that would require *all* the zombies and humans out there!). Still, sample data can be used to draw some conclusions that can be generalized to the broader population. We can imagine that if the humans in our sample generally don't fare well against zombies, this is probably the case for all humans. One way we can use our sample data to understand more about broader phenomena is through resampling—pulling samples from the already collected sample set, and analyzing them to figure out as much as possible about the phenomenon or population the we are trying to learn about.

In this fictional scenario, we don't want to draw too many more samples about zombie-human interactions because doing so probably means putting more humans in more danger. The six sides of the zombie dice represent a sample of the full range of possibilities that might happen when humans meet zombies, and every time we roll a die, we pull a sample from this already existing sample set. Thus, the dice serve as a sort of model—each roll represents the outcome of an independent human-zombie interaction, and we can easily run large numbers of simulations to get a sense of the likelihood of each outcome, should there be a large-scale zombie invasion.

On a side note—two particular kinds of resampling have particularly cool names: jackknifing and bootstrapping.

Save seven to ten minutes at the end of this section to look briefly at some of the data students have collected. On the board, put up tally marks for the data bulleted in the list that follows. You can also improvise histograms (a histogram is another name for a bar graph) by using a sticky note to represent each data point (see the "Histograms and Zombie Data" sidebar).

◇ How many brains a zombie can eat (improvised histogram ranges: maybe 0 to 3, 4 to 7, 8 to 11, or 12 to 15).

◇ How many turns it takes for a certain (red, green, or yellow) zombie to die, on average, or maybe minimum and maximum life spans (a basic histogram here would be a bonus).

◇ The death rate of a certain zombie type (easy fraction for the whole class: for instance, the number of green zombies that died divided by the total number of green zombies).

◇ Other things. Should groups come up with interesting things to report, that's great!

HISTOGRAMS AND ZOMBIE DATA After simulating zombie lives with zombie dice, every student will have determined that every zombie has eaten a certain number of brains (using the "Zombie Modeling" handout). Say that this is our data set:

$$\{6, 8, 11, 12, 4, 13, 7, 6, 2, 1\}$$

To make things easier, let's sort it:

$$\{1, 2, 4, 6, 6, 7, 8, 11, 12, 13\}$$

We can use tally marks to show how many zombies ate how many brains:

0 to 3 brains	4 to 7 brains	8 to 11 brains	12 to 15 brains
II	IIII	II	II

(Two zombies ate 0 to 3 brains.)

A histogram will help us to better visualize the data. If every sticky note represented one zombie, we'd have:

| 0 to 3 brains | 4 to 7 brains | 8 to 11 brains | 12 to 15 brains |

Clearly, most zombies are eating eight to eleven brains in this example!

(*continued*)

It's probably not feasible to use one sticky note per zombie. Look at this example:

0 to 3 brains	4 to 7 brains	8 to 11 brains	12 to 15 brains
6	14	8	4

That would take a lot of sticky notes to represent!

Zombie Mutations, Round 1 (25 minutes)

Now it's time to explore the concept of mutation. Bring out some D20 dice, along with the zombie mutation stickers you prepared ahead of time and the "Mutation Rules" handout, which explains the mutant variants, their prevalence, and how they operate within the game. The story goes that there are now reports coming in of MUTANT ZOMBIES: for example, some that are expert hunters, some that are almost invincible, some that break their legs really easily. We need to learn more about them. Point out that like in real life, some of these mutations are helpful to the zombies, some are harmful, and some don't help out all that much. Some are also more prevalent than others.

In groups of four, have students take turns rolling the D20 to determine the mutations for the zombies at their table. If a student rolls a 3, he or she should create one broken-leg zombie by putting a POW! sticker over the footprints on a zombie die pulled randomly from the zombie dice cup.

Have them hypothesize about how effective these mutations will or won't be. Do a number of rounds here—the goal is to gather data and test hypotheses. This should be fun-filled and feel fast—it's inherently gamelike. Students can own their mad scientist side and their pet zombies, if they like, and engage in direct competition with partners.

They should investigate as many different zombies as possible. There are 18 zombie mutants (3 colors × 6 mutations).

After every round, students should write a couple of sentences summarizing their observations on their "Zombie Modeling" handout. These can be partially fictional and, if you like, can give students an outlet for letting their zombie ideas run wild. (These notes aren't part of the main zombie narrative they're writing.) Should you have extra time, students can write tactical plans for facing some of the most interesting strains. When one encounters a zombie that's better at stalking its prey, how does a person or community evade or resist that zombie differently than when dealing with a normal zombie?

Zombie Mutations, Round 2 (20 minutes)

Here, students will mimic natural selection. In groups of three or four, have them figure out which of their zombie mutations was most successful. They can define success by zombie survivability (which got the fewest POW! stickers) or zombie lethality (which got the most BRAINS stickers). This should take five minutes, maybe a little bit more. Once every group has determined the most successful zombie, they can all share a tidbit of info on it. (For instance, the green stalker zombie ate twenty-nine brains!)

Announce that these zombies have become dominant, and that they will evolve again (now), as organisms do. Have them, once again, roll D20s and mutate their survivor strains. The goal is to see whether any doubly mutated zombies are extra strong. (The answer: probably yes.)

Oh, the Horror . . . (25 minutes)

Students will end by using the data they've collected, and their imagination, to write about another turn of the tide in the zombie war. Now that they've observed some of these new and terrible mutant zombies, and figured out what they're capable of, they should write a story about how these new zombies and their abilities make a comeback (students can opt to create further mutations, but maybe they don't need to—a mutant green hulking stalker is basically invincible and unstoppable), and how they go through civilizations already on the brink. Push them to talk about how the zombie mutations—speed, intelligence, strength—help them counteract the zombie defenses humans have engineered. And, of course, they should write a bit on how some of the humans escape doom yet again, preferably through even more ingenuity.

Session 4: The Day the Zombies Died (!?!)

One of the reasons we use models is that testing the real thing is unethical or implausible. In the case of the zombie apocalypse, it's currently impossible to test the real thing, as there's no one we can infect with zombieism—but even if it were possible, it would be both unethical (to turn a human into a zombie) and implausible (to infect everyone in a city as a test).

This is where technology comes in. Technology has enabled us to do some pretty fun things, and indeed, fun is one of the most common uses of technology. Today, our mobile devices are more powerful than the computers we (adults) grew up with, and a lot of their power goes to social media updates, video games, or video streaming. These, of course, aren't the only ways to use technology. The most powerful computers in the world are used for things like determining how drugs interact with your body, predicting climate changes over time, and simulating the way stars and galaxies are born and die. These are huge.

In this session, via a simple computer simulation, students will get a taste of a practical use of technology beyond creating a slide show for school. They'll tweak the variables in a zombie simulation to assess possible solutions to our fictional zombie crisis, and make recommendations based on their discoveries. (Students won't be creating the simulations themselves, as that's beyond the scope of this lesson. The source code for the simulation is accessible online, though, so those who are motivated can look into it and change things around.)

Preparation

Before class, spend a little time familiarizing yourself with ZombieSim (*http://826national.org /zombiesim*).[1] You'll also need to set up a computer with a projector so the class can see the program run during the lesson.

---

1. ZombieSim is based on "Zombie Infection Simulator" at *http://kevan.org/proce55ing/zombies/*.

Rewriting the Zombie Apocalypse

The Day the Zombies Died
(maybe?)

Let's Reflect

Think back to everything we've learned and everything we've modeled.

What, do you think, are the best ways to fight off the zombies? How can we test this plan?

Congratulations.

Thanks to your engineering efforts two weeks ago, we helped key researchers (and a few test subjects) escape to a CDC lab, where they have created a zombie vaccine.

Moreover, thanks to your research on zombie mutations and countermeasures, our security teams now have better zombie resistance tactics.

A New Model

ZombieSim.

Tiny Town, USA

During your travels, you have come across a small town about to be overrun by zombies. Being the good-hearted person you are, you will come up with a plan to save them.
Use ZombieSim to see how the infection might spread in different versions of Tiny Town, and to test different countermeasures. Don't worry about costs at the moment. Record your results!

Middletown, USA

You've saved Tiny Town!
Now, you've found another town about to be overrun! Thankfully, you've met like-minded anti-zombie strategists here. Report your individual findings to your group, and determine as a group how to best save a medium town.
Resources are hard to come by, so watch your costs, and see if you can keep them down.

The World Needs You

The world's remaining leaders have heard of your success defending against new zombie outbreaks. Now, they want you to determine a plan to save major population centers.
With your groups, create a plan, gather data, and prepare to present your findings to the leaders of the free world.
Don't forget! Resources are very scarce.

What's the plan?

Every group will run their simulation three times; we'll average the number of people saved. Then, we'll divide the cost of the plan by that average, to figure out how much it cost to save each person.

Which plan is best? The most cost-effective? The one that saves the most humans? The one that results in the fewest humans zombified?

The Day the Zombies Died!

Write a story about the last day of the zombie apocalypse.
If the zombies won, you should write about how humanity's last stand failed. If the humans won, instead write about how our plan to fight off the zombies worked.
In either case, you should write about what the world is like after the zombie apocalypse.

Introduction: Let's Think for a Bit (Since Zombies Can't) (15 minutes)

Present students with the following prompt to write about individually, or discuss as a group. Emphasize the modeling portion—after all, we don't want to have to have an actual zombie apocalypse to prepare ourselves for one.

> Think back to everything we've learned and everything we've modeled. What do you think are the best ways to fight off the zombies? How can we test this plan?

The End Is Near, Unless We Can Use ZombieSim to Save It (10 minutes)

Explain that, thanks to students' efforts and engineering in session 2, key researchers (and a test subject) were able to get to a Centers for Disease Control and Prevention bunker, where they have developed a working zombie vaccine. Hooray! Now we finally have a critical tool against the zombies. And thanks to their research, data, and tactical plans, our security forces can better fight back against zombie monstrosities like the green hulking fighter and the green hulking stalker.

But now, it's time to put together a plan to save our remaining cities. How will we know if the plan will work? We can't just test a plan on live people.

Pull up ZombieSim on the screen and demo things briefly. Explain that this is a model for testing strategies and variations on a large scale.

Distribute the "ZombieSim: What's Going on Here?" handout to give students some helpful hints. Then, run the simulation—show how students have to randomize a city, then change settings to initiate the population, then run things one day at a time. They can turn the animation off to speed things up (especially important for the large simulation that is to come).

Saving Tiny Town, USA (15 minutes)

Tell your students that during their travels, they have come across a small town about to be overrun by zombies. Being the good-hearted people they are, they will come up with a plan to save the town. They should use ZombieSim to try out different plans. Distribute copies of the "Zombie Defense Simulations" handout, and instruct students to use it to record their results. (To help guide them, remind them about the importance of isolating variables—see "Variables" in the Science-O-Pedia.)

Saving MediumVille, USA (15 minutes)

Your students have saved Tiny Town!

Now, they've found another town about to be overrun! Thankfully, they've met like-minded antizombie strategists here. (That is, now you're putting students into small groups.) Students should report their individual findings from Tiny Town to their group, and determine together how best to save a medium-size town—again using the "Zombie Defense Simulations" handout to record their experimental data.

At this point, tell students that resources are hard to come by, so they should watch their costs and try to keep them down as much as possible. What antizombie measures offer the best bang for the buck?

Saving the Big City (15 minutes)

Let students know that the world's remaining leaders have heard of their success stopping zombie outbreaks. Now, they want them to determine a plan to save major population centers.

With their group, students should create a plan, gather data, and prepare to present their findings to the leaders of the free world.

Resources are very scarce at this point; don't let your students forget that.

Let's Save the World, Mrs. President (30 minutes)

(If you have a lot of students and groups, and therefore a lot of simulations and presentations to do, you can cut short the "Saving the Big City" section, as there's a tiny bit of overlap.)

Allot ten minutes total for student groups to present their plans to the fictional president. What zombie-control measures are the most important to them? How do they measure their success (for example, fewest humans zombified, most humans alive at the end, lowest cost, fastest zombie eradication, and so on)? Two minutes per group is about right.

In front of the whole class, using ZombieSim, set up a large city with the animation off. Take about twelve minutes to simulate student plans. On a large city with animation off and twenty zombies to start, run each group's plan three times. Determine the average number of humans saved after seven days, and how much it cost to save each person (the plan's cost divided by the average number of humans saved). Get the data up on the board.

After all the simulations are run, use the rest of the time (maybe eight minutes) to discuss what kinds of plans are best, and why. Students should continuously refer to the data they've gathered, both in groups and from the simulations in front of the class. (Although the focus is on the variables they've experimented with during this session, they can definitely refer back to concepts explored in earlier sessions—most relevant are probably disease-control mechanisms from session 1 and survival packs from session 2.) How might they combine aspects of different plans to make an ultimate plan?

The Day the Zombies Died (Maybe?) (20 minutes)

After all that hard work, it's time for a debriefing. Ask students to respond to the following prompt:

> Write a story about the last day of the zombie apocalypse, drawing on the results of the final ZombieSim runs. If the zombies won, you should write about how humanity's last stand failed. If the humans won, instead write about how our plan to fight off the zombies worked.

> You should still write from the perspective of the same character you've been using throughout the lesson in the zombie wasteland. That person can be in the midst of the antizombie uprising, or can even be its architect who's watching from a distance. What is it like implementing these antizombie measures (and any others you may have learned about in earlier sessions) and seeing them in action?

> And no matter what, you should write about what the world is like after the zombie apocalypse.

Should students wrap up early, have them read some of their writing aloud.

FOR YOU TO KNOW (AND YOUR STUDENTS TO DISCOVER)[2]

Using zombieism to study infectious diseases? Really? Although it might initially seem like an off-the-wall idea, it really makes a lot of sense. Scientists routinely use models in their work, but models are similarly important for teaching and learning. In this case, our model, zombieism, provides an engaging context in which to teach students some pretty sophisticated ideas about disease and its spread and prevention. These concepts are traditionally taught in very abstract ways and can thus be perceived as boring. Zombies help bring these ideas to life (pun definitely intended) and give students concrete experiences onto which they can anchor their developing understanding.

---

2. Information is derived from the following sources: "Disease Outbreaks," *http://www.who.int/topics/disease_outbreaks/en/*; "Plague: History," *http://www.cdc.gov/plague/history/*; "Germ Theory," *http://ocp.hul.harvard.edu/contagion/germtheory.html*; "Apostles of Cleanliness," *http://pubs.acs.org/subscribe/archive/mdd/v05/i05/html/05ttl.html*; Markel, Howard, "Life, Liberty and the Pursuit of Vaccines," *New York Times* (February 28, 2011), *http://www.nytimes.com/2011/03/01/health/01smallpox.html*.

(continued)

Disease

Diseases are often divided into two main categories: **infectious** (also known as communicable) diseases and **noninfectious** (also known as noncommunicable) diseases. Briefly, noninfectious diseases include congenital diseases (diseases or conditions that you are born with, such as metabolic disorders like phenylketonuria or nervous system disorders like spina bifida), as well as other diseases that can't be transmitted from person to person, such as asthma, diabetes, and many cancers. Infectious diseases, in contrast, are caused by an infectious agent (most often a **bacterium, virus, fungus,** or **parasite**) and are defined by the fact that they can be transmitted from animal to animal (both within a species and across species). You are probably familiar with many infectious diseases—including those of viral origin, such as colds and the flu; bacterial origin, such as strep throat; and perhaps even parasitic origin, such as malaria. Notably, the preventable childhood illnesses that we typically receive vaccinations against (polio, measles, and pertussis [whooping cough]) are also caused by infectious agents, both viral and bacterial.

Disease Outbreaks

A disease outbreak is formally defined as a higher incidence of a particular infectious disease occurring in a population or region than would otherwise be expected. The flu virus is generally circulating all year long. However, we start to see flu outbreaks (larger numbers of people getting sick from the flu virus) typically when the weather gets cold (and people spend more time in close proximity to one another, indoors). Like the zombie outbreak in the lesson series, disease outbreaks begin with the introduction of the infectious agent into a population. This can happen in a number of ways, among them:

▶ An infected individual (who may be **asymptomatic,** or not showing symptoms) inadvertently transmits a disease to a population. This is probably a very familiar scenario for teachers and parents: a child falls sick at school in the middle of the day (and was infectious before being symptomatic and needing to be sent home), and within several days, many more students in the classroom fall ill. Although annoying when it happens with colds or the flu, it is much more insidious when the disease agent is more dangerous. In the past, very dangerous diseases have found their way into populations with no exposure, and therefore no immunity. The classic example is smallpox, which (along with several other diseases) was introduced to the Americas by European explorers. Because the Native American population had had no previous exposure to smallpox (and therefore no immunity), it devastated entire Native American populations.

▶ Transmission of an infectious disease agent from a **disease reservoir** to the human population. Disease reservoirs are "pools" of infectious agents that can be harbored in either inanimate or living sources. For example, birds are a reservoir for the West Nile virus. This virus can be transmitted to a human when a mosquito first bites an infected bird, then bites a human (the mosquito is called a **vector** in this case, carrying the disease from one population to another). With West Nile, outbreaks typically occur when the mosquito population increases (a warm spell after rainy weather—ideal breeding conditions for mosquitoes).

(continued)

Limiting the Spread of Disease

Throughout history, humans have used several ways to limit the spread of disease, some more effective than others.

Quarantine, from the Black Death to Zombies

Europe was ravaged by multiple Black Death (also called the plague) epidemics during the Middle Ages. The Black Death or plague spread rapidly and was highly lethal (the plague epidemic that began in the 1330s is believed to have killed 60 percent of the European population). Although the cause of the plague was not identified at the time (in fact it would be several hundred years before Anton von Leeuwenhoek built the first microscope and was the first human to realize that there is a universe of microbes that we cannot see with the naked eye), repeated experience with plague epidemics led to organized attempts to limit its spread. Cities began to establish "sanitary cordons" to prevent strangers and particularly traveling merchants from entering the city. In port cities, these cordons included isolating boat passengers, crew, and cargo in buildings separated from the city for forty days.

Quarantine proved a useful strategy to limit disease spread. Quarantine was routinely used in the twentieth century to isolate individuals exposed to such diseases as scarlet fever and measles—and its use continues in times of public health emergencies. Most recently, quarantines were established during the severe acute respiratory syndrome (SARS) outbreak in 2002–2003.

The use of quarantines, although they can be an effective strategy to limit disease spread, is tricky, as quarantines have significant financial implications and raise ethical questions. How do you know who should be quarantined? For how long? Who takes care of them during this time? How do they make up lost time at work or school? and so on. How would this strategy translate to a zombie outbreak?

Washing Away the Filth

The idea that washing hands specifically and sanitation and cleanliness more generally could help limit infection was revolutionary.

In the eighteenth and nineteenth centuries, the second-highest cause of death for women of childbearing age was childbirth fever (puerperal fever). In the 1840s the Austrian physician Ignaz Semmelweis noted that women who gave birth at home with a midwife had much lower rates of childbirth fever than women who gave birth in a hospital (where nearly 40 percent of women giving birth were dying). This got him thinking, and he conducted an experiment in which he had all physicians wash their hands in a bleach solution between patients. Infections decreased by more than 90 percent on his ward. His work provided evidence that doctors were largely responsible for the spread of this disease (though doctors were offended at the thought and were slow to adopt this simple reform), moving from patient to patient without washing their hands (and sometimes even moving unwashed from the autopsy of a patient who died of puerperal fever to a live patient). The importance of hand washing (and sanitation much more generally—think about living in a city in the time

(continued)

before closed sewers carried away waste) is now widely known, and hand washing limits the spread not only of serious infections acquired in hospitals or elsewhere but also of such common illnesses as colds and the flu. Is there any way that sanitation could limit a zombie epidemic? What needs to be cleaned up, and how?

Harnessing Our Own Immune System to Protect Us from Disease

Another revolution in disease prevention was vaccination. Like quarantine and sanitation, early "vaccines" were developed not based on an understanding of biology; instead, they were based on the observation that people who survived infection with a particular disease were immune (protected against another infection) for life. There is evidence that Chinese, Indian, and African cultures deliberately infected nonimmune people with smallpox to generate immunity (this is called inoculation) before the 1600s. This process was controversial and dangerous, as a live virus that carried the risk of a full-on infection was used as the inoculum. Over time, inoculation gained acceptance, and by the late 1700s Benjamin Franklin was promoting inoculation as a way to protect public health. There is evidence that George Washington, John Adams, and other founding fathers all received an inoculation against smallpox.

As our understanding of biology developed, we came to understand that what vaccines do is stimulate our immune system, essentially giving our body a head start in treating disease. Our body is good at recognizing invaders—things that shouldn't be there—but it takes time to mount a defense. Vaccination teaches our immune system what the invader looks like—so that the next time we are exposed to this invader, our immune system is able to react much more quickly. This rapid response protects us from developing a disease, even if we are exposed to an infectious agent.

Vaccination protects not only the individual who receives the vaccine but also that person's community. When there is a critical mass of individuals who are vaccinated, a disease cannot gain a foothold in a community, and individuals who cannot be immunized (newborn infants or immunocompromised individuals who could be sickened by the vaccine) are also protected. This is called **herd immunity.** Herd immunity protects the most vulnerable in our population. Can we use herd immunity to our advantage in our battle against the zombies?

In the past century, widespread vaccination campaigns against what were called childhood diseases have changed the face of childhood in developed countries. Diseases that were once commonplace are now rare—and parents no longer worry about their children suffering and dying before age five of diseases like measles, polio, or diphtheria. That said, because we are now a generation out from having seen this suffering, we are becoming complacent. There are places in the United States where vaccination rates have dropped below the threshold needed for herd immunity, and we are seeing a resurgence of such diseases as measles and pertussis.

It's All About Balance . . .

The biological imperative of a living thing is to reproduce and ensure the continuation of its species. This is true whether you are a virus; a single-celled bacterium; or a complex multicellular creature, such as a human.

(continued)

For an infectious agent to survive and prosper, it must not only infect and reproduce in its first host but also be transmitted to infect other hosts so the cycle can continue. An infectious agent that rapidly kills everyone it infects, without a chance for the infected to pass on the infection, will soon die out. Latency—or a delay between infection and onset of symptoms—is one way that microbes continue their spread. Applied to zombies, zombies that are voraciously hungry and quickly eat the brains of all living humans will soon run out of food (hosts). Similarly, if zombies rapidly convert all humans to zombies, they will also soon run out of brains. There must be a balance. Zombies must be able to infect new humans, and capture others for their brains. But there must be some humans who survive and reproduce—for if not, zombiekind will also be in trouble.

Power in Numbers

The world is teeming with microorganisms, and just as there is tremendous variation among humans (skin, hair, and eye color; height; weight; and so on), there is tremendous variation among microbes—even among those of the same species. This variation helps them survive and thrive in a hostile human environment. Microbes reproduce quickly, and so if a variant is advantageous—helps it grow faster or survive a challenge (such as antibiotic treatment)—the microbes with that advantageous variant (mutation) will outcompete their "siblings." Soon the population will be dominated by the microbes with the advantageous mutation.

You can easily imagine the role of variation in the zombie model. Some zombie variants will have an advantage over their fellow zombies (for instance, being faster), and other variations will provide a disadvantage (for example, zombies with fins instead of legs). Still others will have no significant effect (positive or negative) in the current environment. If the fast zombies are better at infecting humans than normal zombies (and certainly better than fin-legged zombies), soon there will be more fast zombies in the population. For now, being a fast zombie is helpful, but the tables could turn (the key phrase was "in the current environment"), and at some point a different mutation might confer a bigger advantage. Imagine if the humans built an ark or relocated to an island in the middle of the sea . . . which zombies would fare better then?

ZOMBIE-FIGHTING SKILLS

Ask your classmates what their best zombie-fighting skill is, and list them here.

NAME	ZOMBIE-FIGHTING SKILL

ZOMBIE APOCALYPSE BUILDING SUPPLIES

ITEM	WHAT IT REPRESENTS IN THE ZOMBIE WORLD
Craft sticks	Floorboards, furniture, doors, and so on
Plastic sheets (cut from a large plastic garbage bag)	Tarps or other protective covering
Cloth (from old T-shirts or bedsheets)	Bedsheets or other fabric
String	Rope
Individual Bubble Wrap bubbles	Pillows
Aluminum foil	Aluminum siding or roofing
Rubber bands	Hoses
Fishing wire, paper clips	Wire or cable
Duct tape	Duct tape
Bricks	Rooftops
Low-temperature glue gun	Welding
Eggs	Fragile living things (for example, people)
A foam cooler filled with water	A body of water

ZOMBIE APOCALYPSE SURVIVAL SUPPLIES

SURVIVAL SUPPLY	WEIGHT OF SUPPLY	NOTES
MREs (meals, ready to eat)	1 pound	These are military food rations, essentially. If MREs are all you eat, you'll need one or two a day to survive.
Water	8 pounds	Eight pounds is equivalent to 1 gallon of water, which is the recommended amount per day per person for drinking, cooking, washing, and so on.
Other food options?		A small can of food is about ½ pound (8 ounces); a large can is about a pound (16 ounces).
A heavy-duty flashlight	3 pounds	You'll also need extra batteries.
A first-aid kit	3 pounds	
A radio	½ pound	This should be a small, pocket-size transistor.
A sleeping bag	2–4 pounds	It should be insulated.
A hand mirror	1 pound	This item is good for signaling and peeking around corners.
Maps and a compass	1 pound or more	
Rubbing alcohol	2 pounds	This item is used for first aid, and for starting fires.
Matches and a lighter	<1 pound	
Clothing and shoes	2–3 pounds	One complete change of clothes plus footwear is recommended.
Binoculars	1–3 pounds	
A flamethrower	40 pounds	Not a chance!

ZOMBIE MODELING

Type of zombie you're studying: _____

Hypothesis

Describe the zombie. Make an informed guess about how good it is at eating brains, surviving, and so on.

RULES

◇ Each die roll represents an encounter between a zombie and a human.

◇ If you roll a BRAIN, it means the zombie gets a brain.

◇ If you roll a set of FOOTPRINTS, the human gets away.

◇ A POW! means the zombie has been injured.

Observations

Record zombie-human encounter results.

Encounter 1:   Encounter 6:   Encounter 11:

Encounter 2:   Encounter 7:   Encounter 12:

Encounter 3:   Encounter 8:   Encounter 13:

Encounter 4:   Encounter 9:   Encounter 14:

Encounter 5:   Encounter 10:   Encounter 15:

How many brains did the zombie eat? _____   How long did the zombie survive? _____

Conclusion

How dangerous is this zombie? Compare it to other zombie types you and your colleagues have observed.

_____

_____

_____

_____

_____

MUTATION RULES

MUTANT ZOMBIE DICE! In this game, we model how mutation works by using stickers to modify the dice. You'll need two dice: a zombie die and a D20.

The zombie die will serve as your mutant. Now, roll the D20. Based on the number rolled on the D20, place a sticker on your zombie die as directed here:

1, 2: SKULL-LESS ZOMBIE

This zombie's damaged head makes it extra hungry, but also extra vulnerable to damage.

*Replace a **brain** side of the zombie die with a* POW! *sticker.*

3, 4, 5: BROKEN-LEG ZOMBIE

This zombie will hurt itself while chasing after humans.

*Replace a **footprints** side of the zombie die with a* POW! *sticker.*

6, 7, 8, 9, 10: SENSELESS ZOMBIE

This zombie has a reduced ability to sense human brains.

*Replace a **brain** side of the zombie die with a* FOOTPRINTS *sticker.*

11, 12, 13, 14, 15: ESCAPIST ZOMBIE

This zombie isn't entirely mindless, and will actively avoid harm.

Replace a POW! *side of the zombie die with a* FOOTPRINTS *sticker.*

16, 17, 18: STALKER ZOMBIE

This zombie is a skilled, nimble tracker that eventually sneaks up on humans.

*Replace a **footprints** side of the zombie die with a* BRAIN *sticker.*

19, 20: HULKING ZOMBIE

This massive, tumorous zombie is resistant to damage and particularly strong.

Replace a POW! *side of the zombie die with a* BRAIN *sticker.*

ZOMBIESIM: WHAT'S GOING ON HERE?

ZombieSim simulates the zombie infestation reaching a human settlement, ranging from just a hundred people all the way to several thousand. You'll have the chance to try out different zombie resistance measures to see how effective they are in fighting back against the plague and saving humanity. There'll be a lot happening on screen, so here's a guide to what you're seeing.

◇ Black areas represent buildings.

◇ Gray areas represent roads and open areas.

◇ Green dots represent zombies.

◇ Magenta dots represent regular humans.

◇ Pink dots represent humans who are running around and panicking after seeing a zombie or seeing other humans panic.

◇ Blue dots represent any military police you may have in your city.

Here are your zombie resistance options:

◇ We have a vaccine, though it's expensive.

◇ We can give people zombie stunners because that's what they want—it makes folks much more likely to fight zombies, and a bit more successful at eliminating them.

◇ There are training pamphlets and classes on how to avoid zombies and defend against their attacks. And we can call in help and get some of our citizens trained and supplied as troops.

ZOMBIE DEFENSE SIMULATIONS

Simulation number: _____   City size: _____

Plans Enacted

Check all that apply and note the details of each:

☐ Immunization rate: _____   Cost: _____
☐ Defense education rate:_____   Cost:_____
☐ Armed rate: _____   Cost: _____
☐ Troops to start: _____   Cost: _____
☐ Zombies to start: _____

Hypothesis

How do you think your plans will work out? Why?

_____

_____

_____

End Result (After Simulation)

☐ All zombies destroyed   ☐ All humans lost

# of days: _____

# of zombies: _____

# of humans: _____

# of zombies killed: _____

# of humans zombified: _____

# of human casualties: _____

Observations and Conclusions

What worked? What did not? Why? What will you do differently next time? Use the back of the sheet for your writing.

STEM@HOME: ONCE UPON A TIME, PEOPLE DIED FROM THAT

In the last one hundred years, humankind's ability to prevent and treat disease has changed a lot. There were two tremendous advances in medical science that made this possible. The first was the discovery of how to harness and train the human immune system to prevent diseases through the use of vaccines. The second was the discovery of antibiotics—"miracle" drugs that made it possible to cure common bacterial infections—which have saved millions of lives. Most families have stories from their parents' or grandparents' generation of someone in their family getting very sick, or even dying, because of a disease that is now either preventable by vaccines or treatable with antibiotics. 826LA's Julius Diaz Panoriñgan shares his family's story with us here:

As a child in the early 1900s, my grandmother lived with her family in Chicago. She had an older sister named Min. One day, Min's elementary school teacher asked her to bring schoolwork over to a neighbor who was out sick from school. Min dutifully did as she was asked, and had the vivid memory of noticing, when her friend's mother opened the kitchen door, that her sick friend was sitting in the kitchen with her feet in the open oven (this part still doesn't make sense to me).

A couple of days later, the teacher realized that the sick child had diphtheria—a dangerous bacterial infection that can now be prevented by a vaccine—and that by sending Min over with the schoolwork, the teacher had put Min at risk of contracting the disease. Because the disease was so contagious and the risk of death from this disease so high, the teacher called the city public health department and reported the potential exposure. Doctors from the local hospital came out and insisted on taking Min to the hospital (my great-grandfather did not send her willingly; there is a whole story here too), even though she was not yet displaying any symptoms. Min ended up getting diphtheria and survived. The girl next door did not. That Min survived was very possibly because she was in the hospital and received early treatment.

When my great-aunt Min was a child, nearly one in five children under age five with diphtheria died, and nearly one in ten older children with diphtheria died. An antitoxin to diphtheria was first discovered in the late 1890s, but although it counteracted the diphtheria toxin, it was itself toxic, and many children died in the early days of this treatment.

(continued)

STEM@HOME: ONCE UPON A TIME, PEOPLE DIED FROM THAT (continued)

Vaccines that prevent diphtheria were introduced in the 1920s and are so effective that in the four-year period from 2004 to 2008, no children in the United States were diagnosed with the disease.[*]

Aunt Min told me this story herself when she was in her early nineties, and her sharing it gave me a window into a time when families did not assume that their children would survive to adulthood. Because we live in a time with both vaccines and antibiotics, few families in the United States suffer through the death of a child from these preventable infections.

Most families have a story (or many stories) similar to Great-Aunt Min's, about a family member's experience with a childhood disease that is now either preventable or treatable. Julius's family was lucky—Min survived. What about yours?

Talk with your parents and grandparents to ask them about your family's history with such childhood diseases as scarlet fever, diphtheria, measles, whooping cough, or polio. Do they know of anyone who was sickened by these diseases when they were children? What happened? Do they know anyone whose life was saved by antibiotics?

---

[*]"History of Diphtheria," *http://www.historyofvaccines.org/content/timelines/diphtheria*.

APPENDIX

Handy Lesson Links

Follow these links to learn more about each lesson. If a given link doesn't work, try entering the information in a search engine.

The Science of Saving Daylight

Here are videos of brief science talks and experiments:

◇ Tickling rats: *http://www.youtube.com/watch?v=j-admRGFVNM*

◇ More tickling rats: *http://www.youtube.com/watch?v=qObklTM5I2Y*

◇ Bill Nye on prisms (at approximately 1:20–2:29): *http://www.youtube.com/watch?v=gtgBHsSzCPE*

Technically Speaking

There are many different sites that provide printable paper airplane templates. Try . . .

◇ *http://www.funpaperairplanes.com* (for example, the Arrow, Delta, Classic Dart, and Condor are good beginner planes)

◇ *http://www.amazingpaperairplanes.com/Simple.html*

To learn more about what engineers do, visit the following link:

◇ *http://www.science20.com/delay_first_drink_try_explaining_science/what_does_engineer_do*

Here's a look at fictional engineer par excellence, Tony Stark (Iron Man), on the Massachusetts Institute of Technology (MIT) alumni blog:

◇ *https://alum.mit.edu/pages/sliceofmit/2013/05/10/who-is-iron-man/*

It's (Partially) Rocket Science and (Mostly) Ice Cream

The ice cream protocol was put together after looking at a variety of Internet resources like the following:

◇ "How to Make Ice Cream in a Bag": *http://www.ehow.com/how_2042724_make-ice-cream-bag.html*

For some background on avoiding the scientist stereotype, check out the following link:

⬧ *http://www.wired.com/wiredscience/2012/06/opinion-scientist-stereotype/*

To learn more about creating coolers, visit:

⬧ *http://pbskids.org/zoom/activities/sci/keepacube.html*

Planet Oobleck

For more Oobleck recipes, see:

⬧ *http://www.howtosmile.org/record/5805*

⬧ *http://www.lawrencehallofscience.org/kidsite/activities/oobleck/*

To learn more about the activities in session 2, visit:

⬧ *http://seplessons.org/node/94*

For more on Galápagos tortoises and extremophiles—organisms that survive extreme environments, like the freezing cold *inside* glaciers or atmospheres of poison gas—visit:

⬧ *http://www.calacademy.org/teachers/resources/lessons/evolution-and-the-galapagos-tortoise/*

If you'd like more visuals of the discussed organism adaptations, some can be found here:

⬧ *http://www.bbc.co.uk/nature/adaptations*

How to Write Science Fiction

For a great interview with Ray Bradbury, see:

⬧ *http://www.theparisreview.org/interviews/6012/the-art-of-fiction-no-203-ray-bradbury*

Here are a couple of quick reads on the invention of the wheel:

⬧ *http://www.livescience.com/18808-invention-wheel.html*

⬧ *http://www.straightdope.com/columns/read/223/why-did-the-peoples-of-the-new-world-fail-to -invent-the-wheel*

Making Waves

Learn more about Fourier transforms here:

⬧ *http://betterexplained.com/articles/an-interactive-guide-to-the-fourier-transform/*

For more background on timbre, check out:

⬧ *http://music.columbia.edu/cmc/musicandcomputers/chapter1/01_04.php*

Composer John Holland produced an elegant and all-encompassing chart of the acoustic wave spectrum. This gets at the expansive scale of sound waves, way beyond human hearing. Learn more:

⬧ *http://www.johnholland.ws/pdf/AcousticWave.pdf*

Here is a great guide to major musical instrument families:

◇ *http://thebirdfeednyc.com/2012/08/20/musical-instrument-families/*

Go here to see Charlie McDonnell on sound and sense:

◇ *http://www.youtube.com/watch?v=xH8mT2IQz7Y*

For an explanation of waves set to music, see Big Amplitude's "Baby I Love Your Wave" (from *Bill Nye the Science Guy*):

◇ *http://vimeo.com/60132224*

For more on the very useful songs from They Might Be Giants' *Here Comes Science*, see:

◇ "Why Does the Sun Shine?" lyrics: *http://tmbw.net/wiki/Lyrics:Why_Does_The_Sun_Shine%3F _(Science_Version)*
◇ "Why Does the Sun Shine?" music video: *http://www.youtube.com/watch?v=3JdWlSF195Y*
◇ "Why Does the Sun Really Shine?" lyrics: *http://tmbw.net/wiki/Lyrics:Why_Does_The_Sun_Really _Shine%3F*
◇ "Why Does the Sun Really Shine?" music video: *http://www.youtube.com /watch?v=sLkGSV9WDMA*

Here is a fun activity on sound from the Exploratorium:

◇ *https://www.exploratorium.edu/science_explorer/secret_bells.html*

To help visualize sound waves, there are oscilloscope apps that can help illustrate such ideas as wavelength, frequency, and amplitude:

◇ *https://itunes.apple.com/us/app/oscilloscope/id388636804?mt=8*
◇ *https://play.google.com/store/apps/details?id=com.xyz.scope*

Here are links to online hearing tests:

◇ *http://www.audiocheck.net/testtones_hearingtestaudiogram.php*
◇ *http://myhearingtest.net/*

There May Be Bones

For a humorous, insightful look at dinosaurs and birds, check out:

◇ *http://xkcd.com/1104/*
◇ *http://xkcd.com/1211/*

To see bone and skeleton charts, go here:

◇ *http://www.carolina.com/teacher-resources/Interactive/basic-information-on-owl-pellets/tr11103.tr*

For more on two guiding principles pertaining to the complexity of scientific theory, Occam's razor (a model should not be unnecessarily complicated) and Einstein's razor (but the model should explain everything), check out:

⬦ *http://math.ucr.edu/home/baez/physics/General/occam.html*

⬦ *http://decluttering.org/einsteins-razor/*

Water, Water Everywhere, Nor Any Drop to Drink

Here are some directions for making rubber "bending" bones:

⬦ *http://askabiologist.asu.edu/bone-experiments*

This is a brief write-up on making a naked egg:

⬦ *http://www.exploratorium.edu/cooking/eggs/activity-naked.html*

Here are instructions on making cabbage juice indicator, as well as instructions on the basic flow of an experiment:

⬦ *http://www.carolina.com/teacher-resources/Interactive/red-cabbage-guice-homemade-ph-indicator/tr10851.tr*

Here are instructions for creating a salt (ion) tester:

⬦ *http://pbskids.org/zoom/activities/sci/saltwatertester.html*

For a write-up of a colorful acid-base indicator experiment, see:

⬦ *http://iws.collin.edu/mweis/A&P%20Basics/Lab/Basics%20Lab%20Experiments/written%20experiments/2402%20written%20experiments%20for%20basics/apb_lab_acid_base_exercise.htm*

Here are the full National Science Teachers Association (NSTA) safety guidelines:

⬦ *http://www.nsta.org/docs/SafetyInTheScienceClassroomLabAndField.pdf*

This is a fun video on lab safety:

⬦ *https://www.youtube.com/watch?v=VRWRmIEHr3A*

Here's an MIT-produced video on Khan Academy about flocculation:

⬦ *https://www.khanacademy.org/partner-content/mit-k12/mit-k12-materials/v/flocculation*

Here's information on water-based diseases and contaminants from the Centers for Disease Control and Prevention:

⬦ *http://www.cdc.gov/healthywater/drinking/public/water_diseases.html*

⬦ *http://www.cdc.gov/healthywater/drinking/private/wells/diseases.html*

Here are some of the more digestible (relatively speaking) sources of information about specific water contaminants:

◇ Hepatitis A: *http://www.cdc.gov/hepatitis/A/aFAQ.htm*

◇ Giardia: *http://www.cdc.gov/parasites/giardia/gen_info/faqs.html*

◇ Campylobacter: *http://www.cdc.gov/nczved/divisions/dfbmd/diseases/campylobacter/*

◇ E. Coli: *http://www.cdc.gov/ecoli/general/index.html*

◇ Shigella: *http://www.cdc.gov/shigella/index.html*

◇ Cryptosporidium: *http://www.cdc.gov/parasites/crypto/gen_info/infect.html*

◇ Copper: *http://www.atsdr.cdc.gov/toxfaqs/tf.asp?id=205&tid=37*

◇ Arsenic: *http://www.atsdr.cdc.gov/toxfaqs/tf.asp?id=19&tid=3*

◇ Gasoline: *http://www.atsdr.cdc.gov/toxfaqs/tf.asp?id=467&tid=83*

◇ Nitrates and nitrites: *http://www.atsdr.cdc.gov/toxfaqs/tf.asp?id=1186&tid=258*

Here's an EPA experiment that tests the effects of acid (rain) on plants.

◇ *http://www.epa.gov/acidrain/education/experiment7.html*

Learn how the sense of taste works.

◇ *http://www.ncbi.nlm.nih.gov/pubmedhealth/PMH0033701/*

Here are Environmental Protection Agency (EPA) instructions on disinfecting water in an emergency. Boiling is the first and best recommendation; bleach is an alternative.

◇ *http://water.epa.gov/aboutow/ogwdw/upload/2006_09_14_faq_fs_emergency-disinfection-drinking water-2006.pdf*

Here is another resource from the EPA, on public water systems in the United States, including good descriptions of filtration, flocculation, disinfection, absorption, and so on. There are some good images as well.

◇ *http://water.epa.gov/lawsregs/guidance/sdwa/upload/2009_08_28_sdwa_fs_30ann_treatment_web.pdf*

If you're so inclined, you can show students a video of steam distillation. Here are some options:

◇ A sophisticated setup, with great commentary: *https://www.youtube.com/watch?v=DkNmu7uPeyM*

◇ Another sophisticated rig: *https://www.youtube.com/watch?v=00kKPOs_FA4*

◇ A pretty basic setup: *https://www.youtube.com/watch?v=4tY3d6gXwdE*

Here is a solar still video from *Mythbusters*:

◇ *https://www.youtube.com/watch?v=kWxE61WbVCY*

The Science of Superpowers

Session 1

Here is George Ella Lyon's "Where I'm From" poem:

◇ *http://www.georgeellalyon.com/where.html*

Session 2

Paper airplane templates are available at a variety of websites, including:

◇ *http://www.teachengineering.org/collection/cub_/activities/cub_airplanes/cub_airplanes_lesson06_activity1_handout2.pdf*

Hiyao Miyazaki's farewell film, *The Wind Rises,* is a remarkable homage to flight. The trailer has several wonderful scenes of wind, gliders, and airplanes, as well as one of an engineer (the protagonist) designing a plane. It is a nice, accessible visual of airflow (wind) and flight. The trailer is here:

◇ *https://www.youtube.com/watch?v=imtdgdGOB6Q*

Session 3

For a fascinating discussion of the Egyptian pyramids and the engineering design decisions that went into building them, see:

◇ *http://99percentinvisible.org/episode/episode-34-building-pyramids/*

For more information on dome houses, pictures, and storm stories, see:

◇ *http://domeofahome.com/*

Session 4

Engineers used some of the same techniques and some different ones for the landing sequence of the *Curiosity* and *Opportunity* rovers. Here are animations describing the sequence of the *Curiosity* rover (both are narrated, the second by William Shatner):

◇ *http://laughingsquid.com/landing-sequence-animation-for-the-nasa-mars-rover-curiosity/*

◇ *http://www.space.com/16826-mars-rover-landing-star-trek-video.html*

The following video depicts *Opportunity* rover's landing sequence. With this video, be sure to note that it is a mix of simulation (animation) and real audio track of mission control during the landing sequence:

◇ *https://www.youtube.com/watch?v=XRCIzZHpFtY*

The following video shows a crash test using a dummy in a car driven into a wall. In the first sequence, the dummy is not wearing its seat belt. In the second, it is. (*Note:* Instructors should use their best judgment, including considering the ages of the students, to decide if this video is appropriate for their classroom.)

◇ *https://www.youtube.com/watch?v=d7iYZPp2zYY*

The video "Understanding Car Crashes: It's Basic Physics" from the Insurance Institute for Highway Safety provides a great, twenty-two-minute, easily digestible explanation of the physics underlying car crashes and how safety devices mitigate damage and injury. At 6:10, there is a wonderful sequence using an egg as the test dummy.

◇ *http://www.iihs.org/iihs/videos*

Here is an additional link about the physics involved in the "crumple zone":

◇ *http://www.plastics-car.com/Todays-Automobiles/Automotive-Safety/Physics-in-the-Crumple-Zone-2.html*

Here is a discussion of prose poems:

◇ *http://www.poets.org/poetsorg/text/poetic-form-prose-poem*

Infinite Recess

Self-styled recreational mathemusician Vi Hart has videos on a lot of math topics, not just a crazy Möbius strip world. Check her out!

◇ *http://www.youtube.com/user/Vihart*

Here's a Wikipedia article on fractals:

◇ *http://en.wikipedia.org/wiki/Fractal*

To learn more about two of the most well-known fractals, the Sierpinksi triangle and Koch snowflake, respectively, see the following Wikipedia pages:

◇ *http://en.wikipedia.org/wiki/Sierpinski_triangle*

◇ *http://en.wikipedia.org/wiki/Koch_snowflake*

Here's a video on the dragon curve, a fractal that features in the novel *Jurassic Park.* Handily, it introduces a concrete way of making a fractal by folding a strip of paper.

◇ *http://www.numberphile.com/videos/dragon_curve.html*

Here is a fractal app available on the iOS App Store:

◇ *http://fract.al/about*

Here's a zoom-in on the Mandelbrot set, perhaps the most popular fractal:

◇ *https://www.youtube.com/watch?v=0jGaio87u3A*

How does Earth's shape affect its size?

◇ *http://news.discovery.com/space/what-if-earth-was-a-cube-110815.htm*

◇ *http://gizmodo.com/how-gravity-would-be-different-if-the-world-were-a-cube-1492018223*

Here's more on the Klein bottle:

◇ *http://www.math.hmc.edu/funfacts/ffiles/30002.7.shtml*

◇ *http://en.wikipedia.org/wiki/Klein_Bottle*

Here's Nintendo's site for *Super Paper Mario,* with some two- and three-dimensional gameplay:

◇ *http://www.nintendo.com/sites/spm/*

Here's a downloadable PDF of *Flatland:*

◇ *https://github.com/Ivesvdf/flatland/blob/master/oneside_a4.pdf?raw=true*

Here's video of a sphere turning inside out:

◇ *https://www.youtube.com/watch?v=R_w4HYXuo9M*

This is Wikipedia's time travel page:

◇ *http://en.wikipedia.org/wiki/Time_travel*

To learn more about the theory of relativity, go here:

◇ *http://en.wikipedia.org/wiki/Theory_of_relativity*

A massive collection of fiction that involves math has been compiled by Alex Kasman, and can be found here:

◇ *http://kasmana.people.cofc.edu/MATHFICT/*

Rewriting the Zombie Apocalypse
Session 1

This lesson was inspired in part by this article:

◇ *http://www.wired.com/2009/08/zombies/*

Go here for a simulation of a zombie outbreak:

◇ *http://kevan.org/proce55ing/zombies/*

For an example of an activity to demonstrate how disease spreads, see:

◇ *http://www.sciencefriday.com/blogs/09/07/2011/epidemic-the-handshake-game
.html?audience=1&series=1*

This is a cool article about zombie lore:

◇ *http://www.livescience.com/23892-zombies-real-facts.html*

Session 3

Zombie Dice can be purchased, and look something like these:

◇ *http://www.amazon.com/SJG-131313-Zombie-Dice/dp/B003IKMR0U%0AD20*

D20 are twenty-sided die:

◇ *https://www.google.com/search?q=d20&es_sm=91&tbm=isch&tbo=u&source=univ&sa=X&ei=qJWa U8fkLYKhogS9tYKIAg&ved=0CFQQsAQ&biw=1350&bih=644&dpr=0.9*

Session 4

Here is the zombie simulation used in this session:

◇ *http://826national.org/zombiesim*

Self-Assessment Checklists

On the following pages we've provided self-assessment checklists for the lessons' writing assignments. They're divided by elementary, middle, and high school, with checklists for both fiction and nonfiction for the upper grades. Using them will help students evaluate their own work and improve as they go.

ELEMENTARY SCHOOL SELF-ASSESSMENT CHECKLIST

☐ I showed that I know a lot about my topic.

☐ I expressed what I think and feel.

☐ My paper has a main idea.

☐ My ideas are supported.

☐ My paper has paragraphs that flow from one idea to the next.

☐ My paper has a beginning, middle, and end.

☐ I spelled words correctly. When I didn't know how to spell a word, I looked it up.

☐ I used punctuation correctly.

☐ My sentences are complete.

☐ I capitalized words correctly.

☐ I included descriptive details.

☐ I used colorful, energetic, meaningful words instead of bland words like "nice."

☐ I had fun writing it!

MIDDLE SCHOOL SELF-ASSESSMENT CHECKLIST—NONFICTION

☐ My paper has an inventive, original topic.

☐ My paper sticks closely to the topic idea.

☐ My introduction draws the reader in.

☐ My paper is well organized.

☐ My ideas are well supported.

☐ I show the reader that I know a lot about my topic.

☐ My ideas flow logically from paragraph to paragraph.

☐ I included a lot of descriptive detail.

☐ I used colorful, energetic words, instead of bland words like "nice."

☐ I edited out hesitant phrases like "sort of" and "seems to."

- ☐ I wrote in a unique personal voice.
- ☐ I used correct punctuation.
- ☐ I used some advanced punctuation, like semicolons and dashes.
- ☐ I spelled all the words correctly. When I didn't know how to spell something, I looked it up.
- ☐ There are no run-on sentences.
- ☐ My sentence structure is sometimes complex and varied.
- ☐ My paper has a strong conclusion.
- ☐ I proofread my paper.

MIDDLE SCHOOL SELF-ASSESSMENT CHECKLIST—FICTION

- ☐ My introduction draws the reader in.
- ☐ My plot is well thought out and includes an introduction, climax, and conclusion.
- ☐ The characters are well rounded, believable, and interesting.
- ☐ The setting, characters, and plot are well integrated.
- ☐ The action flows logically or naturally.
- ☐ The dialogue is effective and believable.
- ☐ I included a lot of descriptive detail.
- ☐ I used colorful, energetic words, instead of bland words like "nice."
- ☐ I used strong, active language instead of hesitant phrases like "sort of" and "seems to."
- ☐ I wrote in a unique personal voice.
- ☐ I used correct punctuation.
- ☐ I used some advanced punctuation, like semicolons and dashes.
- ☐ I spelled all the words correctly. When I didn't know how to spell something, I looked it up.
- ☐ There are no run-on sentences.
- ☐ My sentence structure is sometimes complex and varied.
- ☐ My ending is strong and fitting.
- ☐ I proofread my story.

High School Self-Assessment Checklist—Nonfiction

- ☐ My paper has a strong, original thesis.
- ☐ My paper sticks closely to my thesis.
- ☐ My introduction draws the reader in.
- ☐ My paper is well organized.
- ☐ My ideas are well supported.
- ☐ I show the reader that I researched my topic well.
- ☐ My ideas flow logically from paragraph to paragraph.
- ☐ I included a lot of descriptive detail.
- ☐ My word choice is inventive and appropriate.
- ☐ I used strong, active language instead of hesitant phrases like "sort of" and "seems to."
- ☐ I wrote in a unique personal voice.
- ☐ I used correct punctuation.
- ☐ I used some advanced punctuation, like semicolons and dashes.
- ☐ I checked my spelling.
- ☐ There are no run-on sentences.
- ☐ My sentence structure is complex and varied.
- ☐ My paper has a strong conclusion that gives the reader something to think about.
- ☐ I proofread my paper.

HIGH SCHOOL SELF-ASSESSMENT CHECKLIST—FICTION

- ☐ My introduction draws the reader in.
- ☐ The plot is well thought out and includes an introduction, climax, and conclusion.
- ☐ The characters are well rounded, believable, and interesting.
- ☐ The setting, characters, and plot are well integrated.
- ☐ The action flows logically or naturally.
- ☐ My story may have multiple subplots.
- ☐ My story may use symbolism or subtext.
- ☐ The dialogue is effective and believable.
- ☐ My story might experiment with different techniques, like magic realism or stream of consciousness.
- ☐ I included a lot of descriptive detail.
- ☐ My word choice is inventive and appropriate. I avoided bland words like "nice."
- ☐ I used strong, active language instead of hesitant phrases like "sort of" and "seems to."
- ☐ I wrote in a unique personal voice.
- ☐ I used correct punctuation.
- ☐ I used some advanced punctuation, like semicolons and dashes.
- ☐ I checked my spelling.
- ☐ There are no run-on sentences.
- ☐ My sentence structure is complex and varied.
- ☐ The ending is effective and fitting.
- ☐ I proofread my story.

Common Core Curriculum Standards for English Language Arts

To help ensure that you're satisfying necessary standards, we've prepared charts to show you which of the Common Core curriculum standards each lesson plan meets. The standards were created as part of the Common Core State Standards (CCSS) Initiative, which aims to align diverse state standards and curricula. You can read the full text of the standards and learn more about them at *www.core standards.org.*

The following is a list of the *writing* English Language Arts standards for grades 5 through 8. An "x" next to the lesson plan indicates that the lesson has the potential to fill the standard, depending on how the instructor implements the lesson.

	Write opinion pieces on topics or texts, supporting a point of view with reasons and information. Introduce a topic or text clearly, state an opinion, and create an organizational structure in which ideas are logically grouped to support the writer's purpose. Provide logically ordered reasons that are supported by facts and details. Link opinion and reasons using words, phrases, and clauses (e.g., *consequently, specifically*). Provide a concluding statement or section related to the opinion presented.	Write informative/explanatory texts to examine a topic and convey ideas and information clearly. ● Introduce a topic clearly, provide a general observation and focus, and group related information logically; include formatting (e.g., headings), illustrations, and multimedia when useful to aiding comprehension. ● Develop the topic with facts, definitions, concrete details, quotations, or other information and examples related to the topic. ● Link ideas within and across categories of information using words, phrases, and clauses (e.g., *in contrast, especially*). ● Use precise language and domain-specific vocabulary to inform about or explain the topic. ● Provide a concluding statement or section related to the information or explanation presented.	Write narratives to develop real or imagined experiences or events using effective technique, descriptive details, and clear event sequences. ● Orient the reader by establishing a situation and introducing a narrator and/or characters; organize an event sequence that unfolds naturally. ● Use narrative techniques, such as dialogue, description, and pacing, to develop experiences and events or show the responses of characters to situations. ● Use a variety of transitional words, phrases, and clauses to manage the sequence of events. ● Use concrete words and phrases and sensory details to convey experiences and events precisely. ● Provide a conclusion that follows from the narrated experiences or events.
THE SCIENCE OF SAVING DAYLIGHT	x		
TECHNICALLY SPEAKING		x	
IT'S (PARTIALLY) ROCKET SCIENCE AND (MOSTLY) ICE CREAM	x	x	x
PLANET OOBLECK		x	x
HOW TO WRITE SCIENCE FICTION		x	x
MAKING WAVES	x	x	
THERE MAY BE BONES	x	x	x
TINFOIL SHIPBUILDING		x	x
WATER, WATER EVERYWHERE, NOR ANY DROP TO DRINK		x	x
THE SCIENCE OF SUPERPOWERS	x		x
INFINITE RECESS			x
REWRITING THE ZOMBIE APOCALYPSE	x	x	x

	Produce clear and coherent writing in which the development and organization are appropriate to task, purpose, and audience. (Grade-specific expectations for writing types are defined in preceding standards for 1–3.)	With guidance and support from peers and adults, develop and strengthen writing as needed by planning, revising, editing, rewriting, or trying a new approach.	With some guidance and support from adults, use technology, including the Internet, to produce and publish writing as well as to interact and collaborate with others; demonstrate sufficient command of keyboarding skills to type a minimum of two pages in a single sitting.
THE SCIENCE OF SAVING DAYLIGHT	x	x	
TECHNICALLY SPEAKING	x	x	
IT'S (PARTIALLY) ROCKET SCIENCE AND (MOSTLY) ICE CREAM	x		
MAKING WAVES	x	x	
THERE MAY BE BONES	x		
TINFOIL SHIPBUILDING	x		
WATER, WATER EVERYWHERE, NOR ANY DROP TO DRINK	x	x	
THE SCIENCE OF SUPERPOWERS	x	x	
INFINITE RECESS	x	x	
REWRITING THE ZOMBIE APOCALYPSE	x		

	GRADE 5		RESEARCH TO BUILD AND PRESENT KNOWLEDGE
	Conduct short research projects that use several sources to build knowledge through investigation of different aspects of a topic.	Recall relevant information from experiences or gather relevant information from print and digital sources; summarize or paraphrase information in notes and finished work, and provide a list of sources.	Draw evidence from literary or informational texts to support analysis, reflection, and research. • Apply *grade 5 reading standards* to literature (e.g., "Compare and contrast two or more characters, settings, or events in a story or a drama, drawing on specific details in the text [e.g., how characters interact]"). • Apply *grade 5 reading standards* to informational texts (e.g., "Explain how an author uses reasons and evidence to support particular points in a text, identifying which reasons and evidence support which point[s]").
THE SCIENCE OF SAVING DAYLIGHT	x		
TECHNICALLY SPEAKING	x		
IT'S (PARTIALLY) ROCKET SCIENCE AND (MOSTLY) ICE CREAM	x	x	x
PLANET OOBLECK	x	x	
HOW TO WRITE SCIENCE FICTION			x
MAKING WAVES	x		
THERE MAY BE BONES	x	x	
TINFOIL SHIPBUILDING	x		
WATER, WATER EVERYWHERE, NOR ANY DROP TO DRINK	x	x	x
THE SCIENCE OF SUPERPOWERS	x		
INFINITE RECESS	x	x	x
REWRITING THE ZOMBIE APOCALYPSE	x		

	GRADE 5: RANGE OF WRITING
	Write routinely over extended time frames (time for research, reflection, and revision) and shorter time frames (a single sitting or a day or two) for a range of discipline-specific tasks, purposes, and audiences.
THE SCIENCE OF SAVING DAYLIGHT	
TECHNICALLY SPEAKING	x
IT'S (PARTIALLY) ROCKET SCIENCE AND (MOSTLY) ICE CREAM	x
PLANET OOBLECK	x
HOW TO WRITE SCIENCE FICTION	x
MAKING WAVES	
THERE MAY BE BONES	x
TINFOIL SHIPBUILDING	
WATER, WATER EVERYWHERE, NOR ANY DROP TO DRINK	x
THE SCIENCE OF SUPERPOWERS	x
INFINITE RECESS	x
REWRITING THE ZOMBIE APOCALYPSE	x

	Write arguments to support claims with clear reasons and relevant evidence.	Write informative/explanatory texts to examine a topic and convey ideas, concepts, and information through the selection, organization, and analysis of relevant content.	Write narratives to develop real or imagined experiences or events using effective technique, relevant descriptive details, and well-structured event sequences.
	Introduce claim(s) and organize the reasons and evidence clearly.	• Introduce a topic; organize ideas, concepts, and information, using strategies such as definition, classification, comparison/contrast, and cause/effect; include formatting (e.g., headings), graphics (e.g., charts, tables), and multimedia when useful to aiding comprehension.	• Engage and orient the reader by establishing a context and introducing a narrator and/or characters; organize an event sequence that unfolds naturally and logically.
	Support claim(s) with clear reasons and relevant evidence, using credible sources and demonstrating an understanding of the topic or text.	• Develop the topic with relevant facts, definitions, concrete details, quotations, or other information and examples.	• Use narrative techniques, such as dialogue, pacing, and description, to develop experiences, events, and/or characters.
	Use words, phrases, and clauses to clarify the relationships among claim(s) and reasons.	• Use appropriate transitions to clarify the relationships among ideas and concepts.	• Use a variety of transition words, phrases, and clauses to convey sequence and signal shifts from one time frame or setting to another.
	Establish and maintain a formal style.	• Use precise language and domain-specific vocabulary to inform about or explain the topic.	• Use precise words and phrases, relevant descriptive details, and sensory language to convey experiences and events.
	Provide a concluding statement or section that follows from the argument presented.	• Establish and maintain a formal style.	• Provide a conclusion that follows from the narrated experiences or events.
		• Provide a concluding statement or section that follows from the information or explanation presented.	
THE SCIENCE OF SAVING DAYLIGHT	x		
TECHNICALLY SPEAKING		x	
IT'S (PARTIALLY) ROCKET SCIENCE AND (MOSTLY) ICE CREAM	x	x	x
PLANET OOBLECK		x	x
HOW TO WRITE SCIENCE FICTION		x	x
MAKING WAVES	x	x	
THERE MAY BE BONES	x	x	x
TINFOIL SHIPBUILDING		x	x
WATER, WATER EVERYWHERE, NOR ANY DROP TO DRINK		x	x
THE SCIENCE OF SUPERPOWERS	x		x
INFINITE RECESS			x
REWRITING THE ZOMBIE APOCALYPSE	x	x	x

	GRADE 6	PRODUCTION AND DISTRIBUTION OF WRITING	
	Produce clear and coherent writing in which the development, organization, and style are appropriate to task, purpose, and audience. (Grade-specific expectations for writing types are defined in preceding standards 1–3.)	With some guidance and support from peers and adults, develop and strengthen writing as needed by planning, revising, editing, rewriting, or trying a new approach. (Editing for conventions should demonstrate command of language standards 1–3 up to and including grade 6.)	Use technology, including the Internet, to produce and publish writing as well as to interact and collaborate with others; demonstrate sufficient command of keyboarding skills to type a minimum of three pages in a single sitting.
THE SCIENCE OF SAVING DAYLIGHT	x	x	
TECHNICALLY SPEAKING	x	x	
IT'S (PARTIALLY) ROCKET SCIENCE AND (MOSTLY) ICE CREAM	x		
PLANET OOBLECK	x		
HOW TO WRITE SCIENCE FICTION	x	x	x
MAKING WAVES	x	x	
THERE MAY BE BONES	x		
TINFOIL SHIPBUILDING	x		
WATER, WATER EVERYWHERE, NOR ANY DROP TO DRINK	x	x	
THE SCIENCE OF SUPERPOWERS	x	x	
INFINITE RECESS	x	x	
REWRITING THE ZOMBIE APOCALYPSE	x		

	Conduct short research projects to answer a question, drawing on several sources and refocusing the inquiry when appropriate.	Gather relevant information from multiple print and digital sources; assess the credibility of each source; and quote or paraphrase the data and conclusions of others while avoiding plagiarism and providing basic bibliographic information for sources.	Draw evidence from literary or informational texts to support analysis, reflection, and research. • Apply *grade 6 reading standards* to literature (e.g., "Compare and contrast texts in different forms or genres [e.g., stories and poems; historical novels and fantasy stories] in terms of their approaches to similar themes and topics"). • Apply *grade 6 reading standards* to literary nonfiction (e.g., "Trace and evaluate the argument and specific claims in a text, distinguishing claims that are supported by reasons and evidence from claims that are not").
THE SCIENCE OF SAVING DAYLIGHT	x		
TECHNICALLY SPEAKING	x		
IT'S (PARTIALLY) ROCKET SCIENCE AND (MOSTLY) ICE CREAM	x	x	x
PLANET OOBLECK	x		
HOW TO WRITE SCIENCE FICTION			
MAKING WAVES	x		
THERE MAY BE BONES	x		
TINFOIL SHIPBUILDING	x		
WATER, WATER EVERYWHERE, NOR ANY DROP TO DRINK	x	x	x
THE SCIENCE OF SUPERPOWERS	x		
INFINITE RECESS	x	x	x
REWRITING THE ZOMBIE APOCALYPSE	x		

	GRADE 6: RANGE OF WRITING
	Write routinely over extended time frames (time for research, reflection, and revision) and shorter time frames (a single sitting or a day or two) for a range of discipline-specific tasks, purposes, and audiences.
THE SCIENCE OF SAVING DAYLIGHT	
TECHNICALLY SPEAKING	x
IT'S (PARTIALLY) ROCKET SCIENCE AND (MOSTLY) ICE CREAM	x
PLANET OOBLECK	x
HOW TO WRITE SCIENCE FICTION	x
MAKING WAVES	
THERE MAY BE BONES	x
TINFOIL SHIPBUILDING	
WATER, WATER EVERYWHERE, NOR ANY DROP TO DRINK	x
THE SCIENCE OF SUPERPOWERS	x
INFINITE RECESS	x
REWRITING THE ZOMBIE APOCALYPSE	x

	Write arguments to support claims with clear reasons and relevant evidence. • Introduce claim(s), acknowledge alternate or opposing claims, and organize the reasons and evidence logically. • Support claim(s) with logical reasoning and relevant evidence, using accurate, credible sources and demonstrating an understanding of the topic or text. • Use words, phrases, and clauses to create cohesion and clarify the relationships among claim(s), reasons, and evidence. • Establish and maintain a formal style. • Provide a concluding statement or section that follows from and supports the argument presented.	Write informative/explanatory texts to examine a topic and convey ideas, concepts, and information through the selection, organization, and analysis of relevant content. • Introduce a topic clearly, previewing what is to follow; organize ideas, concepts, and information, using strategies such as definition, classification, comparison/contrast, and cause/effect; include formatting (e.g., headings), graphics (e.g., charts, tables), and multimedia when useful to aiding comprehension. • Develop the topic with relevant facts, definitions, concrete details, quotations, or other information and examples. • Use appropriate transitions to create cohesion and clarify the relationships among ideas and concepts. • Use precise language and domain-specific vocabulary to inform about or explain the topic. • Establish and maintain a formal style. • Provide a concluding statement or section that follows from and supports the information or explanation presented.	Write narratives to develop real or imagined experiences or events using effective technique, relevant descriptive details, and well-structured event sequences. • Engage and orient the reader by establishing a context and point of view and introducing a narrator and/or characters; organize an event sequence that unfolds naturally and logically. • Use narrative techniques, such as dialogue, pacing, and description, to develop experiences, events, and/or characters. • Use a variety of transition words, phrases, and clauses to convey sequence and signal shifts from one time frame or setting to another. • Use precise words and phrases, relevant descriptive details, and sensory language to capture the action and convey experiences and events. • Provide a conclusion that follows from and reflects on the narrated experiences or events.
THE SCIENCE OF SAVING DAYLIGHT	x		
TECHNICALLY SPEAKING		x	
IT'S (PARTIALLY) ROCKET SCIENCE AND (MOSTLY) ICE CREAM	x	x	x
PLANET OOBLECK		x	x
HOW TO WRITE SCIENCE FICTION		x	x
MAKING WAVES	x	x	
THERE MAY BE BONES	x	x	x
TINFOIL SHIPBUILDING		x	x
WATER, WATER EVERYWHERE, NOR ANY DROP TO DRINK		x	x
THE SCIENCE OF SUPERPOWERS	x		x
INFINITE RECESS			x
REWRITING THE ZOMBIE APOCALYPSE	x	x	x

	Produce clear and coherent writing in which the development, organization, and style are appropriate to task, purpose, and audience. (Grade-specific expectations for writing types are defined in preceding standards 1–3.)	With some guidance and support from peers and adults, develop and strengthen writing as needed by planning, revising, editing, rewriting, or trying a new approach, focusing on how well purpose and audience have been addressed. (Editing for conventions should demonstrate command of language standards 1–3 up to and including grade 7 here.)	Use technology, including the Internet, to produce and publish writing and link to and cite sources as well as to interact and collaborate with others, including linking to and citing sources.
THE SCIENCE OF SAVING DAYLIGHT	x	x	
TECHNICALLY SPEAKING	x	x	
IT'S (PARTIALLY) ROCKET SCIENCE AND (MOSTLY) ICE CREAM	x		
PLANET OOBLECK	x		
HOW TO WRITE SCIENCE FICTION	x	x	x
MAKING WAVES	x	x	
THERE MAY BE BONES	x		
TINFOIL SHIPBUILDING	x		
WATER, WATER EVERYWHERE, NOR ANY DROP TO DRINK	x	x	
THE SCIENCE OF SUPERPOWERS	x	x	
INFINITE RECESS	x	x	
REWRITING THE ZOMBIE APOCALYPSE	x		

	Conduct short research projects to answer a question, drawing on several sources and generating additional related, focused questions for further research and investigation.	Gather relevant information from multiple print and digital sources, using search terms effectively; assess the credibility and accuracy of each source; and quote or paraphrase the data and conclusions of others while avoiding plagiarism and following a standard format for citation.	Draw evidence from literary or informational texts to support analysis, reflection, and research. • Apply *grade 7 reading standards* to literature (e.g., "Compare and contrast a fictional portrayal of a time, place, or character and a historical account of the same period as a means of understanding how authors of fiction use or alter history"). • Apply *grade 7 reading standards* to literary nonfiction (e.g., "Trace and evaluate the argument and specific claims in a text, assessing whether the reasoning is sound and the evidence is relevant and sufficient to support the claims").
THE SCIENCE OF SAVING DAYLIGHT	x		
TECHNICALLY SPEAKING	x		
IT'S (PARTIALLY) ROCKET SCIENCE AND (MOSTLY) ICE CREAM	x	x	x
PLANET OOBLECK			
HOW TO WRITE SCIENCE FICTION	x		
MAKING WAVES	x		
THERE MAY BE BONES	x		
TINFOIL SHIPBUILDING	x		
WATER, WATER EVERYWHERE, NOR ANY DROP TO DRINK	x	x	x
THE SCIENCE OF SUPERPOWERS	x		
INFINITE RECESS	x	x	x
REWRITING THE ZOMBIE APOCALYPSE	x		

	GRADE 7: RANGE OF WRITING
	Write routinely over extended time frames (time for research, reflection, and revision) and shorter time frames (a single sitting or a day or two) for a range of discipline-specific tasks, purposes, and audiences.
THE SCIENCE OF SAVING DAYLIGHT	
TECHNICALLY SPEAKING	x
IT'S (PARTIALLY) ROCKET SCIENCE AND (MOSTLY) ICE CREAM	x
PLANET OOBLECK	x
HOW TO WRITE SCIENCE FICTION	x
MAKING WAVES	
THERE MAY BE BONES	x
TINFOIL SHIPBUILDING	
WATER, WATER EVERYWHERE, NOR ANY DROP TO DRINK	x
THE SCIENCE OF SUPERPOWERS	x
INFINITE RECESS	x
REWRITING THE ZOMBIE APOCALYPSE	x

	Write arguments to support claims with clear reasons and relevant evidence. • Introduce claim(s), acknowledge and distinguish the claim(s) from alternate or opposing claims, and organize the reasons and evidence logically. • Support claim(s) with logical reasoning and relevant evidence, using accurate, credible sources and demonstrating an understanding of the topic or text. • Use words, phrases, and clauses to create cohesion and clarify the relationships among claim(s), counterclaims, reasons, and evidence. • Establish and maintain a formal style. • Provide a concluding statement or section that follows from and supports the argument presented.	Write informative/explanatory texts to examine a topic and convey ideas, concepts, and information through the selection, organization, and analysis of relevant content. • Introduce a topic clearly, previewing what is to follow; organize ideas, concepts, and information into broader categories; include formatting (e.g., headings), graphics (e.g., charts, tables), and multimedia when useful to aiding comprehension. • Develop the topic with relevant, well-chosen facts, definitions, concrete details, quotations, or other information and examples. • Use appropriate and varied transitions to create cohesion and clarify the relationships among ideas and concepts. • Use precise language and domain-specific vocabulary to inform about or explain the topic. • Establish and maintain a formal style. • Provide a concluding statement or section that follows from and supports the information or explanation presented.	Write narratives to develop real or imagined experiences or events using effective technique, relevant descriptive details, and well-structured event sequences. • Engage and orient the reader by establishing a context and point of view and introducing a narrator and/or characters; organize an event sequence that unfolds naturally and logically. • Use narrative techniques, such as dialogue, pacing, description, and reflection, to develop experiences, events, and/or characters. • Use a variety of transition words, phrases, and clauses to convey sequence, signal shifts from one time frame or setting to another, and show the relationships among experiences and events. • Use precise words and phrases, relevant descriptive details, and sensory language to capture the action and convey experiences and events. • Provide a conclusion that follows from and reflects on the narrated experiences or events.
THE SCIENCE OF SAVING DAYLIGHT	x		
TECHNICALLY SPEAKING		x	
IT'S (PARTIALLY) ROCKET SCIENCE AND (MOSTLY) ICE CREAM	x	x	x
PLANET OOBLECK		x	x
HOW TO WRITE SCIENCE FICTION		x	x
MAKING WAVES	x	x	
THERE MAY BE BONES	x	x	x
TINFOIL SHIPBUILDING		x	x
WATER, WATER EVERYWHERE, NOR ANY DROP TO DRINK		x	x
THE SCIENCE OF SUPERPOWERS	x		x
INFINITE RECESS			x
REWRITING THE ZOMBIE APOCALYPSE	x	x	x

	Produce clear and coherent writing in which the development, organization, and style are appropriate to task, purpose, and audience. (Grade-specific expectations for writing types are defined in preceding standards 1–3.)	With some guidance and support from peers and adults, develop and strengthen writing as needed by planning, revising, editing, rewriting, or trying a new approach, focusing on how well purpose and audience have been addressed.	Use technology, including the Internet, to produce and publish writing and present the relationships between information and ideas efficiently as well as to interact and collaborate with others.
THE SCIENCE OF SAVING DAYLIGHT	x	x	
TECHNICALLY SPEAKING	x	x	
IT'S (PARTIALLY) ROCKET SCIENCE AND (MOSTLY) ICE CREAM	x		
PLANET OOBLECK	x		
HOW TO WRITE SCIENCE FICTION	x	x	x
MAKING WAVES	x	x	
THERE MAY BE BONES	x		
TINFOIL SHIPBUILDING	x		
WATER, WATER EVERYWHERE, NOR ANY DROP TO DRINK	x	x	
THE SCIENCE OF SUPERPOWERS	x	x	
INFINITE RECESS	x	x	
REWRITING THE ZOMBIE APOCALYPSE	x		

	Conduct short research projects to answer a question (including a self-generated question), drawing on several sources and generating additional related, focused questions that allow for multiple avenues of exploration.	Gather relevant information from multiple print and digital sources, using search terms effectively; assess the credibility and accuracy of each source; and quote or paraphrase the data and conclusions of others while avoiding plagiarism and following a standard format for citation.	Draw evidence from literary or informational texts to support analysis, reflection, and research. • Apply *grade 8 reading standards* to literature (e.g., "Analyze how a modern work of fiction draws on themes, patterns of events, or character types from myths, traditional stories, or religious works such as the Bible, including describing how the material is rendered new"). • Apply *grade 8 reading standards* to literary nonfiction (e.g., "Delineate and evaluate the argument and specific claims in a text, assessing whether the reasoning is sound and the evidence is relevant and sufficient; recognize when irrelevant evidence is introduced").
THE SCIENCE OF SAVING DAYLIGHT	x		
TECHNICALLY SPEAKING	x		
IT'S (PARTIALLY) ROCKET SCIENCE AND (MOSTLY) ICE CREAM	x	x	x
PLANET OOBLECK			
HOW TO WRITE SCIENCE FICTION	x		
MAKING WAVES	x		
THERE MAY BE BONES	x		
TINFOIL SHIPBUILDING	x		
WATER, WATER EVERYWHERE, NOR ANY DROP TO DRINK	x	x	x
THE SCIENCE OF SUPERPOWERS	x		
INFINITE RECESS	x	x	x
REWRITING THE ZOMBIE APOCALYPSE	x		

	GRADE 8: RANGE OF WRITING
	Write routinely over extended time frames (time for research, reflection, and revision) and shorter time frames (a single sitting or a day or two) for a range of discipline-specific tasks, purposes, and audiences.
THE SCIENCE OF SAVING DAYLIGHT	
TECHNICALLY SPEAKING	x
IT'S (PARTIALLY) ROCKET SCIENCE AND (MOSTLY) ICE CREAM	x
PLANET OOBLECK	x
HOW TO WRITE SCIENCE FICTION	x
MAKING WAVES	
THERE MAY BE BONES	x
TINFOIL SHIPBUILDING	
WATER, WATER EVERYWHERE, NOR ANY DROP TO DRINK	x
THE SCIENCE OF SUPERPOWERS	x
INFINITE RECESS	x
REWRITING THE ZOMBIE APOCALYPSE	x

Next Generation Science Standards

The Next Generation Science Standards (NGSS) were developed in 2013 by a consortium consisting of the National Research Council, the National Science Teachers Association, the American Association for the Advancement of Science, the nonprofit organization Achieve, and twenty-six states. They aim to define academic standards in the sciences, and to promote students' interest in pursuing the sciences. On the following chart, standards are indicated by grade level in parentheses: (5) for fifth grade, (MS) for middle school. You can read the full text of the standards and learn more about them at *www.nextgenscience.org/next-generation-science-standards*.

LESSON	DISCIPLINARY CORE IDEAS	SCIENCE AND ENGINEERING PRACTICES	CROSS-CUTTING CONCEPTS	SCIENCE, TECHNOLOGY, SOCIETY, AND THE ENVIRONMENT
	LS2.A — Interdependent Relationships in Ecosystems: The food of almost any kind of animal can be traced back to plants. Organisms are related in food webs in which some animals eat plants for food and other animals eat the animals that eat plants. (5) • Predatory interactions may reduce the number of organisms or eliminate whole populations of organisms. (MS)	Asking Questions (and Defining Problems); Developing and Using Models; Analyzing and Interpreting Data / Planning and Carrying Out Investigations	Energy and Matter — The transfer of energy can be tracked as energy flows through a natural system. (MS)	
There May Be Bones	LS2.B — Cycle of Matter and Energy Transfer in Ecosystems: Matter cycles between the air and soil and among plants, animals, and microbes as these organisms live and die. Organisms obtain gases, and water from the environment, and release waste matter (gas, liquid or solid) back into the environment. (5) • Food webs are models that demonstrate how matter and energy is transferred between producers, consumers, and decomposers as the three groups interact within an ecosystem. (MS)	Constructing Explanations and Designing Solutions; Engaging in Argument from Evidence; Obtaining, Evaluating, and Communicating Information		
Making Waves (Sound and Instrument Building)	PS4.A — Wave Properties: A simple wave model has a repeating pattern with a specific wavelength, frequency, and amplitude. • A sound wave needs a medium through which it is transmitted. (MS)	Asking Questions and Defining Problems; Constructing Explanations and Designing Solutions; Engaging in Argument from Evidence	Structure and Function — Substructures have shapes and parts that serve functions. (5) • Students design structures to serve particular functions by taking into account properties of different materials and how materials can be shaped and used. (MS); Patterns — Similarities and differences in patterns can be used to sort, classify, communicate and analyze simple rates of change for natural phenomena and designed products. (5) and Patterns can be used as evidence to support an explanation (5) • Patterns in rates of change and other numerical relationships can provide information about natural and human designed systems." and "Patterns can be used to identify cause and effect relationships. (MS)	
	ETS1.A — Defining and Delimiting Engineering Problems: Possible solutions to a problem are limited by available materials resources (constraints). The success of a designed solution is determined by considering the desired features of a solution (criteria). Different proposals for solutions can be compared on the basis of how well each one meets the specified criteria for success or how well each one takes the constraints into account. (5) • The more precisely a design task's criteria and constraints can be defined, the more likely it is that the designed solution will be successful. Specification of constraints includes consideration of scientific principles and other relevant knowledge likely to limit possible solutions. (MS)	Asking Questions and Defining Problems; Planning and Carrying Out Investigations	Cause and Effect — Cause and effect relationships are routinely identified, tested, and used to explain change. (5)	

Lesson	Disciplinary Core Ideas		Science and Engineering Practices	Cross-Cutting Concepts	Science, Technology, Society, and the Environment
	ETS1.B	Developing Possible Solutions: A solution needs to be tested, and then modified on the basis of the test results, in order to improve on it.		Scale, Proportion, and Quantity	
				The observed function of natural and designed systems may change with scale and proportional relationships among different types of quantities provide information about the magnitude of properties and processes. (MS)	
		Defining and Delimiting Engineering Problems: Possible solutions to a problem are limited by available materials resources (constraints). The success of a designed solution is determined by considering the desired features of a solution (criteria). Different proposals for solutions can be compared on the basis of how well each one meets the specified criteria for success or how well each takes the constraints into account. (5)		Scale, Proportion, and Quantity	The observed function of natural and designed systems may change with scale. (MS)
	ETS1.A	• The more precisely a design task's criteria and constraints can be defined, the more likely it is that the designed solution will be successful. Specification of constraints includes consideration of scientific principles and other relevant knowledge likely to limit possible solutions. (MS)	Asking Questions and Defining Problems		Small changes in one part of a system might cause large changes in another part. A nd: Stability might be disturbed either by sudden events or gradual changes that accumulate over time. (MS)
			Planning and Carrying Out Investigations	Stability and Change	
Tinfoil Shipbuilding		Developing Possible Solutions: At whatever stage (of design) communicating with peers about proposed solutions is an important part of the design process, and shared ideas can lead to improved designs. (5) • A solution needs to be tested, and then modified on the basis of the test results, in order to improve on it. (MS)	Developing and Using Models		
	ETS1.B	Optimizing the Design Solution - Optimizing the Design Solution: Different solutions need to be tested in order to determine which of them best solves the problem, given the criteria and constraints. (5) • The iterative process of testing the most promising solutions and modifying what is proposed on the basis of the test results leads to greater refinement and ultimately to an optimal solution. (MS)	Cause and Effect		• Cause and effect relationships are routinely identified, tested, and used to explain change. (5) • Cause and effect relationships may be used to predict phenomena in natural or designed systems. (MS)
			Stucture and Function		
	ETS1.C			Sucture and Function	Structures can be designed to serve particular functions by taking into account properties of different materials and how materials can be shaped and used. (MS)

(continued)

LESSON	DISCIPLINARY CORE IDEAS	SCIENCE AND ENGINEERING PRACTICES		CROSS-CUTTING CONCEPTS
The Science of Saving Daylight		Asking Questions and Defining Problems	Planning and (Carrying out) Investigations · Constructing Explanations and Designing Solutions	Cause and Effect: • Cause and effect relationships are routinely identified, tested, and used to explain change. (5) · • Cause and effect relationships may be used to predict phenomena in natural or designed systems. (MS)
		Analyzing and Interpreting Data	Engaging in Argument from Evidence · Obtaining, Evaluating and Communicating Information	
	Forces & motion - The role of the mass of an object must be qualitatively accounted for in any change of motion due to the application of a force. (MS)			Cause and Effect: Cause and effect relationships are routinely identified and used to explain change. (5) · • Students classify relationships as causal or correlational, and recognize that correlation does not necessarily imply causation. and They understand that phenomena can have more than one cause. (MS)
	PS2.A Motion & Stability: Forces and Interactions: Types of Interactions: The gravitational force of Earth acting on an object near Earth's surface pulls that object towards the planet's center. (5)		Using Mathematics and Computational Thinking	
	PS2.B Relationship between energy and forces: Then two objects interact, each exerts a force on the other, and these forces can transfer energy between them. (MS)	Planning and Carrying Out Investigations	Analyzing and Interpreting Data	
	PS3.C			Structure and Function: Substructures have shapes and parts that serve functions. (5) · • Students model complex structures and systems and visualize how their function depends on the shapes, composition, and relationships among its parts. They design structures to serve particular functions by taking into account properties of different materials and how materials can be shaped and used. (MS)
Technically Speaking	Developing possible solutions: There are systematic processes for evaluating solutions with respect to how well they meet the criteria and constraints of a problem and A solution needs to be tested, and then modified on the basis of the test results in order to improve on it. (MS)		(Obtaining, Evaluating, and) Communicating Information	Stability and Change: Change is measured in terms of differences over time and may occur at different rates. (5) · • Students explain stability and change in a designed system by examining changes over time and considering forces at different scales. Students learn that changes in one part of a system might cause large changes in another part. (MS)
	ETS1-B Optimizing the Design Solution: Although one design may not perform the best across all tests, identifying the characteristics of the design that performed the best in each test can provide useful information for the redesign process: that is some of those characteristics may be incorporated into the new design. (MS)	(Constructing Explanations) and Designing Solutions	Asking Questions and Defining Problems	
	ETS1-C		Developing and Using Models	

Lesson	Disciplinary Core Ideas	Science and Engineering Practices	Cross-Cutting Concepts	Science, Technology, Society, and the Environment
		(Constructing Explanations) and Designing Solutions	Interdependence of Science, Engineering, and Technology	Engineering advances have led to important discoveries in virtually every field of science, and scientific discoveries have led to the development of entire industries and engineered systems.
How to Write Science Fiction				The use of technologies and any limitation on their use are driven by individual or societal needs, desires, and values; by the findings of scientific research; and by differences in such factors as climate, natural resources, and economic conditions. Thus, technology use varies from region to region over time.
			Influence of Engineering, Technology, and Science on Society and the Natural World	
	Definitions of Energy: The term "heat" as used in everyday language refers both to thermal energy (the motion of atoms or molecules within a substance) and the transfer of that thermal energy from one object to another. In science, heat is used only for this second meaning; it refers to the energy transferred due to the temperature difference between two objects. (MS) • Temperature is a measure of the average kinetic energy of particles of matter. The relationship between the temperature and the total energy of a system depends on the types, states, and amounts of matter present. (MS)		Energy and Matter (Session 1, 2)	• Energy can be transferred in various ways and between objects. (5) • The transfer of energy can be tracked as energy flows through a designed or natural system. (MS) • Energy may take different forms (e.g. energy in fields, thermal energy, energy of motion). (MS)
PS3.A (Session 1)		Asking Questions and Defining Problems (Session 1,2)		
		Planning and Carrying Out Investigations (Session 1,2)		
		Constructing Explanations and Designing Solutions (Session 2)	Cause and Effect (Session 1, 2)	• Cause and effect relationships are routinely identified and used to explain change. (5th) • Cause and effect relationships may be used to predict phenomena in natural or designed systems. (MS)

(continued)

Lesson	Disciplinary Core Ideas	Science and Engineering Practices	Cross-Cutting Concepts	Science, Technology, Society, and the Environment
It's (Partially) Rocket Science and (Mostly) Ice Cream	**PS1.B** (Session 1) Chemical Reactions: • When two or more different substances are mixed, a new substance with different properties may be formed. (5) • Some chemical reactions release energy, others store energy. (MS) **PS3.B** (Session 1, 2) Conservation of Energy and Energy Transfer: Energy is spontaneously transferred out of hotter regions or objects and into colder ones. (MS) • The amount of energy transfer needed to change the temperature of a matter sample by a given amount depends on the nature of the matter, the size of the sample, and the environment. (MS) **ETS1.A** (Session 2) Defining and Delimiting Engineering Problems: Possible solutions to a problem are limited by available materials and resources (constraints). The success of a designed solution is determined by considering the desired features of a solution (criteria). Different proposals for solutions can be compared on the basis of how well each one meets the specified criteris for success or how well each takes the constraints into account. (5) • The more precisely a design task's criteria canbe defined, the more likely it is that the designed solution will be successful. Specification of constraints includes consideration of scientific principles and other relevant knowledge that is likely to limit possible solutions. (MS)	Developing and Using Models (Session 3) Analyzing and Interpreting Data (Session 2) Obtaining, Evaluating, and Communicating Information (Session 2, 3, 4)	Structure and Function (Session 2) Systems and Systems Models (Session 2)	• Structures can be designed to serve particular functions by taking into account properties of different materials and how materials can be shaped and used. (MS) • A system can be described in terms of its components and their interactions. (5) • Systems may interact with other systems; they may have subsystems and be part of larger complex systems. (MS)

LESSON	DISCIPLINARY CORE IDEAS	SCIENCE AND ENGINEERING PRACTICES	CROSS-CUTTING CONCEPTS	SCIENCE, TECHNOLOGY, SOCIETY, AND THE ENVIRONMENT
	Developing Possible Solutions: At whatever stage (of design) communicating with peers about proposed solutions is an important part of the design process, and shared ideas can lead to improved designs. (5)			
ETS1.B (Session 2)	• Tests are often designed to identify failure points or difficulties, which suggest the elements of a design that need to be improved. (5) • A solution needs to be tested and then modified on the basis of the test results in order to improve it. (MS) • Sometimes parts of different solutions can be combined to create a solution that is better than any of its predecessors. (MS)			
	Optimizing the Design Solution: Different solutions need to be tested in order to determine which of them best solves the problem, given the criteria and constraints. (5) • A solution needs to be tested and then modified on the basis of the test results in order to improve it. (MS) • Sometimes parts of different solutions can be combined to create a solution that is better than any of its predecessors. (MS)	Engaging in Argument from Evidence (Session 2)		
ETS1.C (Session 2)				

(continued)

LESSON	DISCIPLINARY CORE IDEAS	SCIENCE AND ENGINEERING PRACTICES	CROSS-CUTTING CONCEPTS	SCIENCE, TECHNOLOGY, SOCIETY, AND THE ENVIRONMENT
ETS1.A (Session 1)	Defining and Delimiting Engineering Problems: Possible solutions to a problem are limited by available materials and resources (constraints). The success of a designed solution is determined by considering the desired features of a solution (criteria). Different proposals for solutions can be compared on the basis of how well each one meets the specified criteris for success or how well each takes the constraints into account. (5)	Asking Questions and Defining Problems (Session 1)		
	• The more precisely a design task's criteria canbe defined, the more likely it is that the designed solution will be successful. Specification of constraints includes consideration of scientific principles and other relevant knowledge that is likely to limit possible solutions. (MS)	Planning and Carrying Out Investigations (Session 1, 2)		
	Developing Possible Solutions: At whatever stage (of design) communicating with peers about proposed solutions is an important part of the design process, and shared ideas can lead to improved designs. (5)	Constructing Explanations and Designing Solutions (Session 1, 2)	• Cause and effect relationships are routinely identified and used to explain change. (5) • Cause and effect relationships may be used to predict phenomena in natural or designed systems. (MS)	
ETS1.B (Session 1)	• Tests are often designed to identify failure points or difficulties, which suggest the elements of a design that need to be improved. (5)		Cause and Effect (Session 1)	
	• A solution needs to be tested and then modified on the basis of the test results in order to improve it. (MS)		Structures can be designed to serve particular functions by taking into account properties of different materials and how materials can be shaped and used. (MS)	
	• Sometimes parts of different solutions can be combined to create a solution that is better than any of its predecessors. (MS)		Structure and Function (Session 1)	

Lesson	Disciplinary Core Ideas	Science and Engineering Practices	Cross-Cutting Concepts	Science, Technology, Society, and the Environment
	ESS2.A (Session 1)			
Planet Oobleck	• Earth's major systems are the geosphere (solid and molten rock, soil, and sediments), the hydrosphere (water and ice), the atmosphere (air), and the biosphere (living things, including humans). These systems interact in multiple ways to affect Earth's surface materials and processes. (5)	Developing and Using Models (1)		
		Obtaining, Evaluating, and Communicating Information (Session 1, 2)	Systems and Systems Models (Session 1, 2)	
			• A system can be described in terms of its components and their interactions. (5)	
			• Systems may interact with other systems; they may have subsystems and be part of larger complex systems. (MS)	
			Connections to Engineering, Technology, and Applications of Science (Session 1)	The uses of technologies and any limitations on their use are driven by individual or societal needs, desires, and values; by the findings of scientific research; and by differences in such factors as climate, natural resources, and economic conditions. Thus technology use varies from region to region and over time. (MS)
	Organisms, and populations of ecosystems are dependent on their environmental interactions both with other living things and with non-living factors. (MS)		• Technologies extend the measurement, exploration, modeling, and computational capacit of scientific investigations. (MS)	
	LS2.A (Session 2)			
	Natural Selection: Both natural and artificial selection result from certain traits giving some individuals an advantage in surviving and reproducing leading to predominance of certain traits in the population. (MS)			
	LS4.B (Session 2)		Patterns (Session 2)	Students identify similarities and differences in order to sort and classify natural objects and designed products. (5)
	Adaptation: Adaptation by natural selection acting over generations is one important process by which species change over time in response to changes in environmental conditions. (MS)			
	LS4.C (Session 2)			

(continued)

Lesson	Disciplinary Core Ideas	Science and Engineering Practices	Cross-Cutting Concepts	Science, Technology, Society, and the Environment
Water, Water, Everywhere	LS2.B Cycles of Matter and Energy Transfer in Ecosystems: Matter cycles between the air and soil and among plants, animals, and microbes. Organisms obtain gases, and water, from the environment, and release waste matter (gas, liquid, or solid) back into the environment. (5)	Constructing Explanations and Designing Solutions (1,2,3)	Systems and System Models — A system can be described in terms of its components and their interactions. (5) Cause and Effect	Influence of Science, Engineering, and Technology on Society and the Natural World — All human activity draws on natural resources and has both short and long-term consequences, positive as well as negative for the health of people and the natural environment. (MS)
	ESS2.C The Roles of Water in Earth's Surface Processes: Nearly all of Earth's available water is in the ocean. Most fresh water is in glaciers or underground; only a tiny fraction is in streams, lakes, and the atmospheres. (5)		Cause and effect relationships are routinely identified and used to explain change. (5) Cause and effect relationships may be used to predict phenomena in natural or designed systems. (MS)	Influence of Engineering, Technology and Science on Society and the Natural World — Engineers improve existing technologies or develop new ones to increase their benefits, decrease known risks, and meet societal needs. (5)
	ESS3.A Natural Resources: Humans depend on Earth's land, ocean, atmosphere, and biosphere for many different resources. Minerals, fresh water, and biosphere resources are limited, and many are not renewable or replaceable over human lifetimes. (MS) Human Impacts on Earth Systems: Human activities in agriculture, industry and everyday life have had major effects on the land, vegetation, streams, ocean, air, and even outer space. But, individuals and communities are doing things to help protect earth's resources and environments. (5)	Asking Questions and Defining Problems (Session 1,2,3) Obtaining, Evaluating, and Communicating Information (Session 2,3)	Structure and Function — Structures can be designed to serve particular functions byraking into account properties of different materials, and how materials can be shaped and used. (MS)	Influence of Science, Engineering, and Technology on Society and the Natural World — The uses of technologies and any limitations on their use are driven by individual or societal needs, desires, and values: by the findings of scientific research; and by differences in such factors as climate, natural resources, and economic conditions. Thus technology use varies from region to region and over time. (MS)
	ESS3.C • Human activities have significantly altered the biosphere, sometimes damaging or destroying natural habitats (and causing the extinction of other species.) (MS)			

LESSON	DISCIPLINARY CORE IDEAS	SCIENCE AND ENGINEERING PRACTICES	CROSS-CUTTING CONCEPTS	SCIENCE, TECHNOLOGY, SOCIETY, AND THE ENVIRONMENT
	Defining and Delimiting Engineering Problems: Possible solutions to a problem are limited by available materials resources (constraints). The success of a designed solution is determined by considering the desired features of a solution (criteria). Different proposals for solutions can be compared on the basis of how well each one meets the specified criteria for success or how well each takes the constraints into account. (5)	Analyzing and Interpreting Data (Session 1,2,3)	Engaging in Argument from Evidence (Session 1,2,3)	
ETS1.A	• The more precisely a design task's criteria and constraints can be defined, the more likely it is that the designed solution will be successful. Specification of constraints includes consideration of scientific principles and other relevant knowledge that are likely to limit possible solutions. (MS) Developing Possible Solutions: Testing a solution involves investigating how well it performs under a range of likely conditions.	Planning and Carrying Out Investigations (Session 1,2,3)		
ETS1.B	• At whatever stage, communicating with peers about proposed solutions is an important part of the design process and shared ideas can lead to improved designs. (5) • A solution needs to be tested and then modified on the basis of the test results in order to improve it. (MS) • Sometimes parts of different solutions can be combined to create a solution that is better than any of its predecessors. (MS)			

(continued)

Lesson	Disciplinary Core Ideas	Science and Engineering Practices	Cross-Cutting Concepts	Science, Technology, Society, and the Environment
	ETS1.C			
	Optimizing the Design Solution: Different solutions need to be tested in order to determine which of them best solves the problem, given the criteria and constraints. (5)			
	• Although one design may not perform the best across all tests, identifying the characteristics of the design that performed the best in each test can provide useful information for the redesign process - that is, some of those characteristics may be incorporated into the new design.			
	• The iterative process of testing the most promising solutions and modifying what is proposed on the basis of the test results leads to greater refinement and ultimately to an optimal solution. (MS)		• Some systems appear stable, but over long periods of time will eventually change. (5)	
			• Change is measured in terms of differences over time and may occur at different rates. (5)	
Rewriting the Zombie Apocalypse	LS4.B		Stability and Change	
	Natural Selection: Natural selection leads to the predominance of certain traits in a population and the suppression of others. (MS)		• Explanations of stability and change in natural or designed systems can be constructed by examining the changes over time (and forces at different scales). (MS)	
		Developing and Using Models (Session 1,2,3,4)	• Small changes in one part of a system may cause large changes in another part. (MS)	
			• Stability may be disrupted either by sudden events or gradual changes that accumulate over time. (MS)	
	LS4.C		A system can be described in terms of its components and their interactions. (5)	
	Adaptation: Adaptation by natural selection acting over generations is one important process by which species change over time in response to changes in environmental conditions. Traits that support successful survival and reproduction in the new environment become more common; those that do not become less common. Thus the distribution of traits in a population changes. (MS)	Analyzing and Interpreting Data (Session 1,2,3,4)	Systems and Systems Models	
		Using Mathematics and Computational Thinking (Session 3,4)	• Models can be used to represent systems and their interactions: such as inputs, processes and outputs - and energy, matter, and information flows within systems. (MS)	
			• Models are limited in that they only represent certain aspects of the system under study. (MS)	
	LS3.B		Structures can be designed r o serve particular functions by taking into account properties of different materials, and how materials can be shaped and used. (MS)	
	Variation of Traits: In addition to variations that arise from sexual reproduction, genetic information can be altered because of mutations. Though rare, mutations may result in changes to the structure and function of proteins. Some changes are beneficial, others harmful, and some neutral to the organism. (MS)		Structure and Function	

LESSON	DISCIPLINARY CORE IDEAS	SCIENCE AND ENGINEERING PRACTICES	CROSS-CUTTING CONCEPTS	SCIENCE, TECHNOLOGY, SOCIETY, AND THE ENVIRONMENT
ETS1.A	Defining and Delimiting Engineering Problems: Possible solutions to a problem are limited by available materials resources (constraints). The success of a designed solution is determined by considering the desired features of a solution (criteria). Different proposals for solutions can be compared on the basis of how well each one meets the specified criteria for success or how well each takes the constraints into account. (5) • The more precisely a design task's criteria and constraints can be defined, the more likely it is that the designed solution will be successful. Specification of constraints includes consideration of scientific principles and other relevant knowledge that are likely to limit possible solutions. (MS)	Asking Questions and Defining Problems (Session 1,2,4) Planning and Carrying Out Investigations (Session 1,2,3,4)	Scale Proportion, and Quantity Proportional relationships among different types of quantities provide information about the magnitude of properties and processes. (MS) Cause and effect relationships are routinely identified, tested and used to explain change. (5) Phenomena may have more than one cause, and some cause and effect relationships in systems can only be described using prwobability. (MS)	
ETS1.B	Developing Possible Solutions: Testing a solution involves investigating how well it performs under a range of likely conditions. • At whatever stage, communicating with peers about proposed solutions is an important part of the design process and shared ideas can lead to improved designs. (5) • A solution needs to be tested and then modified on the basis of the test results in order to improve it. (MS) • Sometimes parts of different solutions can be combined to create a solution that is better than any of its predecessors. (MS)	Constructing Explanations and Designing Solutions (Session 2,3,4)	Cause and effect Patterns	
ETS1.C	Optimizing the Design Solution: Different solutions need to be tested in order to determine which of them best solves the problem, given the criteria and constraints. (5) • Although one design may not perform the best across all tests, identifying the characteristics of the design that performed the best in each test can provide useful information for the redesign process - that is, some of those characteristics may be incorporated into the new design. • The iterative process of testing the most promising solutions and modifying what is proposed on the basis of the test results leads to greater refinement and ultimately to an optimal solution. (MS)	Obtain, Evaluate, and Communicate Information (Session 2,3,4) Engaging in Argument from Evidence (Session 4)	Patterns can by used to identify cause and effect relationships. (MS) • Patterns of change can be used to make predictions. (5) • Patterns can be used as evidence to support an explanation. (5) • Patterns in rates of change and other numerical relationships can provide information about natural and human designed systems. (MS) • Graphs, charts, and images can be used to identify patterns in data. (MS)	

(continued)

Lesson	Disciplinary Core Ideas	Science and Engineering Practices	Cross-Cutting Concepts	Science, Technology, Society, and the Environment
				People's needs and wants change over time, as do their demands for new and improved technologies. (5) • Engineers improve existing technologies or develop new ones to increase their benefits, decrease known risks, and meet societal demands. (5) • Engineering advances have led to important discoveries in virtually every field of science and scientific discoveries have led to the development of entire industries and engineered systems. (MS)
Science of Superpowers	**LS1.B** (Session 1) Growth and Development of Organisms: Genetic factors as well as local conditions affect the growth of the (adult plant). (MS) • Organisms reproduce either sexually or asexually and transfer their genetic information to their offspring. (MS) Inheritance of Traits: Genes are located in the chromosomes of cells, with each chromosome pair containing two variants of each of many distinct genes. Each distinct gene controls the production of specific proteins, which in turn affects the traits of the individual. Changes (mutations) to genes can result in changes to proteins which can affect the structures and functions of the organism and thereby change traits. (MS) • Variations of inherited traits between parents and offspring arise from genetic differences that result from the subset of chromosomes (and therefore genes) inherited. (MS) **LS3.A** (Session 1) Variation of Traits: In addition to variations that arise from sexual reproduction, genetic information can be altered because of mutations. **LS3.B** (Session 1) Though rare, mutations may result in changes to the structure and function of proteins. Some changes are beneficial, others harmful, and some neutral to the organism. (MS)	Planning and Carrying Out Investigations (Session 2,4) Engaging in Argument from Evidence (Session 2) Constructing Explanations and Designing Solutions (Session 2, 3, 4)	Scale, Proportion, and Quantity (Session 1, 4) Natural objects and/or observable phenomena exist from the very small to the immensely large or from very short to very long time periods. (5) Time, space, and energy phenomena can be observed at various scales using models to study systems that are too large or too small. (MS) Systems and System Models (Session 2, 4) Stability and Change (Session 2, 3) Substructures have shapes and parts that serve functions. (5) * Structures can be designed to serve particular functions by taking into account properties of different materials, and how materials can be shaped and used. (MS) Structure and Function Relationships (Session 2, 3, 4) Cause and Effect (Session 2, 4) Cause and effect relationships are routinely identified and used to explain change (5). • Cause and effect relationships may be used to predict phenomena in natural or designed systems (MS).	Influence of Engineering, Technology, and Science on Society and the Natural World (Session 2, 3, 4)

Lesson	Disciplinary Core Ideas	Science and Engineering Practices	Cross-Cutting Concepts	Science, Technology, Society, and the Environment
PS2.A (Session 2)	Forces and Motion: The motion of an object is determined by the sum of the forces acting on it; if the total force on the object is not zero, its motion will change. The greater the mass of the object, the greate the force needed to achieve the same change in motion. For any given object, a larger force causes a larger change in motion. (MS)		A system can be described in terms of its components and their interactions. (5) • A systems is a group of related parts that make up a whole and can carry out functions its individual parts cannot. (5) • Models can be used to represent systems and their interactions – such as inputs, processes and outputs, - and energy and matter flows within systems. (MS) • Systems may interact with other systems; they may have sub-systems and be part of larger complex systems. (MS)	
PS2.B (Session 2)	Types of Interactions: The gravitational force of Earth acting on an object near Earth's surface pulls that object toward the planet's center. (5) • Gravitational forces are always attractive. There is a gravitational force between any two masses, but it is very small except when one or both of the objects have a large mass. (MS)		Explanations of stability and change in natural or designed systems can be constructed by examining the changes over time and forces at different scales. (MS) • Stability might be disturbed either by sudden events or gradual changes that accumulate over time. (MS)	
ETS1.A (Session 3, 4)	Defining and Delimiting Engineering Problems: Possible solutions to a problem are limited by available materials and resources (constraints). The success of a designed solution is determined by considering the desired features of a solution (criteria). Different proposals for solutions can be compared on the basis of how well each one meets the specified criteris for success or how well each takes the constraints into account. (5) • The more precisely a design task's criteria canbe defined, the more likely it is that the designed solution will be successful. Specification of constraints includes consideration of scientific principles and other relevant knowledge that is likely to limit possible solutions. (MS)	Asking Questions and Defining Problems (Session 2, 3, 4) Mathematical and Computational Thinking (Session 2) Developing and Using Models (Session 2, 3, 4)	Energy and Matter: Flows, Cycles, and Conservation (Session 4) Energy can be transferred in various ways and between objects. (5) • Elthin a natural or designed system, the transfer of energy drives the motion and/or cycling of matter. (MS) • The transfer of energy can be tracked as energy flows through a designed or natural system. (MS)	

(continued)

LESSON	DISCIPLINARY CORE IDEAS	SCIENCE AND ENGINEERING PRACTICES	CROSS-CUTTING CONCEPTS	SCIENCE, TECHNOLOGY, SOCIETY, AND THE ENVIRONMENT
	Developing Possible Solutions: Tests are often designed to identify failure points or difficulties, which suggest the elements of the design that needs to be improved. (5)			
ETS1.B (Session 2, Session 4)	• At whatever stage, communicating with peers about proposed solutions is an important part of the design process, and shared ideas can lead to improved designs. (5)			
	• A solution needs to be tested, and then modified on the basis of the test results, in order to improve it. (MS)			
	• Sometimes parts of different solutions can be combined to create a solution that is better than any of its predecessors. (MS)			
	Optimizing the Design Solution: Different solutions need to be tested in order to determine which of them best solves the problem, given the criteria and constraints. (5)	Obtaining, Evaluating, and Communicating Information (Session 2)		
ETS1.C (Session 2, 4)	• The iterative process of testing the most promising solutions and modifying what is proposed on the basis of the test results leads to greater refinement and ultimately to an optimal solution. (MS)			
PS2.A (Session 4)	Forces and Motion: The motion of an object is determined by the sum of the forces acting on it; if the total force on the object is not zero, it's motion will change. The greater the mass of the object, the greater the force needed to achieve the same change in motion. (MS)			
PS3.B (Session 4)	Conservation of Energy and Energy Transfer: When th emotion energy of an object changes, there is inevitably some other change in energy at the same time. (MS)			
PS3.C (Session 4)	Relationship between energy and forces: When two objects interact, each one exerts a force on the other that can cause energy to be transferred to or from the object. (MS)	Developing and Using Models		
Infinite Recess		Asking Questions and Defining Problems	Analyzing and Interpreting Data (Session 2)	
		Planning and Carrying Out Investigations		

Student Survey

In the student survey that follows, we have included a sample set of questions that can be used to ask your students about their experience taking part in a given lesson. This tool is not meant to be used to gauge advances in learning or content knowledge, but rather is designed to help you, the instructor, learn how your students felt about the lesson and enable you to incorporate their suggestions the next time you teach it.

STUDENT SURVEY

How could this lesson be better?

Lesson name: _____ Date: _____

How true are the following statements about this lesson?

(For the first three questions, please check the appropriate column.)

		NOT TRUE AT ALL	NOT VERY TRUE	SOMEWHAT TRUE	VERY TRUE
1.	I had fun doing this lesson.				
2.	The lesson made me want to learn about the topic we covered.				
3.	I learned new things in this lesson.				

4. What did you like most about this lesson?

5. What (if anything) would you change about this lesson?

6. What new things did you learn during this lesson?

Thanks for filling this out!

826 Centers and Staff

826 National *established 2008*
Chief Executive Officer: Gerald Richards
Board President: Terry Wit

44 Gough Street, Suite 206
San Francisco, CA 94103
(415) 864-2098
www.826national.org

826 Valencia *established 2002*
Serves: San Francisco Unified Public School District
Store: Pirate Supply Store
Executive Director: Bita Nazarian
Board Chair: Matt Middlebrook

826 Valencia Street
San Francisco, CA 94110
(415) 642-5905
www.826valencia.org

826NYC *established 2004*
Serves: New York City Public Schools
Store: Brooklyn Superhero Supply Co.
Executive Director: Joshua Mandelbaum
Board Chair: Jon Scieszka

372 Fifth Avenue
Brooklyn, NY 11215
(718) 499-9884
www.826nyc.org

826LA *established 2005*
Serves: Los Angeles Unified School District
Store: The Time Travel Mart
Executive Director: Joel Arquillos
Board Chair: Jodie Evans

Mar Vista
12515 Venice Boulevard
Los Angeles, CA 90066
(310) 915-0200
www.826la.org

Echo Park
1714 West Sunset Boulevard
Los Angeles, CA 90026
(213) 413-3388
www.826la.org

826CHI *established 2005*
Serves: Chicago Public Schools
Store: The Wicker Park Secret Agent Supply Co.
Executive Director: Kendra Curry-Khanna
Board Chair: Hilary Hodge

1276 N. Milwaukee Avenue
Chicago, IL 60622
(773) 772-8108
www.826chi.org

826michigan *established 2005*
Serves: Ann Arbor Public Schools, Ypsilanti Public School District, Lincoln Consolidated
Schools, Willow Run Community Schools, and Detroit Public Schools
Store: Liberty Street Robot Supply and Repair
Executive Director: Amanda Uhle
Board Chair: Joseph Malcoun

115 East Liberty Street
Ann Arbor, MI 48104
(734) 761-3463
www.826michigan.org

826 Boston *established 2007*
Serves: Boston Public Schools and greater Boston area school districts
Store: Greater Boston Bigfoot Research Institute
Executive Director: Daniel Johnson
Board Chair: Kevin Whalen

3035 Washington Street
Roxbury, MA 02119
(617) 422-5400
www.826boston.org

826DC *established 2010*
Serves: District of Columbia Public Schools
Store: The Museum of Unnatural History
Executive Director: Joe Callahan
Board Chair: Tara Greco

3233 14th Street NW
Washington, DC 20010
(202) 525-1074
www.826dc.org

INDEX